MANCHU
PRINCESS,
JAPANESE
SPY

ASIA PERSPECTIVES

Weatherhead East Asian Institute,
Columbia University

Kawashima Yoshiko, around 1933   *Courtesy Hokari Kashio*

Phyllis
Birnbaum

MANCHU PRINCESS, JAPANESE SPY

SPY The Story of

Kawashima Yoshiko,

the Cross-Dressing

Spy Who Commanded

Her Own Army

Columbia University Press
New York

ASIA PERSPECTIVES: HISTORY, SOCIETY, AND CULTURE

A Series of the Weatherhead East Asian Institute, Columbia University

CAROL GLUCK, EDITOR

FOR ASHOK

CONTENTS

CONTENTS

MAIN CHARACTERS

Chizuko: Yoshiko's assistant

Doihara Kenji: notorious agent provocateur of the Kwantung Army, whose many dark acts furthered Japanese advances in China; said to be one of Yoshiko's financial backers

Fuku: Yoshiko's adoptive mother; wife of Kawashima Naniwa

Fukunaga Kosei: only surviving daughter of Hiro and Pujie

Ganjurjab: son of Mongol military leader Babujab; married Yoshiko in 1927

Harada Tomohiko: Naniwa's relative, who knew Yoshiko in her youth

Hiro: *see* Saga Hiro

Itō Hanni: speculator, Yoshiko's lover

Iwata Ainosuke: ultranationalist activist and Yoshiko's onetime suitor

Jin Bihui: another name for Kawashima Yoshiko

Jin Moyu: Yoshiko's younger sister

Kamisaka Fuyuko: author of 1984 biography of Yoshiko

Kawashima Naniwa: Yoshiko's adoptive father

Kawashima Renko: Yoshiko's niece; adopted by Kawashima Naniwa

Kawashima Shōko: Yoshiko's grand-niece, Renko's daughter

Kawashima Yoshiko: also known as Aisin Gioro Xianyu, Eastern Jewel, Radiant Jade, Jin Bihui

Kosei: *see* Fukunaga Kosei

Mariko: Yoshiko's fictional counterpart in Muramatsu Shōfū's novel *The Beauty in Men's Clothing*

Matsuoka Yōsuke: foreign minister of Japan 1940–1941

Moriyama Eiji: ultranationalist and Yoshiko's onetime suitor

Muramatsu Shōfū: author of best-selling novel about Yoshiko, *The Beauty in Men's Clothing*

Muramatsu Tomomi: Muramatsu Shōfū's grandson; also wrote about Yoshiko

Naniwa: *see* Kawashima Naniwa

Ogata Hachirō: Yoshiko's assistant in the latter part of her life

Prince Su: Yoshiko's father; also known as Shanqi

Pujie: younger brother of "Last Emperor" Puyi; husband of Saga Hiro

Puyi: last emperor of the Qing dynasty

Renko: *see* Kawashima Renko

Saga Hiro: aristocratic Japanese wife of Pujie

Sasakawa Ryōichi: controversial entrepreneur and Yoshiko's benefactor

Shōfū: *see* Muramatsu Shōfū

Shōko: *see* Kawashima Shōko

Sonomoto Kotone: became close friend of Yoshiko's in 1939, in Fukuoka

Su Bingwen: warlord who staged a rebellion against the occupying Japanese

Tada Hayao: officer in Kwantung Army, Yoshiko's lover

Tanaka Ryūkichi: officer in Kwantung Army, Yoshiko's lover

Terao Saho: author of 2008 biography of Yoshiko

Tomomi: *see* Muramatsu Tomomi

Tōyama Mitsuru: prominent ultranationalist leader of Gen'yōsha, a group
   dedicated to Japan's expansion

Wanrong: Puyi's wife

Xianli: Yoshiko's older brother

Yamaga Tōru: Yoshiko's "first love"; later worked for Japan's Special Service
   Agency

Yamaguchi Yoshiko: famed singer-actress, known in China as Li Xianglan and
   in Japan as Ri Kōran

Zhang Zuolin: also known as Chang Tso-lin; powerful warlord assassinated by
   the Japanese in 1928

CHRONOLOGY

1865	Birth of Kawashima Naniwa, Yoshiko's adoptive father
1904–1905	Russo-Japanese War
1907	Approximate date of Yoshiko's birth
1911	Revolution in China brings down the Qing dynasty
1912	Republic of China established, Qing emperor Puyi abdicates
	Prince Su and family flee from Beijing to Lushun
1915	Approximate date of Yoshiko's arrival in Japan as Naniwa's adopted daughter
1922	Death of both Yoshiko's father, Prince Su, and her mother
1925	Puyi flees from Beijing to Japanese concession in Tianjin
1927	Yoshiko marries Ganjurjab
1928	Warlord Zhang Zuolin assassinated
1931	Manchurian Incident
	Puyi leaves Tianjin for Manchuria, soon joined by his wife, Wanrong
1932	Shanghai Incident
	Establishment of Manchukuo
	Warlord Su Bingwen seizes a railway line in Manchukuo, leading to Hulunbuir Incident
1933	Battle of Rehe
	The Beauty in Men's Clothing published
1937	Start of Sino-Japanese War
1940	Japan signs Tripartite Pact with Germany and Italy
1941	Japanese-Soviet Neutrality Pact signed
	Pearl Harbor
1945	Soviets invade Manchukuo
	Japanese defeated in Second World War
	Yoshiko arrested
1948	Yoshiko executed in Beijing

A NOTE ON THE TEXT

C hinese and Japanese names are generally written with the family name first, followed by the given name. I usually refer to individuals by their family names, but in cases where a family name can refer to more than one person, the given name is used. For example, Kawashima Yoshiko is usually referred to as Yoshiko; Aisin Gioro Xianli is referred to as Xianli.

For Chinese people and places I've generally used the pinyin system of romanization, except for those better known in other forms, for example Chiang Kai-shek. In the few quotations from older English-language works and translations, I've kept the Chinese and Japanese names and places as printed in the originals.

Chinese and Japanese traditionally count their ages using a system different from the one used in the West—a child is one on the date of birth and two the following New Year's Day—but they now also use the Western system. Frequently it is hard to determine which system is being used. For this reason, I have left the ages as cited in the original documents. Yoshiko's age is particularly difficult to determine, with many different dates cited by contemporaries and biographers.

MANCHU
PRINCESS,
JAPANESE
SPY

1

BORN TO CHAOS

I don't want to die with humans. But I'll be happy if I die
with monkeys. Monkeys are honest. Dogs too.

—KAWASHIMA YOSHIKO

On a March morning in 1948, the prisoner emerged just as the sun
was coming up. She had expressed a wish to die quietly, without
the fanfare that had often accompanied her every move. She had
also wanted to wear a white Japanese robe for her last moments, but this
request was denied. "On March 25, I will be executed," she had written to her
adoptive father. "Please tell young people to never stop praying for China's
future." As she was brought out to the Beijing prison yard, the prison official
announced the charges against her and confirmed her identity. She died,
kneeling, a bullet to the back of her head. Later on, the official reported that
she had not flinched in the slightest.

In rambling letters she had written from prison, she took pride in
her tranquil state of mind. She had not weakened under the pressures
of the trial, nor did she fear the outcome. "They'll probably execute me.
The court ruling says that I am a big spy, that I tried to use the Japanese
to bring the Qing dynasty back to power. They say I sold China to the
enemy. They'll execute me since this is what they have in their heads.
I feel like thanking them—was I really such an important person? Excuse
me—I ask them—please show me some proof. That's when the monkey
show really gets going."

In these letters, she went out of her way to praise her adoptive father,
who had formed her ideas. She believed that she had honored his teachings
by dedicating her life to her people, as he had urged. She had ridden her
horse to Rehe, commanding troops against those who stood in her way.

Wounded in battle, she had looked ahead to the benefits a victory would bring—a return of her clan to power and an end to chaos for all Chinese. She told her father not worry about her, for she had lived as she wished and credited him with giving her courage. "I am truly calm and clear in my mind, as befits your daughter. I am proud of myself." If not for his instruction, she would have had nothing, not the glory, not the toil for her people. And without that, what worth did life possess? "For me," she wrote in her warrior style, "there's not much difference between being exonerated or executed."

One shot to the head at close range ended her life that morning in 1948 and the exploits that had earned her international celebrity. A gruesome photo showed her dead, body laid out for public view, face covered with blood. It was the last of a woman who had been, for some, a traitor, and for others, a liberator—or for others still, a lonely and unstable figure, perhaps mad.

But was it the end? Almost as soon as the photo of her corpse was presented to the public, the questions began. Had she really died that morning in the courtyard of Beijing's Number 1 Prison? Only two Western journalists had been allowed to witness the execution, and they were outsiders who could not be trusted to verify the facts. A reporter from the Associated Press wrote about seeing the fabled woman fall before his own eyes, but skeptics wondered whether he could identify her correctly. The Chinese reporters, expecting to be present at the great event, had been barred from the prison that morning. Denied entry to the execution, they raised a ruckus. If government officials had nothing to hide, why weren't Chinese journalists allowed to identify the deceased? When a family member sought to put an end to the controversy by asserting that the hands of the corpse in the photograph were unmistakably Yoshiko's, few took notice. Nothing was distinct in the photograph, so how could anyone profess to identify the hands?

The questions never found satisfactory answers, and the rumors gained new, persuasive details as the years passed. Why, money could purchase anything in China, and her family was rich and well connected. They could have easily bribed an official to fake an execution. Later on, a woman came forward to claim that it was not the famed spy who had died that morning but her own poor, ailing sister. The woman's family had been promised a lot of money if the sister died in the prisoner's place. While some of the money had been paid beforehand, the woman complained that her family never received the rest.

And so the gossip spread. In a country as vast as China, even someone well-known as—depending on whose side you're on—the "Mata Hari of the East" or "Joan of Arc of the Manchus" could have set up a secret life in a remote region. She was spotted whipping up mischief in Mongolia and then Korea. Just recently, Chinese researchers came forward to insist that until 1978 she had lived on in Changchun, in China's Northeast, where she had many connections. According to these reports, she had become more interested in Buddhism as she had aged, often visiting a nearby temple. In her youth, she had been known for her tomboyish ways, and some Changchun residents swore that they had definitely seen her not so long ago climbing trees in the neighborhood.

*

No matter when or where she died, this woman, who went by various names, shows no sign of disappearing from history anytime soon. While the details of her life are often disputed, few doubt that a more serene start might have produced a more serene end. But quiet was not to be her lot as she faced dynastic upheavals and alleged sexual abuse. Born in China and raised in Japan, she finished belonging to neither place.

As Aisin Gioro Xianyu, she started out in Beijing as the fourteenth daughter of a Manchu prince, whose legacy included unfulfilled dreams of a coup d'état and thirty-eight children. After the Manchu Qing dynasty fell in 1912, the prince plotted to bring about its return to power. His supply of children abundant, he thought nothing of giving Xianyu to a Japanese friend who promoted his political causes.

As Kawashima Yoshiko, she settled down into a life in Japan, where she startled the neighbors by riding horseback, as befit a Manchu princess, to her country school. She also soaked up her adoptive father's beliefs about how she must devote herself to bringing the Manchus back to their former glory. This goal, impelling her to storm off to battle, suited her hot, erratic temperament.

As Commander Jin, she built a reputation as a spy who liked to dress as a man and became the heroine of a best-selling novel. With her short, handsome haircut and military uniforms, she was credited with unconfirmed exploits, among them riding horseback again, this time as leader of her own army. Renown intoxicated her, and she branched out into other areas where her qualifications were just as dubious. She recorded what she declared were genuine Mongolian folk songs, but she made up the lyrics and themes herself.

If her ideas were sometimes sublime, her colleagues were not. While trying to promote the Manchus, she got involved in promoting the puppet Manchu state the Japanese had set up in Manchuria. That's one of the reasons why Yoshiko was tried for treason in China after the Japanese were defeated. By then, her myth had captured the imagination of the public worldwide. Either she had lost her teeth and her man's wardrobe by 1948, when Chiang Kai-shek had her executed at dawn. Or, she did not really die that day but in the nick of time was swept off to a waiting plane, to begin a new life in places unknown.

*

No matter that her death remains a question to this day, the celebrity spy still has a way of turning up time and again. For a government seeking to whip up its citizens' patriotic fervor, recounting her past deeds can stir the crowds. It is a tricky business, however, for her aims were contradictory, and so she can be held up as an example by both sides. To the Chinese, she continues to offer a case of all-purpose evil as a Chinese traitor who caused damage that can never be forgotten. They blame her for starting a war in Shanghai and for otherwise assisting the Japanese occupation; they do not fail to bring up her childhood rape and later unquenchable sexual thirst. While there is substance to some of these charges, her Chinese accusers go too far when they blame her for masterminding the bombing of a certain warlord's train as it passed under a bridge in Shenyang. In fact, she had no expertise in explosives and was far more qualified for her role as a dance hall girl in Shanghai. It is impossible that the young woman who won a first prize for her waltz carried out that spectacular assassination.

For Japanese, the story takes on another look entirely. In Japan, as Kawashima Yoshiko, she is accepted as almost one of their own since she spent much of her youth in the country. Therefore, in Japan they take a more wistful view of Yoshiko's escapades. They emphasize her psychological problems, and once they start along this line—childhood woes, abandonment, solitude—there is much to consider. The Japanese tend to forgive her wartime activities and have no interest in the assassination plot. For the

Japanese, Yoshiko has been wronged over and over, by her birth father, her adoptive father, the entire Japanese military establishment, other males who took advantage of her beauty and her daring. Finally, she was wronged by carelessness: there are claims she would not have faced execution if a certain form had been filled in when she was a young girl. By the time anyone got around to worrying about this form, she was on trial for her life. "Poor Yoshiko," her niece lamented upon learning of her death. "That one piece of paper would have saved her."

This Chinese-Japanese spy has also been taken up by the moviemakers, most notably Bernardo Bertolucci in his 1987 film *The Last Emperor*. She makes her first appearance in the film at the Tianjin residence of Puyi, the exiled "Last Emperor" who was her distant relative. Dashing in men's clothes, she arrives in a pilot's leathers, and more dashingly, she identifies herself as "Eastern Jewel," another of her names. Eastern Jewel quickly establishes her contempt for convention when she dismisses the institution of marriage and becomes the empress's opium supplier.

"Oh, I know everything," she tells the empress. "I know Chiang Kai-shek has false teeth. I know his nickname, 'Cash My Check.' I'm a spy and I don't care who knows it."

When Emperor Puyi strides into the room, Eastern Jewel welcomes him with an enthusiastic, uncousinly embrace. Since Puyi's consort has just left him, Eastern Jewel volunteers to serve as substitute. Puyi, however, declares that she's not his type.

Unfazed, Eastern Jewel moves on to political intrigue.

★

As Bertolucci's film and other, more reliable sources make plain, Yoshiko's fame was tangled up in the Japanese occupation of China, which started in Manchuria in 1931 and went on until the Japanese defeat in 1945. During those years, Yoshiko moved between China and Japan with ease, undaunted by the differences in language and customs of her two home countries. She also did not seem to fear the peril of her unusual circumstances, and this insouciance in the face of danger proved either her immense courage or her utter misunderstanding of current events.

To justify their aggressions, the Japanese claimed that they were liberating China from imperialist Western powers. Britain and France, among others, had foisted degrading treaties upon China and "carved up the Chinese melon" by taking control of swaths of land. In the course of their "liberation" of China, the Japanese proved themselves more bloodthirsty imperialists than the Westerners, all the while spouting slogans about the all-Asian heaven they were creating. Ruthless in their usurpation of Chinese territory, they eventually advanced from Manchuria down along much of China's east coast.

A princess of Manchuria with strong Japanese influences, Yoshiko thrived and fell on that turmoil. As China and Japan continue to argue about the terrible events of those years, she has taken her place in the never-ending debate. Was she just a gullible victim in the butchery going on around her? Could she have avoided being drawn into the "paradise" the Japanese claimed to be creating in China? Once drawn into that "paradise," did she bear any responsibility for that regime's cruelty?

Yoshiko's supporters now say that she was just a lonely woman, discarded by her birth father and looking for affection. Others, less sympathetic, point out that not every lonesome woman rides off on horseback to assist foreign invaders or does undercover work for the occupiers of her native land.

2
LITTLE SISTER

A picturesque film-drama figure, half tomboy, half heroine, flits
through the Japanese press these days with the nickname "the
Manchukuo Joan of Arc." Yoshiko Kawashima is her name, and there
are about her many strange circumstances that make her appealing
to a nation which takes deep pride in the army and its exploits.

Yoshiko has been a spy for the Japanese, has been photographed
riding with the Manchukuo troops to war and has been featured in
newspaper stories and in a novel. When she visited Tokyo recently,
a waitress at a café asked her whether she was a boy or girl. "I am half
boy and half girl," she is reported to have replied. Soon afterward she
broadcast an address in which she said she was now a man, and as a
man she proceeded to advise Japanese women against bobbed hair
and foreign dress.

Yoshiko Kawashima is Manchu by birth. Her father (according
to the versions of her history which find currency in Japan) was a
Manchu prince. . . . After the revolution her father fled from Tientsin
to Port Arthur, aided by a Japanese ronin or freelance, who had
been mixing in China's troubled politics.

—*NEW YORK TIMES*, SEPTEMBER 17, 1933

Although at her trial Yoshiko claimed to be younger than commonly
believed and may not have died when the Chinese government said
she did, it is absolutely certain that she has not made any public pro-
nouncements since her execution date. Until recently, the closest anyone
could get to seeing Yoshiko was her sister Jin Moyu, who, in fact, provided a
good place to start. Born in 1918, Jin was the youngest of their father, Prince
Su's, thirty-eight children from five mothers. Waspish always, Jin had her own

view of the family, easily mixing fashion commentary with pointed remarks about her siblings. Over her long life—she died in 2014—she learned that certain personal characteristics could be life threatening. In particular, outspokenness mixed with a noble class background in China could guarantee at the very least a prison stay and at the worst, execution at dawn.

Both Yoshiko and Jin Moyu were daughters of Prince Su's fourth consort, and, like many in the family, both lived for long periods in China and Japan. This ensured the divided loyalties that brought disaster to both of them. Yoshiko was (supposedly) shot in 1948, while Jin spent fifteen years imprisoned in China, accused of being an enemy of the Chinese Revolution because of her infamous older sister and her own Japanese associations. Philosophical in her old age about what she had endured, Jin never forgot her complicated history.

"I'm Chinese," she wrote in her autobiography *I Was Born a Qing Princess*, "but I've been Japanized in my approach to things and my way of thinking. . . . I never studied anything about Communism or Socialism. I am totally apolitical. . . . I have never spent even one day in Chinese schools. From primary school to college, I went to Japanese schools. All my friends are Japanese." Although Jin was persecuted in China because of her ties to Japan, she remained proud of her Japanese ways. When she was eighty, she opened a Japanese-language school in Beijing where she lived, bedridden and combative, into her old age.

"Look," Jin once scolded me over the phone, speaking in her fluent, blunt Japanese, "I can't worry about the past. I came from the kind of family I came from and can't do anything about it. I don't want to spend my life going over and over what I could have done. I suffered. I survived. And now here I am." She was more inclined to talk about the differences between Japanese and Chinese cooking: "If you ask me, Chinese cooking has much more variety. But you can't beat Japan when it comes to the beautiful dishes they use to serve the food." She next moved on to her health: "I have diabetes but I don't feel a bit sick. It's really nothing. I don't even worry about sugar. You know, when you're ninety years old, you don't really worry about anything. Americans are too picky about what they eat."

While Jin chatted at length about food and health, she avoided talking about Yoshiko, whose activities brought her family years of harassment by both the Nationalists and the Communists. Relations between the sisters did not end cordially, but even so, it would have been risky for her to express any kind of affection for Yoshiko, whom Chinese authorities still denounce whenever her name comes up.

Still, in 2007, Jin Moyu seemed to go out of her way to evoke the ghost of this disgraced sister when she was interviewed on "The Eighty-eight-Year-Old Princess," a Chinese television program about her own life. Never mentioning Yoshiko except to say that her big sister called her "Shrimp," Jin nonetheless had no qualms about reviving her older sister's personal style. She turned up for her television appearance in male clothing head to toe and preened in her mannish suit, shirt, and shoes. Jin's getup, accompanied by a boyish hairstyle and deep chuckles, seemed to announce that this was a version of Yoshiko reconstituted for the twenty-first century. With her smart trousers and sassy replies, Jin used her experiences, not to foment political unrest, but to offer self-help advice to her Chinese audience.

"Don't cry after something bad happens," Jin Moyu urged. "This is useless. You have to go beyond your own problems and try to attain a higher spiritual level. This means you must control your anger and sadness in the proper way by not letting those feelings surface. Otherwise, you may hurt others. So, I say, swallow these emotions." Her voice rough, Jin enjoyed downplaying the strengths that had pulled her through a privileged youth as a Manchu princess from a deposed dynasty, the family's life in exile after the Qing's fall, two marriages, trouble with the cook at her home-style Beijing restaurant, a long prison stay.

"Somehow or other I am a person who adapts well to a new environment," she said, grinning at the understatement. "I stole corn bread buns while in prison since everyone around me was very, very hungry. I took pity on them. That's why I stole food for them."

In her autobiography, Jin Moyu was willing to take up the matter of her sister Yoshiko in more detail. Jin did not grow up with Yoshiko, who was about eleven years older; by the time Jin was born in Lushun, Yoshiko had already been sent to her new home in Japan. In 1927, when she was nine, Jin met her sister for the first time. Yoshiko had come for her marriage in Lushun, where her Chinese family lived.

"I never met Yoshiko until she arrived in Lushun," Jin wrote, "but I'd heard stories about her. Her beauty had been obvious since she was small. Also she was good at telling lies, and Mother always scolded her about that. Mother was absolutely against sending Yoshiko to Japan. I heard that even on her deathbed, Mother said, 'Please bring Yoshiko back.'"

At first Jin Moyu was dazzled by Yoshiko's glamour, for she didn't dress like a man in those days before her marriage. "Yoshiko had her hair in loose waves, with a curl on each cheek, a hairstyle I'd never seen before. She wore a pure white fur jacket over her skirt. When she walked around the quiet Lushun of those days, she really stood out."

This fashionable older sister was also trouble.

> One day I went to the store to buy some things and bumped right into my sister Yoshiko at the entrance. That day too you could tell it was Yoshiko from way off since she was wearing her pure white jacket and skirt. On top of that, she didn't seem at all ashamed of fully exposing her legs, which were as shapeless and thick as a daikon radish. (She was small and had pretty hands and feet, but her calves were like daikon). She had high heels on.
>
> I thought to myself, "Oh, no, here she is," but by then it was too late.
>
> My sister noticed me right away and called out, "So tell me, Shrimp, what are you doing here?"
>
> "I came to buy biscuits for the dog."
>
> I started to go into the shop, but my sister wouldn't let me go. "I'll wait for you, and we can go home together."
>
> Also she had something in her hand, and when I took a closer look, I saw that it was Lion's Toothpaste. I don't know what she had done to that toothpaste, but the contents had oozed out of the top and stuck to her palm. When she saw what had happened, she let out with a loud laugh of surprise, not at all concerned about where she was.
>
> Gradually a crowd gathered. I quickly ran into the store.

After the Japanese created their puppet state in Manchuria, Yoshiko established herself in Changchun, their capital city. Since Jin Moyu attended middle school there, she used to visit Yoshiko often and remembers her sister driving a Ford V-8 around town. Once when Jin fell ill, she left her dormitory without permission to convalesce at Yoshiko's home. A teacher came searching for the missing pupil, but Yoshiko was not the sort to apologize for breaking school rules.

"What's this all about?" Yoshiko said with a loud laugh. "Our Shrimp ran away and came here. . . . Shrimp is not so strong and gets a fever easily. This really worries me. I'll feed her some of her favorite foods for two or three days, and then I'll send her back."

Though Jin Moyu appreciated the freedom of Yoshiko's household, the rest of the family was not at all pleased about the growing closeness between the two sisters. Clearly Yoshiko was not their first choice when it came to selecting a person to mold young minds. Yoshiko frequented the dance halls each night, and young Jin, eager to follow her example, mastered the waltz and tango. The two sisters danced together for practice.

"Why, Chizuko," Yoshiko exclaimed to her assistant, marveling at her sister's natural dancing skills, "she's even better and lighter on her feet than you."

Jin took to accompanying her sister to the dance hall on Saturdays and even acquired her own following. She started to mimic Yoshiko's boyish style, dressing in a black velvet jacket with red lining, matching velvet shorts, white shirt, and red necktie. Apparently alarmed by these goings on, Jin's older brother soon shipped her off to school in Japan.

"Come back soon!" Yoshiko said in sadness at their parting.

The two sisters had their final encounter when they were both living together in Beijing in the summer of 1945, just after Japan's defeat. By then Yoshiko was no longer the celebrity spy in the Ford V-8 sought after by journalists and military bigwigs but a shunned has-been strongly connected to the losing side.

"Yoshiko invited me to live with her many times," Jin Moyu wrote. "But I had a look at the people around her and her general attitude toward life, and from that time on, I was totally disappointed with what she was doing. Since there was no way I could accept her invitations, I turned her down." As Jin and others learned, spurning Yoshiko came at a price:

A little while later, Yoshiko suddenly came to see me along with some low-life Chinese I'd never seen before. She burst into my room with a sword and went wild

"Apologize!" she said.

I of course had nothing to apologize for. "If you have something you want to talk about, then sit down quietly over there and we can have a conversation."

"I didn't get your kind of education," Yoshiko replied. "You really do talk a lot, don't you? Do you take me for a fool?"

When Yoshiko started smashing the glass shelves and windows, people from the main house heard what was going on. They got alarmed and rushed over. I of course hadn't shouted or cried out until then. I'd decided that I would shout for help if she struck me with the sword.

When a servant at last yelled that my brother had come home, Yoshiko was surprised and stopped smashing things.

"What on earth are you doing?" my brother asked her. "If you have something to say, come into my room." He took her away, and I followed behind. He was very angry. "Just tell me why you're subjecting us to this kind of vulgar display?"

After a few moments' silence she suddenly said to me, "Why didn't you come over for my birthday?"

In 1948 Jin was not overcome with grief when she learned of Yoshiko's execution. "I looked at the newspaper photograph of Yoshiko's fallen body and for a long while felt very complicated emotions. But to be completely honest, I didn't shed a single tear. Rather I thought that meeting her end this way perhaps was just like her and so was a good thing."

3
ROYALTY IN EXILE

The clean, cool fragrance of fresh-cut gardenias in a jade bowl caressed us like the smooth silk of the Oriental tapestry on the wall. The dusty, burning glare of the noisy, crowded Tianjin street which we had just left seemed miles away as we sank into the velvety depths of a huge sofa. We tried to accustom our squinting eyes to the palm-shaded dimness of the Princess' reception room.

Across the expanse of Oriental rugs, a well-dressed Chinese family was sitting stiffly on straight-backed, highly-polished chairs. . . .

Sounds of a mild commotion in the hall outside riveted our eyes on the door at the back of the room. With a heavy click, it burst open, to admit a huge Chinese attendant, followed by a small, young-looking Chinese girl (or could it be a boy?), in brown knickers and a bright orange sweater.

She nonchalantly swaggered down the length of the cushiony carpet, impatiently motioning the several men, who reverently rose as she entered, to sit down again and be comfortable. With utter lack of ceremony, she plopped down into a large ebony chair, crossed one leg over her knee, brushed back her straight boyish-bobbed hair, and lighted a cigarette.

—WILLA LOU WOODS

Yoshiko did not get around to starting work on her autobiography *In the Shadow of Chaos* until 1937, and by that time she was living in China's Tianjin, where she ran a restaurant known for its Genghis Khan hot pot. She was only about thirty years old, but even so, the years of fame were behind her. Physically too, she was in decline. There was the trouble with her back that sent her off to Japan for cures, the bullet fragments—from wartime battles or a suicide attempt—still lodged in various parts of her body, and the addictions, either to painkillers or opium or both, that further weakened her. At thirty, she was already prepared to look back and shape her legend for posterity.

By then Yoshiko had become a seasoned interview subject who had spoken of her adventures to countless reporters and fans; one Japanese author had, with her assistance, already written a popular novel based on her life. Her mixture of fact and fiction was always masterful, and that is why her mother had complained about her precocious skill for telling lies. As a result, her recollections are inaccurate, self-serving, at times even hallucinatory. On top of that, her words were edited by those who had a stake in making sure that their side came out looking good. The result is an unreliable heap of facts presented with varying degrees of bravado. Yet even this jumble cannot bury Yoshiko, and she manages to strut out of the mess as she tells her story, a woman forced to the sidelines but still trying to make her case.

Yoshiko's autobiography takes up a dramatic moment at the beginning, when she narrates a childhood memory. She is about five years old, and though she is on a ship bound for places unknown, she claims to remember the sea breezes, and the smells of paint and people. Suddenly she is awakened from her sleep by a servant who is singing a sad lullaby as the waves beat against the ship. Crying, the servant hugs her tightly.

"Why are you crying?" the young Yoshiko wonders. "What's the matter?"

The servant's only reply is a tearful wail. "Oh, Princess, Princess!"

The scene is well chosen, since it marks the event that would transform Yoshiko's life. She and the large entourage of family and servants—estimates range from fifty to two hundred people—were aboard the ship en route from their Beijing mansion to exile in Manchuria, after the fall of the Qing dynasty. Her father, Prince Su, had been a prominent official in the imperial regime and firmly against the emperor's abdication. With the end of the Qing, the more than two-hundred-fifty-year rule of the minority Manchus ended, and the majority Han Chinese took over, establishing the Republic of China in 1912.

When Prince Su had fled Beijing, he disguised himself as a poor merchant and made his way to Lushun, in Manchuria, which was then under Japanese control. The Japanese military provided him with protection during his getaway, realizing that the prince would prove useful to their plans for expansion in Manchuria; in fact they had him in mind as the future head of the puppet state they planned to establish there. Nowadays the prince's family takes pains to insist that he did not rush willingly into cooperation with the Japanese. "My father wanted to go to Hōten [Shenyang]," his son Xianli says, "raise the Qing flag there and, together with [the warlord] Zhang Zuolin, bring down Yuan Shikai," head of the new Republic of China. These plans were thwarted when the Japanese arranged for the destruction of a bridge along the way, making the prince's journey there impossible.

Even so, once out of Beijing, Prince Su expressed defiance of the new regime in a poem, "I will not tread upon the soil of the Republic." The Japanese also provided him with a residence in Lushun, and Yoshiko, along with the rest of the household, traveled by ship to join him.

As they established themselves in the Japanese-held port, Prince Su, a Manchu prince in exile, and his family could not have found the atmosphere congenial. One temporary resident of the house remembers the prince in those days as "small, with dark skin, fat. He had a big head and many wrinkles on his face. He had not cut off his queue." Since the Manchus, a minority nationality from the north, had ruled China for centuries, it was long argued that they had assimilated into Han culture. Nowadays this view has been challenged by evidence that the Manchus did not blend in so thoroughly and instead maintained their distinctiveness throughout their reign. The prince would seem to have exemplified the sort of Manchu who followed the ancient ways, not only in his traditional Manchu queue and robes but also in his devotion to Manchu practices and to the revival of the regime.

The prince may have been delighted to get away from all those Han Republicans pouring into Beijing, but Lushun, once known as Port Arthur, put him and his family in the emotional heart of Japanese Manchuria. This port had been the site of fierce battles during the Russo-Japanese War, and in 1904 the legendary General Nogi Maresuke was renowned for having led Japanese forces to victory, incurring more than fifty thousand casualties along the way. That crucial win, achieved with the spilling of much Japanese blood, gave the Japanese control of Lushun and other territory in Manchuria, and also whetted the Japanese appetite for more of China. "Here, many hundreds of miles from home," went the popular song that kept alive the memory of the Japanese sacrifices, "in the glow of faraway Manchuria's red twilight, my friend lies under a stone at the end of a field."

In addition, Japan's victory in the Russo-Japanese War came to be seen as a major military and psychological triumph of an Asian nation over a European power. As this sank in, the Japanese took great pride in the contrast between their ascendance and the decline of China, their formerly venerated neighbor. Japanese admiration of Chinese civilization, which dated back centuries, had shifted to contempt at China's backwardness. After the Meiji Restoration, Japan had modernized with remarkable speed, wielding its new power in the region, which culminated in the defeat of mighty Russia; all this while China could not shake off old ways and unite to move forward. "At the time of the war against China [in the 1930s]," a Japanese wrote, "the patriotism of Japanese developed to extremes that had never been known before. They despised the Chinese, scorned them as effeminate, and they were hateful to them."

As such attitudes grew, Yoshiko and her large family moved into a two-story red-brick building on a Lushun hilltop; this was a former Russian hotel that had been ceded to the Japanese after the Russo-Japanese War. The Japanese military never let Prince Su out of their sight, keeping him under close surveillance. "The Japanese police wanted to protect my grandfather," his grandson writes, "and some bodyguards had been sent over by the Japanese government who kept watch on him day and night. . . . Grandfather liked to go fishing and would get a big group of family members together and go to the harbor at Lushun to fish from a small boat. . . . Of course a police guard accompanied him."

Their big red house on the hill survives, shabbily, although the once-splendid view from the second floor has lost the fight with development and pollution. "You can say that I grew up looking out at the Laohuwei Peninsula from the veranda of that house," Jin Moyu has written, in happy remembrance. There was not enough space to spread out, and so the family created a royal dormitory, with the children crammed together. The prince also had to adjust to straitened conditions. A devotee of Chinese opera, he had built a stage in his Beijing mansion for private performances. In Lushun, he was reduced to hobbies that did not require such a large private arena and so concentrated on Chinese chess and calligraphy.

It was not only the leisurely pursuits of royalty in retirement that kept him busy since the prince also was intent on toppling the Republic and returning the Qing dynasty to power. Never mind that the Qing dynasty had been unable to put an end to foreign incursions into China, widespread opium addiction, official corruption, military incompetence, and economic disarray, among other problems: Prince Su never ceased preparing for the day when he and his family would be back in Beijing, restored to their former royal status. Until his death, he remained wholly committed to this dream of a Qing restoration.

The various plots never succeeded, and there is a sense that the organization of uprisings was not the prince's forte. He proved, however, adept at organizing his family, which, given the crowd, was no small achievement. "In the Lushun house there was a large eating area," begins the description in Yoshiko's autobiography. "Three times a day at the sound of a bell, we all emerged from our rooms and headed there. You know, we were in all close to fifty people, and so when we came out of our rooms and went off to eat all together, there was a lot of commotion. After we finished eating, we'd often stay in our seats and have a family conference or father would give a talk."

The prince exhorted his exiled family to ready themselves for better days to come. "Looking back at those days in Lushun," Yoshiko wrote, "what I clearly remember is my father's specialty, the historical tale 'Putuo's Barley and Rice.'" This tale—featuring setback in battle, suffering, eventual triumph—was one of the inspirational tales the prince related to his army of children after dinner. "With the world in today's state of ruin," Prince Su said in his hortatory mode,

> I must say that it is an unexpected happiness that our family has not had to endure the misfortune of being torn apart, and we are able to enjoy our days here all together in this room. All of us have hands and feet that we can use for our own benefit. Up until now we have in our idle way used the hands and feet of others to do our work. We should have been ashamed of this kind of life, which goes against the Heavenly Way. Our present life may feel restricted as compared with the way we lived before, but it is really a life that accords with the Heavenly Way.

He went on to describe the fate of Gaozu, founder of the Han dynasty, whose troops were beaten back to the banks of the Putuo River. Wind and rain battered him, he was starving, but with just a handful of barley and rice donated by a kindly farmer and a drink of river water, Gaozu revived, going out again to give his all to the fight.

"If each of you," the prince urged his brood, "can live each day with the same spirit as Gaozu, who conquered his hunger with just a handful of grains, you will not find our life here restricted or unsatisfactory."

Though the prince, in this account, deserves credit for trying to boost morale with such myths, it would have been understandable if Yoshiko and the rest of the prince's children found the idea of survival on a handful of grains an alien concept. After all, they had just been pulled out of their sprawling mansion in Beijing with its two hundred Chinese and Western-style rooms, at least ten courtyards, gardens, stable, and other necessities of the imperial life. There's a story of how the prince used to air out his holdings of gold and silver each summer, filling up the whole courtyard for a week. Though only fragments of the mansion are still standing off a bustling Beijing alley—where current residents inhale the pollution and dust blown in from the Gobi Desert—it is still possible to get a sense of the prince's great wealth on that city block. This is despite the present Chinese government's lack of interest in preserving the former Beijing mansion of the prince, who did them no favors by collaborating with the Japanese.

All about the prince's old neighborhood, there is definite proof of the transience of glory on this earth, since most of the old mansion buildings have been torn down. Until recently, a sock factory occupied the prince's land. Now the old courtyard serves as part vegetable market, part distribution center for newspapers and bottled water. Two begrimed rows of rooms remain from the original mansion, almost hidden amid watermelon stands. A drunken resident from the outer courtyard is the only person who will come out to attest to Prince Su's former eminence.

"My building used to be part of the mansion," the man boasts as he invites visitors in to see his squalid room and filthy cot. "This was the side court for the servants."

★

Even with the shift in their circumstances in Lushun, Yoshiko's family was determined to adapt. Anxiety about the future may have blown in through their house's many windows, but there were the consolations of a lively household and family solidarity. Some of Yoshiko's siblings would look back on those days as an idyll amid the blooms of sweet-smelling flowers and trees. "All around it was quiet and sometimes small birds would come flying over, singing in joy, *chi-chi-*. We children felt that we were in a forest and played there to our hearts' content." In later decades, Prince Su's descendants would be hounded by successive Chinese regimes for their aristocratic backgrounds, their family's collaboration with the Japanese, and their own pro-Japanese activities. They would experience public disgrace, long prison terms, torture, execution.

"Our life in Lushun was simple," Prince Su's granddaughter remembered later, "but I absorbed lessons there that served me well as an adult, and so I think it was a good experience. If I had been brought up in luxury in Prince Su's mansion, I would not have had the courage nor the spiritual strength to endure the lengthy period of suffering in years to come."

In the old days, Manchu warriors had ridden on horseback across the northern steppes, fending off the enemy hordes with bows and arrows. The Kangxi emperor himself, whose reign began in the seventeenth century, was an ace at hitting the bulls-eye. Mindful of such achievements, the prince constructed an archery range in the garden. "Since ancient times," Prince Su told his children, "the men of our family had to learn the art of archery starting at age ten. Each year there were tests, and the most fervent and able practitioners were given bows as prizes. Shooting off arrows with a bow is not only a discipline for the body, it is also a way to discipline the mind. Only when the heart and mind are one will you be able to hit the target."

At home, the prince himself taught his children the Chinese classics and calligraphy, and a Japanese tutor was responsible for Japanese and math. Hardiness definitely a priority, the prince had his brood trek up and down the snowy Lushun hills, where tens of thousands of Japanese soldiers had been mowed down in combat during the Russo-Japanese War.

"They wore Japanese clothes and spoke Japanese," a Japanese woman observed when she met some of the prince's daughters in Lushun. "If you encountered them on the street, you would never dream that these children were Their Highnesses, the princess daughters of Prince Su, who had wielded such power during the Qing dynasty." The children attended Japanese schools, and while the heavy dose of Japanese schooling met the prince's high educational standards, it marked the children from then on as outsiders in Chinese society and partisans of Japan.

Meantime, in between archery practice and math classes, the prince did not forget that he had a dynasty to restore to power. Manchuria was not only the ancestral land of the prince's Manchu ancestors but also the very region where the Japanese were pushing to expand their presence in China. There was no getting away from the overlapping yet divergent ambitions of the prince and his Japanese hosts as they contemplated the possibilities. For the Japanese, a takeover of Manchuria would provide security against Russia in the north and a base for possible military activity in the future. There would be the benefit of Manchuria's natural resources, business opportunities, and wide-open spaces for the impoverished in Japan's overpopulated farm regions.

In order to achieve their goals, the Japanese were eager to convince the rest of the world that Manchuria, along with Inner Mongolia, was a distinct region, with its own culture and peoples, and certainly not part of China, with its mainly Han Chinese population. Some Japanese went so far as to say that the Manchus and Mongols were closer to Japanese than to Han Chinese. Plans were on for an "independence" movement that would "liberate" Manchuria and Mongolia from China and establish a new regime, under Japanese guidance.

Prince Su had a different plan in mind as he accepted Japanese assistance. He too wanted to establish an independent Manchu-Mongol regime, but he hoped this would eventually lead to the return of Manchu rule in all of China. His participation in these restorationist schemes consumed him. "Prince Su's home in Port Arthur," writes Christopher Dewell, "became a de facto headquarters for quasi-clandestine independence movement plots with the constant coming and going of various Japanese, Chinese, Manchu, and Mongol parties." Currency and armbands with imperial dragon designs were kept in the house, as were firearms and explosives, all in preparation for a Qing return. Dewell calls the home in Lushun "a busy conspirators' lair." Notable among the prince's advisers was his close Japanese friend Kawashima Naniwa, who served as secret liaison to the Japanese government in Tokyo and its army in China.

Almost always pictured in his Manchu robes and queue, Prince Su seems to have been the sort of preoccupied family head who would give no thought to his daughter's emotional well-being when considering his dynastic goals. And so, around 1915, the little girl named Aisin Gioro Xianyu, the prince's fourteenth daughter, was sent from Lushun to the Tokyo home of his loyal comrade Kawashima Naniwa. She would henceforth be known as Naniwa's adopted daughter, with the new Japanese name Kawashima Yoshiko. Her birth date is not certain, but she was probably about eight years old.

Yoshiko about six years old, in Qing-dynasty-era clothes

Courtesy Wada Chishū

There is much speculation about the reasons behind the prince's decision to give this daughter to Kawashima Naniwa, who himself says that the prince took pity on him for his childlessness and for his wife's increasingly unsound behavior. "He told me that he was sending me a toy," Naniwa recalled.

Concern for Naniwa's domestic woes may have played a part in this decision, but the prince's own circumstances must also be taken into account. Around that time, as he sat practicing calligraphy on the red Lushun house's veranda with its superb view, the prince may have seen disaster coming his way through the morning mists of Laohuwei. In Lushun, he was under Japanese control regarding his home and his safety. His recent insurrection, which was to have established a new Manchu-Mongol state, had come to nothing. The Japanese government had officially denied any role in this plot, although it had clandestinely supplied arms and manpower. The government had abruptly withdrawn its support halfway into the conflict and shifted its backing to the Chinese Republic.

As a result of this change in policy, Prince Su's faithful fellow plotter Naniwa had to leave China and return to Japan. With Naniwa out of China, there was no guarantee that Prince Su would continue to receive this friend's attention. Sending his daughter to Naniwa would be a way to strengthen their bond and their mutual commitment to the Qing resurgence.

Her older brother remembers the moment when Yoshiko, already a lively child, left the family:

> Yoshiko went up to my father's room on the second floor to say good-bye. She wore Chinese clothes and had a white ribbon in her hair.
>
> She was crying. "I don't want to go to Japan."
>
> When she saw her daughter weep, Yoshiko's mother kept on caressing her. "You be a good girl. Don't cry."

The horse and buggy soon arrived to take her away, and the whole family gathered to bid Yoshiko farewell. Her brother never forgot their mother's sadness that day.

Later on Yoshiko did not have a clear memory of Prince Su, her birth father, but she could easily recall her bewilderment and helplessness as a little girl facing those who had complete control over her future.

"One day I was asleep in bed in my father, Prince Su's, mansion in Lushun, and the next day I found myself in Moji [Japan]. I was taken away without knowing what was happening to me."

4

CONTINENTAL ADVENTURER

Water, sky; sky and water, clouds; these gave way to land, seemingly
floating in the water; this was the mainland of China. This was to be
my second homeland, one that had appeared so often in my dreams.

—MIYAZAKI TŌTEN

K awashima Naniwa's reputation has been assaulted from various
quarters over the years, and mention of his name can still bring on
a lot of yelling. That kind of roughing up, however, does not take
place within hearing of his small circle of surviving fans, who would not
tolerate such insults. Led by those from Naniwa's birthplace in Nagano Prefecture, these admirers continue to view his legacy with reverence and hold
up his activities as an example to all. There are of course those in Nagano
who object to this, but they have the good sense to avoid a wrangle. In the
decades since Naniwa's death, his supporters have continued to extol the
native son, who traveled widely but returned home at the end, ever true to
his visionary ideals.

Among the contingent of Naniwa's devotees, few make their position
more plain than Wada Chishū, a retired journalist, who was born in Nagano
City. Like his hero Naniwa, he lived for some time in Tokyo, but Wada was
not won over by the marvels of that metropolis. Instead, he returned to the
shimmering landscapes of his home, to Nagano's pines and bamboo on gently sloping mountains, and the springtime gift of mountain cherry trees.
Wada found Tokyo also lacking in an aspect crucial to a Nagano native:
Tokyo may be the center of the universe, but Wada couldn't find any decent
hot springs. Nagano is known for its piping hot natural baths, and according
to Wada, those around Tokyo are tepid.

"No competition in Tokyo at all," he told me. "I wasted my money."

In his seventies now, Wada Chishū is an impressive sight as he climbs about the mountains of Nagano, in search of vegetables or a cedar planted by Naniwa himself. He does not appear to have heard about what can happen if ageing human bones smash against mountainsides.

"I climb mountains every day here. It's just a part of my life. Worry about breaking bones? Not at all. I worry more about snakes, and there are a lot of them around. I should have worn boots today but I forgot. . . . The secret of my health? Alcohol. I drink every night. I start with two glasses of beer and then drink three cups of *shōchū*, straight. Every night."

On the front of his business card, Wada describes his occupation as a "researcher on Kawashima Naniwa," and on the back he offers ringing praise of his subject:

> Patriotic man of high principles, Kawashima Naniwa (1865–1949) was born in the city of Matsumoto in Shinshū [the old name for the region]. He lived life on a large scale. He served as a Chinese translator, composed many poems in Chinese. . . . As an expert on China, he was involved in forming our nation's policies on that continent both overtly and covertly.

Clearly Naniwa could not ask for a more positive assessment, and Wada followed up on this with a series of articles about Naniwa in a local newspaper. Here is one of Wada's summations of Naniwa's policies regarding Japan's role in Northeast China:

> Kawashima's idea in those days was to forge an independent state with a shining culture in Manchuria and Mongolia, which basically had no leadership, and to establish an ideal government there. . . . As a result, there would be an end to the chaos of world war. And with the development of this country in an ideal fashion, both Japan and China would benefit, assuring their futures.

Wada's position represents one extreme in analyses of Naniwa's contributions; detractors use the same evidence to reach other conclusions, labeling Naniwa an ultranationalistic betrayer of China, and worse. Floating about these different interpretations, though, are certain facts that are not under dispute. For example, it is certain that, more than once, Naniwa, acting as an agent of the Japanese government, supplied arms and expertise to those aiming to set up an independent state in Manchuria and Mongolia. It is also certain that Naniwa was given Yoshiko to raise by her father Prince Su, that he took the Manchu Yoshiko into his home, and that he became the single most important influence on her life. In Yoshiko's ideas and sorrows, Naniwa's hand is everywhere evident. He also certainly had his own plans for her upbringing, emphasizing her Manchu heritage and inculcating in her his own very special view of world affairs: "Manchuria is the very nerve center of East Asia's life and death struggle," he wrote. Evaluations of Kawashima Naniwa's achievements vary, but Wada and other commentators agree that this was no ordinary father.

Wada wonders at how a man of Naniwa's small stature—he was just five feet tall and weighed eighty-eight pounds—could have found the energy to go back and forth between Japan and China throughout his life. In 1875, when he was ten years old, his family moved from Nagano to Tokyo. Naniwa himself has conceded that he was a weakling when growing up. "By nature, I was a nervous boy, fragile as glass, affected by the slightest disturbance and very easily shattered." Bullied by his classmates and ashamed of his cowardice, he took the easy way out by skipping school. With nothing else to do, he passed his days lolling about in the woods or playing with the birds. One Sunday, a missionary's son happened to invite him to a service at the Russian Orthodox church in Tokyo, known as the Nikolai Cathedral, where he was exposed to Christianity for the first time. The sermon, which informed him about the omniscience of God, gave Naniwa a fright. "God can see into a person's good and bad sides," the sermon warned. "Even if you do something bad deep down in a hole where humans will not notice, it will be visible to God."

Sure now that his naughtiness was about to be exposed, Naniwa returned home in tears. His mother was disgusted by his sniveling since she had been promised a more radiant son. "You are a child made with the moon and the sun inside you," she once informed him. "It is said that long ago the mother of [the great warrior] Toyotomi Hideyoshi dreamed that the sun had entered her breast when she became pregnant with him. When I became pregnant with you, both the sun and the moon became a part of you. I dreamed one night that the moon and the sun appeared lined up side by side in back of the peak of Higashiyama. . . . So you must become more eminent than Hideyoshi." The mother lived to regret instilling in Naniwa such grand notions, especially when she was close to starvation and he abandoned her by sailing off to meet his destiny in Shanghai. His adopted daughter, Yoshiko, too would feel the devastating effects of Naniwa's determination.

Yet Naniwa's account of his own beginnings—his timidity as a child, his mother's outsized expectations—leads up to his larger message of personal grit and single-minded dedication that are essential to such life stories. Because spinelessness did not suit a young man carrying around inside him both the sun and moon, Naniwa determined to build himself up. Of samurai stock, he did not have to look far for lessons about stoicism and physical courage. He began to fight back against the bullies at school, but soon that challenge did not suffice. He next took to throwing himself in the frozen waters of a forest lake at night and under a waterfall, to test his endurance. "Absolutely naked, I sat in prayer beneath the waterfall and fought against the cold." Along with immersions in the freezing lake and the waterfall came other tests of his bravery, like facing down foxes. He climbed mountain peaks and meditated alone in remote temples.

Thus Naniwa was ready when China beckoned. He eventually joined the ranks of the Japanese men known *tairiku rōnin*—"continental adventurers"— who, for an assortment of reasons, made China the center of their lives. In 1919, an exasperated contributor to the *New York Times* described these Japanese in China as "those gentlemen who are conspicuous by the lack of wealth, occupation, and profession, but have a lot of big political ideas." Others would define their activities more charitably and see them as Japanese idealists who wanted to assist in lifting China out of backwardness. There were also those *rōnin* who were freelance operatives in China, seeking only to benefit their native country by enlarging Japan's presence there. Whatever their motives, these Japanese *rōnin* were a disorderly bunch who become known for things as diverse as aiding Chinese revolutionaries or leading murderous mobs to kill Chinese protesting against the Japanese in China or organizing drug-trafficking rings.

One also gets the idea that no matter what spurred the *rōnin* on, a small country like Japan cramped their style. China in those days was inspiring, deep, troubled, vast; a certain type of restless Japanese man was eager to be let loose there. Miyazaki Tōten, one of the best known of the China *rōnin*, provided critical help to revolutionary Sun Yat-sen in the struggle to overthrow the Qing dynasty and establish the Republic of China in 1912.

Miyazaki's autobiography is a rollicking mixture of high principles, high spirits, and profligacy.

> I imagined myself entering the Chinese continent in front of a host of Chinese, a general mounted on a white horse in white raiment. When I thought about this I would cry for joy and fortify myself with saké. At other times, when I dreamed of the trials of the Chinese revolution, the white-robed general would fall victim to the enemy assassin's dagger. And when I dreamed of tragedy I would end up heading for the geisha house singing a gambler's song. Ah, that white-robed general on his white horse, he was not the real me but a phantom of my high ambition, a make-believe figure. I couldn't get away from such illusion; I was not yet a stable, mature individual single-mindedly pursuing my purposes. Instead, at that point I was a make-believe figure, the phantom. Certainly I had high ideals, but I lacked the morality appropriate to them. Consequently spirit did not match with morality, and will wandered apart from resolve so that they could not proceed in tandem. I hadn't come to realize that half my life was made up of saké and sex.

As he toiled on behalf of Sun Yat-sen, Miyazaki neglected his wife and children back in Japan. More than one commentator has observed that while the Japanese *rōnin* took naturally to certain Chinese customs, the Chinese emphasis on family responsibility did not make a big impression on them.

*

During Naniwa's youth, conditions in China looked bleak to Japanese observers, with Western powers stripping China of resources and sovereignty. Not only were the Japanese angered by this treatment of another Asian country, they also feared that Japan might next be overtaken by the rapacious West. "Many in Asia were being increasingly dogged by the detestable pressure of the white race," Naniwa wrote of the period. "Many had already pretty much lost their independence under this occupation. Asian people had sunk so deep as to become their slaves, and only a few countries like China, Korea, and Japan remained free. Our indignation gave rise to the idea that we had to rally against this chaos. Japan was the first to promote the idea that, first of all, we must stop the ruin of China." As a statement of his intentions, this presents only one side of his ambitions, the side—emphasized by writers like Wada—that sought only the uplift of China. Less-sympathetic analysts emphasize Naniwa's other facets: there was also the Naniwa who believed that Japan had to establish itself in China before other powers seized everything.

With the resolve that he had shown sitting under waterfalls, Naniwa began a study of China. His birthplace was Matsumoto, which had once been an important town in Japan's old feudal regime, a history still remembered in the city's wonderful castle. Solid grounding in Chinese classics had been an essential element in the educational system of the old days, and there were centers of Chinese learning still functioning in Matsumoto when Naniwa was young. Then there were the Matsumoto natives lauded for bringing back news of China, in particular army general Fukushima Yasumasa, who eventually became Naniwa's patron. Fukushima had achieved the status of national hero, an icon of Japanese male might, when he set out alone on horseback in February 1892 and rode for sixteen months from Berlin to Vladivostok, collecting intelligence along the way.

Still, in the 1880s, when Naniwa was a student, learning Chinese was not a popular choice among Japanese youth; Western languages promised more opportunity to the ambitious. "Those were the days when everyone in Japan was trying to be very up-to-date," Naniwa wrote, "and you were disdained as a barbarian if you couldn't read Western works written horizontally across the page." When one of his relatives berated him for sticking to Chinese rather than French and English, Naniwa became enraged, as he often did: "Swallows and sparrows can't comprehend the dreams of the great phoenix. I won't step foot in this house again until I have succeeded."

Although Naniwa was not a star pupil at his language school, he immersed himself in Chinese history and culture. When his behavior became too disruptive, he was confined to his quarters or forced off the premises, again exhibiting the explosive nature more suited to a roving *rōnin* than an ordinary citizen of Japan. Naniwa claims that school authorities misjudged him. "I was the rowdiest of the rowdy but I never stooped to low behavior. I used to beat up the weaklings who frequented the pleasure quarters." Through it all, he remained stalwart in his refusal to learn English, registering a lifelong resistance to Western influences. "I'll show you how I can achieve much in life without knowing even the 'A' of 'AB.'"

Ignoring all advice, Naniwa left his language school without graduating and made plans to go to China. Before departing, he had to contend with his poverty-stricken parents, "blessed with many children"—they had ten—who begged him to stay at home in Tokyo. He was the oldest son, and traditions of filial piety demanded that he renounce his own desires for his family's sake, but Naniwa seems to have had little regard for this old-fashioned Confucian concept.

He scrounged around to collect his travel expenses and at last took a boat to Shanghai in September 1886, explaining that if he did not go now, his future would amount to nothing. He urged his virtually penniless parents to hold out for just a little while longer and in later writings at least had the decency to say that he had felt qualms about leaving his relatives at the dock. "Weeping blood in my heart," he took off anyway, dashing off some Chinese poetry to commemorate the occasion.

★

Once he reached China, Naniwa released the full might of a personality kept at a lower pitch in Japan. He had temper tantrums, which foiled his attempts to earn money, and was belligerent with strangers. His extreme restlessness and irascibility flourished in this foreign land still ruled by a Manchu dynasty; soon he was sporting Chinese clothes and a queue. In seeking to fulfill his ambitions, mere theories in Tokyo, he became involved in escapades possible only in a big country like China, where no one could keep an eye on him.

Following Naniwa's early activities in China gives a clear sense of what Yoshiko later faced under his tutelage. A conventional life had perhaps never been possible for her since family connections and world history made inevitable her involvement in Sino-Japanese politics. Others can imagine a more ordinary fate. "Yoshiko was outstandingly gifted," her niece once said. "She dropped out of high school, but she taught herself things like calligraphy, haiku, and painting. Everyone talked about how good she was in all of these. She was talented with her hands too—she did wonderful work in sewing, knitting, tea ceremony, flower arrangement. The food she cooked was delicious. If she had become a wife in an ordinary household, she'd have led a happy life and would now be surrounded by grandchildren."

Yoshiko never imagined such a rosy future, nor did she consider herself much of a catch: "If in the end the restoration of the Qing dynasty turns out to be a hopeless fantasy, I'll end up married to some lame or blind Japanese man."

Yoshiko's speculations fail to take into account the potency of Naniwa's personality, which so affected her choices. Family and history nudged Yoshiko in certain directions definitely, but so did Naniwa, who, despite repeated failures, had enough plans and energy to power the activities of the next generation.

Naniwa next went to Tianjin, where he found out that his promised job had been taken by someone else. Alone, abroad, and with little money, he could not bring himself to coax his would-be employer to reconsider his decision. Rather, he stormed off in one of his fits of temper ("I don't need your help!") from his only potential source of income. Modifying his itinerary, he took a long nighttime ride in a horse-drawn carriage to catch a ship that would take him back to Shanghai. Once at the dock, he discovered that the ship would not be going to Shanghai and that he had contracted malaria. Feverish from his illness, he managed to get to Shanghai at last, and there he became acquainted with a Japanese naval officer who was on a secret mission to investigate the state of China's coastal defenses. Derring-do despite malarial fevers was a point of pride for Naniwa, and we next find him aboard another ship accompanying the Japanese officer on his next assignment.

Once they disembarked, Naniwa's temper got in the way of the secret mission's success. He hired a local Chinese to guide him to the coast, and over lunch Naniwa requested a taste of the guide's bean-stuffed rice ball. Refused even though he offered one of his own rice balls in exchange, Naniwa became furious and knocked the Chinese guide to the ground. Back on his feet, the Chinese fled from this violent foreigner.

Naniwa finally found his way back to the ship on his own and was preparing supper with the crew when the Chinese guide appeared, this time accompanied by a vengeful, club-wielding gang. The whole crew under assault from the gang's clubs as well as rocks and bottles picked up along the way, the hotheaded Naniwa took out a shotgun and was about to shoot the attackers. Those fearing a mass slaughter urged him to restrain himself;

finally he went along with the idea that the better course of action was a quick escape from the area.

Although such stories are presented as jolly exploits, they show Naniwa unable to control himself even when a cool head was crucial. For anyone searching for evidence, these incidents can provide clues about why later, more complex projects ended in failure.

*

In Shanghai, Naniwa came in contact with other like-minded Japanese who met regularly to discuss the dire state of affairs in China. He came to accept the prevailing view that Russia, seeking to acquire a warm-water port in Manchuria, posed the greatest threat to Japan. If the Russians took over Manchuria, they would eventually advance further into China and go on to take over Korea too. It was only a matter of time before the Russians turned their attention to Japan. In Naniwa's view, Japan had to immediately establish a stronghold against the Russians in Manchuria; if the Japanese government could not rouse itself to act against this imminent danger, he was prepared to take over the job.

In 1889 Naniwa set off with two friends on a hike to Manchuria, where he intended to implement his ideas. Dressed like Chinese coolies from their ragged clothes to the bamboo shoulder poles the three comrades used to carry their possessions, they also brought along a pistol and a Japanese sword. Beautiful and ridiculous in Naniwa's later description, this scheme had them winning over the hearts and minds of the people, living alongside them in harmony, and raising pigs and sheep together. Moreover, Naniwa says he planned to convince the local bandit gangs to join his crusade, and together they would rise up to beat off the Russian threat by building a new Manchu-Mongol state. It was Naniwa's dream that the Japanese government would gradually join in to repel the Russians. Afterward, the people of Manchuria and Mongolia would reward these efforts by supporting a lasting Japanese presence in the region.

When Naniwa fell ill again, he urged his companions to carry out the mission without him. "You just leave me here and proceed on your own. Even though I may die here, you will fulfill my deepest wishes if you carry out my plan." Rejecting this plea, his friends decided to give up on creating an independent state for the time being. One member of the band returned to Japan because his father had died; the other left to prepare for study in France. Alone and ill, Naniwa at last headed back to Tokyo to convalesce. He vowed to fulfill his dreams at a later date.

*

In recounting these escapades, Naniwa strives to create a winning impression of a youth with a noble mission in mind. The mature Naniwa remained true to his original purpose, but his spontaneous, low-budget efforts gave way later to violent, government-funded assaults on Manchuria and Mongolia.

In his dream of expanding his operations, Naniwa got a big break in 1900 when—according to Naniwa—he single-handedly saved the Forbidden City from destruction. An antiforeign secret society known as the Boxers had been killing Chinese Christians and then moved on to Beijing, where they started murdering foreigners. Foreign troops were summoned to put an end to the Boxers' siege. When the German contingent threatened an assault on the Forbidden City, Naniwa was serving as Chinese translator for the Japanese forces in Beijing.

"Leave the Forbidden City to me!" was Naniwa's cry as he kept the Germans at bay and saved the palace, as well as the members of the Qing royal family and their entourage, who were trapped inside.

With this deed, Naniwa earned the gratitude of the imperial family and, in particular, of Prince Su, who was awed by Naniwa's professional abilities. Thus began that personal and political alliance between this Japanese man and the Manchu prince that would have far-reaching consequences. "Prince Su depended too much on Naniwa," the prince's great-granddaughter mused recently, looking back on the effects of this friendship on Chinese history and her own family. With Prince Su's patronage, Naniwa secured prominent posts in last-ditch reformist projects of the Qing dynasty. In a more lasting role, he became an important behind-the-scenes agent of the Japanese government, which publicly denied any involvement in Chinese affairs.

Those wondering about the character of the Japanese man entrusted with bringing up the Chinese child Yoshiko must also take an interest in his shifting attitude toward China and its people. As a young man, Naniwa had starry-eyed views about the relations between China and his native land: "The proper way for Japan and China to interact should not be based

Kawashima Naniwa and Prince Su   *Courtesy Hokari Kashio*

on capitalistic exploitation, nor on invasions by militarists, but rather their exchanges must be based on a humanism founded on brotherly love that is mutually beneficial."

But Naniwa's affection for China, where he had won the respect of powerful Manchu officials and made himself extremely useful, soured as time passed. He got into the habit of saying things like "China is like a wrecked car" or "[The Chinese people] are like sand, completely incapable of forming a strong union on their own."

Eventually his view of China settled into vituperative disdain. In 1928, he lost his temper in print and wrote, "I often say that Prince Su's family is like China in miniature; if you want to know China, just study them. Prince Su was a great person, rare among men in China, but his more than twenty children don't resemble him at all. It's ironic, but in their stupid vulgarity they are perfect examples of the Chinese mentality."

5
A NEW LIFE IN JAPAN

When I was thirteen I started to attend Atomi Girls School.
I was a gentle, one might even say frail, princess.

—KAWASHIMA YOSHIKO

O nce she became a celebrity, Kawashima Yoshiko avoided going into details in public about her life with Naniwa. Instead she was coy in her descriptions, getting her points across through innuendo. In her twenties, Yoshiko reviewed her youth for the Japanese women's magazine *Fujin kōron*, emphasizing her confused state after she was suddenly removed from her home in China and passed along to Kawashima Naniwa in Japan. She keeps it brief, but, again, her pathetic state is clear. "They took away my Chinese clothes and dressed me in a Japanese crepe robe and long vest. My hair was cut into a short Japanese style with bangs in front. . . . In those days the Japanese called Chinese 'Chinks' . . . and so I didn't have anyone to play with. But now when I look back on myself—though I know it's strange of me to say such a thing—I don't think that I was a hateful person."

Naniwa always maintained that Yoshiko's adjustment to Japan had gone smoothly. He liked to boast about how he had taken in a Chinese princess, whose father, a Manchu prince of the fallen Qing dynasty, had been his intimate friend, a blood brother really, with whom he had shared a fondness so deep that they had overcome differences of nationality, custom, language. He had aided this royal prince for much of his life, stood by his side in good fortune and painful exile.

Naniwa of course wanted to present himself as a benefactor, a builder of bridges between China and Japan. The adoption of Yoshiko fit nicely into this, for he could claim yet another act of magnanimity in leaving Prince Su with one less child to support; he would also be helping Yoshiko, who—in accordance with the belief that grew within him as he aged—would be blessed with the chance to grow up in clean and enlightened Japan rather than dirty, sleazy China. Over the years, Naniwa took in many more of Prince Su's children on a temporary basis, and in true colonialist's style, he bragged of his concern for their futures, how he enrolled them in Japanese schools and advised the boys in their choice of professions.

Prince Su's descendants, who eventually became involved in financial disputes with Naniwa and his heirs, have other explanations for Naniwa's willingness to take their family members into his home. They point out that Naniwa lived like a rich man in Japan though he did not have a job or income of his own, and depended upon the money he received from Prince Su for raising these children, as well as other funds that came his way because of his connection to the family. "Naniwa was loose about women and money," one commentator notes.

Yoshiko's distress under Naniwa's care emerged gradually, though looking back from the perspective of today, her pain seems inevitable. But today of course is not yesterday, when even royal children, and especially women, were expected to remain stoical in the face of any manner of personal catastrophe. Emotional collapse, violence, shredding a rival's clothing—these were not the stuff of behavioral primers of the time. But when such incidents reached the public eye, the newspapers strove to accommodate a curious public, especially when the person involved was a former Qing princess living in Japan. Throughout Yoshiko's life, her dramas received extensive coverage.

After her arrival, Yoshiko found herself under the supervision of Naniwa's wife, Fuku, whose mental health had worsened because of her husband's infidelities, his hot temper, and frequent absences. Fuku had been married off to Naniwa after one of his adventures in China, and though her parents had been put off by his ill-mannered behavior and had at first balked at the match, they eventually agreed to let their daughter marry this man they had sized up as frugal and serious, as well as rude and sixteen years her senior.

After their marriage Naniwa and Fuku had lived together in Beijing, enjoying the special privileges accorded those with close ties to the ruling dynasty. When the Qing dynasty fell, Naniwa still was occupied for a while in his schemes to bring about the dynasty's return, but for Fuku, the good times ended when they were ordered back to Tokyo. Her life with Naniwa became intolerable, and the neighbors still remember her mental problems;

Yoshiko in Japanese clothes

Courtesy Hokari Kashio

she left proof of her ferocious unhappiness when she scratched her face out of the official photographs taken while she was in China.

"Once Fuku was back in Japan," Naniwa's highly partisan biographer writes, in the bland tone he adopts for this woman's emotional collapse,

> the tensions she had been feeling quickly eased. She was extremely tired and took to her bed. Her fatigue fed upon her terrible sluggishness and attacked her without pause. . . . She also lacked any understanding of her husband's work and sometimes was very cold to him. Kawashima was very busy working for his independence movements and often would return home late. For days, he might be away from home. As his time away increased, his wife's criticisms multiplied, and she'd confront him with her complaints. . . . Wearied by his endeavors, bumping up against complex problems, Kawashima finally would start shouting, though he did not really mean it. There was no peace, and an increasingly fierce storm raged through their lives.

Although Yoshiko tended to skip over her early days in Japan, we can get some idea about how she was first received in Naniwa's home from the accounts of her niece Renko, who was six years younger. Renko was brought to Naniwa's home from China some years later and also became the focus of Fuku's attention. Renko paints a portrait of a mother figure whose personal misery fueled zealous cleanliness. As soon as Renko walked into Naniwa's house, Fuku took her to task for making a mess. "What are you doing? Your footprints are making marks on the tatami. Take off your socks and clean up those footprints." Fuku managed to collect herself enough to bring out a decent dinner—"You must be hungry after your long trip. Be sure to eat a lot"—but soon enough, she was back to irritation when she insisted that Renko, exhausted after her long trip, help with the dishes. "Cleaning up after a meal is a woman's job," Fuku announced. What followed was a detailed lesson in putting items away in just the right place. "Look at the way you've piled these things up! It's all wrong. Teacups and plates must be stacked separately. Otherwise they will fall over. You don't even know that?"

If Fuku was a trial to the children in the house, then Naniwa presented them with other problems as the years passed. He had left for China for the first time in 1886, with dreams of fomenting those great changes in China, establishing a new regime in the Northeast and thereby bringing great benefit to his homeland. He had been the trusted secret liaison between the Japanese government and Manchu royalists seeking to return to power. Over the years, these and other endeavors decisively and publicly failed. Once at the forefront of the "independence" movement in Manchuria and Mongolia, he was gradually tossed aside by Japanese officials, who no longer relied on the services of amateurs like him. It has been speculated that Naniwa "lost his balance" after his failed attempts to set up a Japanese-backed regime in Manchuria and Mongolia.

Naniwa also eventually lost his hearing, and deafness made him even more ill-tempered and dependent upon others. Harada Tomohiko, a young relative, offers this portrait of Naniwa in retirement:

> In those days, right-wing hotheads set the tone in Kawashima's house. . . . Weirdos and strange China *rōnin* connected to [the ultranationalist group] Gen'yōsha infested the place. The live-in students and the rest saw themselves as heroic types in training for great deeds. The world of these hotheads seemed idiotic to me, but from their point of view I was just some heretic.

In addition, this relative could not find much good to say about his private moments with Naniwa:

I used to get emergency telegrams from Naniwa to come and help him with something. In those days only inns or businesses or rich people had phones. Even if people lived close to each other, forty or fifty minutes away, they'd send a telegram when they wanted something.

"Now what?" I'd ask myself and go over.

You couldn't say it was anything very important. He'd ask me to prepare a batch of ink for him or straighten out the calligraphy paper. When Naniwa was in a cheerful mood, he could be a really good old guy. He'd narrow his eyes, let out with a good laugh, and tell some stories. He didn't really have many interesting stories, and mostly he gave little lectures. As I said before, he couldn't hear, and so I'd have to write down my answers or anything else I wanted to say. It was a real pain.

While I was writing, he would warn me about various things: "Today's Tokyo Imperial University is a den of socialists—a place where lots of germs all get together. Don't you dare associate with them."

"Yes, yes," I'd say, looking at him meekly.

"And don't drink any liquor. Your father used to be an interesting person, but alcohol ruined him. Don't fall into the same trap."

Naniwa didn't like to drink liquor. After a few drinks his face would become bright red.

6

MANCHU PRINCE, JAPANESE WIFE

The Kwantung Army hoped that Pujie would marry a Japanese girl
for the sake of friendship between the two countries. . . . Clearly they
intended to bring Pujie completely under their control.

—PUYI

Around this point in descriptions of Yoshiko's childhood, Saga Hiro is
often brought in for comparison. It is easy to see why. From a noble
family, Hiro was born in Tokyo in 1914, and so she was about seven
years younger than Yoshiko. Unlike Yoshiko, she did not become known for
dressing like a man, gain a reputation as a spy, or get herself executed as the
sun was coming up. But both faced dislocation and danger; their futures
were settled by powerful males, who gave no thought to their welfare.

Yoshiko, a Manchu by birth, was shipped off to Japan as a child; Hiro was
a Japanese forced into a marriage with a Manchu prince and then sent to live
in Manchuria. The contrast is neat. For both women, there were language
problems, foreign customs to be taken in, adjustments to food and weather.
And both had political issues to consider: Yoshiko kept up her loyalty to the
Manchu cause from the start, spurred on by Naniwa. Hiro seems to have
taken more time to sort out her loyalties, though, finally, she lived out her
life in China.

Yet the similarities between the two women go only so far. The Manchu
Yoshiko had a difficult time from early on, wrenched from her father's mansion in Beijing to exile in Lushun and then on to a life in Japan, where she
was distant from everything familiar. Spared such experiences, the Japanese
Hiro spent her youth on a Tokyo estate with her family, who were related to
the Japanese emperor. The two women were opposites also when it came to
their manners. Yoshiko spoke her mind too often, ranting about both petty

Marriage of Saga Hiro and Aisin Gioro Pujie, 1937

Courtesy Fukunaga Kosei

and consequential matters. Restraint rarely eluded Hiro, and upon being suddenly ordered to marry a Manchu prince, she obeyed: "I will leave the matter to you," she dutifully told her family. One unstable and promiscuous, the other a marvel of propriety and strength, they both took part in momentous events far from home.

The writings of the two women also show the divergent impressions each wished to make on the public. Yoshiko can be bitter in her descriptions of her personal and political predicament. She was used, abused, discarded, a victim of epic connivance, and won't let anyone forget it. Saga Hiro, on the other hand, uses her autobiography, *Vicissitudes of a Princess*, to create a more refined atmosphere, feeding her readers' fascination for the upper crust by providing a close-up view of royalty in Japan and Manchuria. She is assisted by rich material, which includes her dissection of the formal kowtow she was obliged to perform while pregnant and in high heels (kneel three times, touch forehead to floor nine times). In such passages, Hiro manages to transform her experiences into a riveting romance about the years with her beloved prince in a far-off land, culminating in her hair-raising flight to safety after the war.

But then again, after insisting that the two princesses are quite different, we must return to their similarities. In fact Kawashima Yoshiko and Saga Hiro have both been offered up again and again, to perform the same role for the Chinese and Japanese: the two life stories have enough soap opera elements to keep the focus on their emotional highs and lows rather than on the hell of war, which sent these women off to god-knows-where in the first place.

Hiro's appeal to her public is more straightforward than Yoshiko's, because Hiro was a woman who did her duty. She was bred to become a proper and aristocratic Japanese wife. As a young woman she showed some pluck in deciding to put off marriage and continue her studies in Western painting. Instructed by a well-known artist, she enjoyed the Bohemian atmosphere at his painting school. Yet Hiro was no rebel and embraced the conventions of her class. She could not have expected to pursue her artistic ambitions any longer than it took to get her married off into a Japanese family with a lineage comparable to her own.

Hiro may have been able to stall her parents' plans for her marriage for a little while, but she did not stand a chance when the Japanese army stepped in. One day in 1936, when Hiro thought she was going to attend a performance of Kabuki with her mother and grandmother, a Japanese general came to pay her family a visit at their Tokyo home. Apparently, the general had just the man for her—the Manchu prince Pujie, who was the younger brother of Emperor Puyi. For their enterprise in Manchuria, the Japanese wanted to emphasize the union of the Japanese and Manchus by this marriage of the Japanese Hiro and a Manchu royal. Her grandmother wept and vowed to block the army's plans, but in the end, the family had to accede to their demands.

"We refused the offer that had been made," Hiro wrote later. "But that did not put an end to it. Behind the proposal lurked the Kwantung Army, which in those days took pride in its great power."

According to the sweet tale, officers from the Kwantung Army, Japan's military force in Manchuria, selected Saga Hiro from a pile of photographs of well-born Japanese women and urged Pujie to marry her. Here's the romance again, for Pujie, who was studying at Japan's Army Academy and spoke Japanese, happened to be a fan of Takarazuka, Japan's all-female drama troupe; he saw a resemblance between the photo of Saga Hiro and one of his favorite stars. That was all it took to set up the first meeting between Pujie and Hiro at her parents' Tokyo home.

Their love story remains perfect for mass-market distribution, especially since it is usually stripped of troubling moral issues like Pujie's willingness to go along with the Japanese military and his prominent public role in the sham regime the Japanese set up in Manchuria. Instead, the couple's romance has been shaped to invite, and get, the tears that flow with each dramatization. Years later, with wars, a lengthy prison stay, and tragedies behind him, Pujie still savored that moment when he first met his future wife:

> Unexpectedly, for both of us it was love at first sight, and I agreed to make Saga Hiro my wife. At the start, this was a marriage that the Kwantung Army had arranged on its own, but it turned into a marriage in which a husband and wife shared a deep love for each other and many hardships, joy, and sadness. Over the years, we two would frequently talk about who had been responsible for bringing us together as a married couple, inseparable for our entire lives. In any event, because we were brought together, there is no denying that she brought me countless days of happiness. Nor can I forget that the first half of my life, with its many vicissitudes, brought her immense pain.

7
SCHOOL DAYS

In this world there are many women who are not allowed to be free, and many women who don't know what freedom is. Even when such women follow a fated path chosen by others and become unhappy, they must themselves take responsibility for what happens.

—MURAMATSU SHŌFŪ

Kawashima Yoshiko had trouble adjusting to her new home in Japan, and when she did not respond well, she could silence anyone who had thought that this child could be wrenched from her family against her will at age eight without psychological damage. She lived first in Naniwa's spacious Tokyo home with its extensive grounds—no Qing mansion, but splendid by most standards, especially for an owner without a certifiable source of income. "Just tell me, where did he get all that cash?" was the battle cry of Prince Su's family in years to come. Two hundred cherry trees bloomed by the stone pillars out front, and there was so much land that it was "quite a walk" to the front door.

Once established inside her new residence, Yoshiko looked as if she definitely belonged elsewhere. A visitor was struck by her oddness—she wore a satin top and Japanese-style pleated trousers of purple damask, with a big ribbon stuck on. She went to her Japanese school in this outfit and definitely stood out among the other students all dressed in navy serge. "What country are you from?" Yoshiko was asked, and in her response, she cleverly sidestepped what would be her lifelong problem of figuring out whether she belonged to China or Japan: "I came from inside my mother's stomach."

Naniwa soon brought Akabane Matsue into the household as a tutor since Yoshiko needed to learn Japanese customs and language in a hurry. During her childhood and after, Yoshiko would be able to look to only this woman for maternal affection. "The only person who will break down with tears of grief when she hears that I have died," Yoshiko wrote shortly before her execution, "who will truly mourn that I am gone, is Mother Akabane." Akabane was a daring character for those times, traveling on her own to New York City, where she studied at Columbia University. Back in Japan, she dedicated herself to assisting foreign students.

Quick to see that Yoshiko presented her with a new and challenging cause, Akabane lived in Naniwa's house and shared a room with her student. There was no doubt in Akabane's mind that Yoshiko was exceptional, sensitive, and wise beyond her years.

> On a day when I knew that I had to scold her about something she'd done, I waited for her to return from school. Perhaps she could tell what was coming from the expression on my face because she avoided me until bedtime, and I put off saying anything to her. I'll give her a talking-to tomorrow morning, I thought, and went to sleep.
>
> The next morning when I'd awakened she was sitting very straight on the floor in her nightclothes waiting for me to wake up.
>
> Then she looked at me and apologized. "Sensei, please forgive me."
>
> That really surprised me.

Naniwa, Yoshiko, and her family members   *Courtesy Hokari Kashio*

This sensitive pupil continued to haunt Akabane, who, long after leaving Naniwa's employ, claimed deep insight into Yoshiko's character. Her insistence upon the engaging nature of the young girl she always addressed as "Princess" continued even after Yoshiko's more antisocial traits grabbed everyone's attention. Indeed, in the months that preceded Yoshiko's execution, when there was still hope that she would be spared, Akabane wore herself out trying to obtain a pardon. She collapsed when she learned about Yoshiko's death, and later on, still mourning, she became a chaplain to death row prisoners.

*

In 1921, when she was fourteen, Yoshiko moved again, this time because of Naniwa's sputtering career as nation builder in Manchuria. Still hoping to engineer another plot, Naniwa tried to earn money in oil field development and next decided to use the excellent water from his birthplace to make "Princess Z Champagne Cider." To this day, Yoshiko's Chinese family rages that these unsuccessful ventures were funded by money that rightly belonged to Prince Su.

Naniwa moved back to his hometown in Matsumoto, where he had much time to reflect upon his depleted finances and his thwarted insurgencies. One can say that he returned to a place well suited to contemplation. Surrounded by the Japan Alps, Matsumoto offers much country charm, far removed from the roar of Tokyo. The genuine medieval castle, one of the few extant in Japan, is visible at many spots around town—up the hill, down on the plains, from a distant Shinto shrine, and up close, always magnificent against the sky at any time of day.

With remnants of Japan's feudal past on display, Matsumoto remains very much a provincial city. Even today, the arrival of a Chinese princess relocated to Japan would seriously jar the residents; almost a century ago, when Yoshiko moved in, she must have caused a stir.

Yoshiko was left to make the adjustment to another new city more or less on her own, for Naniwa's wife, Fuku, had left the house, unconsoled by the pleasures of raising a daughter and undone by her husband's absences and philandering. Fuku would return from time to time, but she went to live with her own family within three years of Yoshiko's arrival in Japan, leaving Naniwa as Yoshiko's sole guardian.

Though there were many people living in the house, visitors, and an ever-replenishing supply of Naniwa's young disciples, Yoshiko spent much of the time by herself. When she did go out, she showed signs of a child who lacked parental supervision and spent too much time with the crude young men hanging around Naniwa. In their comments, contemporaries quickly move from descriptions of her beauty to shock at her headstrong, tomboyish behavior. Such descriptions have usually been offered decades after she achieved renown as an undercover agent in men's clothes, and so these memories may have been edited to suit what she would become. But then again, perhaps these acquaintances from her youth remember accurately that, even back then, Yoshiko took to boys' ways.

At least it can be said that, either from sadness or an inherent obstreperousness, Yoshiko sought notice in a household where schemes about such things as how to get control of Manchuria were the most acceptable topics of conversation. One classmate remembers being shocked by Yoshiko's spoken Japanese, for she often used the sort of rough language reserved for men. "Two student teachers, from the school next door, always worked at our elementary school," one of her female classmates remembered, "and they'd join us at the playground. We'd respectfully address them as 'Sensei,' but Yoshiko would call out to them with 'Hey, you.'" This could have reflected the sort of Japanese Yoshiko heard in Naniwa's home, which was full of his ill-mannered young male disciples, all eager to follow his footsteps to China. In picking up a new language, Yoshiko may simply have been mimicking their insolent style. Still, since she heard enough examples of female Japanese elsewhere and was surely corrected when she used the male style, her early preference for male Japanese seems noteworthy.

"She would one moment look so beautiful," another contemporary recalls, "with the mouth like a pomegranate flower and her pearly teeth, but then the next moment she would let out with a really incredible sound that was like a croaking toad. Everyone passing by turned around to see what had happened. Even as a young child I wondered about these boyish habits of hers, which did not go well with her lovely appearance and was most unbecoming of a princess."

Then again, a childhood acquaintance remembers Yoshiko as beautiful as a doll, with an aristocratic bearing, a silky white complexion dotted with freckles, and shiny, braided black hair parted down the middle. As befitted her royal station, she was carried to school on the back of a chubby servant when it rained or snowed. "It did not look like an easy way to get to class." In addition, she had two cars at her disposal and a driver.

★

Around Matsumoto, Yoshiko was known as Naniwa's "adopted daughter," but she was not legally a member of his family since he never entered her name into his family register—an omission that later became a life-and-death issue for her. In the years since then, there has been much speculation about why Yoshiko's name was never entered in the register; the most credible guess has Naniwa unwilling to transform Yoshiko into an official Japanese citizen, which registry entry would have achieved, since he wanted her to remain a Manchu and a symbol of the Qing resurgence. Still, his actual reasons remain unknown.

With no legal status in Japan, she could not be officially enrolled by public school authorities, who got around that by allowing her to attend school as an auditor. Feeling herself more a guest than an ordinary student, she did not take her classes seriously, and others remember her disobedient behavior. "It was as if a lustrous crane had alighted upon a rubbish heap." Never the pliant, eager-to-please newcomer, she went to Matsumoto Girls High School on her horse—which she claimed was a descendant of Napoléon's favorite mount—and thereby brought Manchu warrior traditions to the streets of Matsumoto. One of her classmates never forgot her first impression of the school's newest student.

> She really stood out. Think of it—she came to school on a horse! The first time I saw Yoshiko she was dismounting. In those days, not many people rode horses. The Fiftieth Regiment [stationed in Matsumoto] was made up of infantry, and only important officials like the battalion commander or the company commander rode horseback. The only woman who rode horseback was Yoshiko. She'd arrive in her riding clothes on her auburn horse. *Ta-ta-ta-ta*, you could hear the sound as she came riding in, an indescribably wonderful sight.

High school student Yoshiko with her horse

Courtesy Hokari Kashio

Although Yoshiko was criticized for her misconduct, some classmates remember her as an isolated figure, off by herself and humming Chinese songs. "My clowning," she wrote in a letter, "ruins the study time of the other students. But I am (and my enemies will laugh at this), in my heart, not enjoying myself at all." After a while, she refused to attend Asian history class because of the Japanese teacher's denigrating remarks about China. Another teacher discovered her drinking tea with the janitor when she should have been in class. "The teacher is so insulting," Yoshiko explained. "That really bothers me."

The gloom deepened when her father died in Lushun in 1922, followed immediately by the death of her mother. There are accounts that have the mother committing suicide in her grief over her husband's death, while others state that she was pregnant with her eleventh child at the time Prince Su became ill. Busy nursing her husband, she took medicine to induce abortion, and this eventually killed her.

Naniwa and Yoshiko rushed to Lushun for Prince Su's funeral, a solemn, momentous occasion, and an enormous blow to the entire Qing restoration movement. Without the prince's financial and emotional support, the Manchus could not easily contemplate a return to power. Hundreds of mourners dressed in white gathered in the prince's Lushun home. The funeral procession went along the streets at such a slow and stately pace that an entire day passed before the last vehicle reached the station, where the coffin was transported to Beijing for burial. Many came to pay their respects along the way, and as his daughter Jin Moyu wrote, "Even though the Qing dynasty was no more, the funeral rituals were carried out as befit Prince Su of the Qing."

In the aftermath, Naniwa claimed to have been made head of the household in accordance with the prince's will, and this started the squabbles over his handling of the family's assets. One of Prince Su's sons argues that Naniwa, in fact snatching these powers without any sanction from the prince, was again eager to maintain his ties to the family, who remained a source of funds for him.

Front and center in the disputes was a market in Dalian that had been rented, with the help of Naniwa and the Japanese military, on behalf of Prince Su, to provide an income for his large family. Merchants rented stalls and hawked mostly used wares—carpenter's tools, soiled leopard skins, faded Chinese clothes, and the like. The place had been nicknamed "Thieves Market," since it was said that burgled goods were put on sale there almost immediately. The rents from this enterprise made for a lucrative investment, and Prince Su's numerous relatives came to depend on the income, which was dispensed by Naniwa. Eventually the prince's family charged him with bungling and outright criminality, forged documents, among other outrages. Although Naniwa later said that the family would have starved without his astute management of their property, Prince Su's descendants considered Naniwa and his cohorts a pack of looters.

The loss of both her parents was devastating to Yoshiko, and she expressed her feelings in a frequently quoted poem: "I have a home but cannot return there. I have tears but cannot speak about them." She remained in China for some time to participate in the death ceremonies, but when she returned to Matsumoto, she was refused readmission to her school. There had been complaints about Yoshiko's behavior in class and her rough, masculine language. She was considered "disruptive to order" and a bad influence on the others. The horse got blamed too, for it had caused a commotion one day after breaking free of the cherry tree where it had been tied.

Officially, Yoshiko's reenrollment was denied by the new school principal, who had been installed while Yoshiko was away. He insisted that she go through the required application procedures before registering again, procedures the former school head had brushed aside. In her memoirs, Yoshiko writes that the school refused her because she had not been entered into Naniwa's family register.

Upon hearing of the school's demand for proper procedures, Naniwa, who had been worn down by the shock of Prince Su's death, showed that he still had strength enough to have a fit. "That's just a roundabout way of saying that they won't let a Chinese enroll in the school. Since there's such an obstinate principal in charge of the school, I'm the one who's going to refuse to allow you to attend." As often happened in Naniwa's life, his temper vaporized all sensible options, leaving him with little else but the satisfaction of having told everyone off.

At the same time, journalists, who already had grudges against the new principal, enthusiastically attacked him over his decision. "Uncivilized Principal of Girls' High School in Matsumoto, Nagano Prefecture, Refuses Entry to Foreigner" went one headline in a newspaper from faraway Tokyo. Though this marked Yoshiko's debut as the focus of media attention, the principal did not relent. In fact he later wrote that by refusing her, he had "rid the school of a nuisance without getting my hands dirty."

In the end, Naniwa decided to educate Yoshiko at home. This saved her from the stubborn principal but also meant that she was stuck in the house all day. The deaf Naniwa could also make use of her as a secretary, having her record conversations he could not hear himself. Along the way, he inculcated into Yoshiko the ideas of "discipline and stoicism," concepts important in achieving independence for Manchuria but not so obviously essential to this troubled teenager's development.

*

It's important to pause here, to imagine Yoshiko being tutored alone in her adoptive father's home by Matsumoto's hot springs. These were the days she spent acquiring her paltry formal education, but it was also a period that molded her character. Until this point, Yoshiko had only been an unfortunate minor character in the much larger catastrophe then developing between Japan and China. Her fate was pitiable but not unheard of. Throughout history, princesses and their ilk had been bartered away at the convenience of their male family members, swept off forever because of the larger political aims their sacrifices served.

Under Naniwa's tutelage, Yoshiko acquired a sense of purpose that would set her apart from the usual female pawn. She learned to take pride in her Manchu heritage, in particular her royal lineage, and decided to devote herself to the aid of her fellow Manchus, who had experienced persecution and impoverishment after the fall of the Qing. In that way, she would take up their cause where her birth father Prince Su had left off.

Yoshiko grasped the notion of her special destiny with enthusiasm, though her meager education, cut short early, left her susceptible to the influence of others' ideas: certainly she lacked a deep understanding of history or of the contemporary conflicts that would soon feature her participation. At a very young age, according to her autobiography, she envisioned herself as the Manchu's Joan of Arc. "That day on the way home from school I bought *The Story of Joan of Arc* and stayed up until ten o'clock at night reading the whole thing. As I was reading, I kept thinking, 'I also want to become Joan of Arc.' . . . The next day I went to school rubbing my sleepy eyes and started acting like Joan of Arc, telling everyone things like, 'If I had three thousand soldiers, I'd take China.'"

While such quixotic dreams are usually just the stuff of childhood, they took hold of Yoshiko and endured. Her isolation in a foreign country surely gave her much time to strengthen such beliefs, but there was also Naniwa, who had his own reasons for encouraging this Manchu princess in her vision of herself as liberator of her people.

In addition, Yoshiko always stands out because of her desire to keep others informed about each new turn in her story. Her early experiments in going public with her secrets were clumsy but show the flair for publicity that she would later put to good use.

In the appeals she began to issue from inside Naniwa's home, Yoshiko started out small, choosing to express her true feelings to a young family tutor. She wrote him lugubrious letters, sometimes calling herself, in English, "Little Dove" or "Your Servant"; she called the tutor "White Rose," and

Naniwa's house was "Cold Home." Trapped and alone, she sought solace in the countryside. "Tonight is a dark night," she wrote. "A child who has lost her parents wants to see them but cannot even see their shadows. It is a dark night. It won't protect me. It won't console my sad, lonely heart." In the darkness of that night, she also saw the other facts clearly.

> Sacrifice! I am a sacrifice, as I told you the other day! Did you understand? I am the sacrifice of Prince Su's whole family. I have come here as their substitute. For the sake of my younger brothers. "Instead of just having me look after your children, send me a daughter to keep for myself" [Naniwa told my father,] and with those words, my whole future was ruined.

Yoshiko detailed her other complaints, and these were more alarming. When recounting incidents of Naniwa's physical assaults, she did not surprise the tutor, who was well aware of the adoptive father's violent temper. In fact, the tutor had interceded on those occasions when Naniwa had gone after Yoshiko with a shovel. That's why she did not hesitate to tell him about the latest episode.

> I was hit today too. I just serve as an outlet for his anger. When he gets angry at others, he has gotten into the habit of hitting me. Sometime in the future I'll definitely have a chance to show you where he hit me. This is certainly not something he's doing to further my education. If it were a question of my education, and I did something wrong, all he'd have to do is tell me about it, and I'd understand.

Naniwa's supporters try to justify his behavior, but they only make things worse. "This 'patriot' had entered his old age, having lost a lifetime's worth of dreams. His emotions got the best of him, and it seems so very human that he would thrash that young girl, who was a keepsake from his great friend."

Yoshiko supplies her own view of the situation:

> They won't let go of me for even a second. They keep me near them. They are always really worried that I will run away. They forced me to come here [to Japan] and say that they can't very well send me back. They worry that this child, who has grown big, knows what they have done. They know that

I am against them. They are afraid that I will tell the world about what's happened. They think that I will definitely say bad things about them if I leave the house. So they don't let me talk to anyone. . . . I don't have anyone who is on my side in the whole world. . . .

If suicide is a shame to my parents, then I will go back to China. That would be a big relief to me. I'd like to tell them that I will kill myself if they don't send me back, but they wouldn't believe me and probably wouldn't send me back anyway.

Even if I returned to China, I can't speak the language. I have no parents, no siblings.

8

THE BEAUTY IN MEN'S CLOTHING

I had the best of intentions and wrote the novel to help her out.

—MURAMATSU SHŌFŪ

Long afterward, the writer Muramatsu Shōfū often talked about the shocking encounter. In 1954, nine years after Japan's defeat in the war, he visited a Tokyo dance hall with some friends. Although he had not stepped into that particular establishment for some time, upon entering he was, as always, cheered by the lively goings-on. By then, Shōfū was about sixty-five, well-known for his novels, travelogues, and sexual escapades, many spiced up with a racy mix of Japan and China. More than two decades before, he had caused a stir with his best-selling novel *The Beauty in Men's Clothing*, which was based on Kawashima Yoshiko's life. Shōfū had long been a habitué of dance halls, and that night he followed his usual practice in picking out a partner. With the casual air he had perfected over the years, he ambled toward the back of the hall where his potential women partners had collected. He had his hands in his pockets as he walked by and finally made his choice.

Shōfū next went back to his seat, but a stranger approached, calling out his name. The man, about forty, portly, with a gleam in his eyes, addressed Shōfū in a rough and drunken manner.

"I was with Kawashima Yoshiko in China. I want to have a word with you about her."

Hoping to avoid trouble, Shōfū aimed for graciousness. "Oh, so you knew Kawashima Yoshiko? Then I also have some things I'd like to talk to you about." He next found himself in the stranger's grip, led to a more secluded section of the dance hall like a criminal under arrest.

Although the man's best days were behind him, Shōfū could see that nine years back, when this stranger had known Yoshiko, he would have been attractive enough to meet her standards. The stranger said that he'd been living in China with Yoshiko at the time of Japan's defeat, and that they'd also been together during their arrests and trials.

"So tell me, what do you think of Kawashima Yoshiko?" the man belligerently inquired. Shōfū had only begun to answer when the man exploded with a shout, "You killed Kawashima Yoshiko!"

Though Shōfū was taken aback, this was not the first time he had been blamed for Yoshiko's death. When he had learned of her execution, he'd been shocked, but, after thinking about the matter further, he realized that Yoshiko had never been the type destined to die peacefully on her futon. He also believed that she would have preferred execution to facing the denunciations of her wartime activities that would surely have engulfed her postwar.

But then, about a year after Yoshiko's death, a Japanese returning from China had brought Shōfū some disturbing news: scenes from his novel *The Beauty in Men's Clothing* had been taken as fact by the Chinese judges at her trial and used to convict Yoshiko of treason. As a result, the Chinese generally believed that Shōfū's novel had caused her death. Though upset for a time, Shōfū told himself that this might be mere rumor and pushed the matter from his mind.

Now here, once again, came the same accusation in the Tokyo dance hall and this time from a more persistent informant. Overcome by astonishment and guilt, Shōfū felt impelled to explain to the stranger how he had come to write *The Beauty in Men's Clothing*. "I had been interested in Kawashima Yoshiko for a long time, but I didn't meet her until the Shanghai Incident in 1932. That's when I agreed to write a novel about her." In the 1930s, the Japanese military imposed strict censorship on all publications, and so, he explained, he had not been able to write about Yoshiko's activities as he had wished. Under the circumstances, he had to take liberties with the facts, and, sometimes aided by Yoshiko, he made up sensational undercover assignments she had supposedly carried out in order to improve upon the real story.

"So you can say that *The Beauty in Men's Clothing* was a collaborative work by Kawashima Yoshiko and myself."

Readers of *The Beauty in Men's Clothing*, Shōfū claimed, were not supposed to be so convinced by his imaginings that they mistook the novel's
fictional heroine for the real thing. To Yoshiko's misfortune, undiscriminat-
ing readers included the Chinese judges at her trial.

*

Muramatsu Shōfū was one of those writers whose stamina attests to the
amazingly robust constitutions of some Japanese literary figures. How do
they do it? He sustained a prolific literary output year after year despite a
private life that was, at the very least, exhausting. Bravura sexual dramas,
financial reverses, international intrigue—the works. In his youth, Shōfū
earned a reputation for fiction on Japanese themes, with an emphasis on the
passionate aspects.

"When it comes to historical fiction, there's always Mori Ōgai," an editor told him, referring to one of Japan's most esteemed authors. "But there's
nothing sexy in Ōgai. Your works are meticulously documented, the writing
is tight, and there's a lot of sex. So I think you're better than Ōgai."

Shōfū's connection to Kawashima Yoshiko can be traced back to the
time when he decided to move beyond the pleasure quarters of Japan and
investigate China. His inspiration was another esteemed writer, Akutagawa
Ryūnosuke, who had traveled to China on a journalism assignment in
1921 during a period of profound intellectual and political upheaval there.
Though Akutagawa had been physically done in over the course of this visit
(he was hospitalized twice), he was moved by China's troubled situation.
Akutagawa's impressions of China were mixed: "The specialties of this place
are new ideas and typhoid."

But Akutagawa had been in a more positive mood the day he inspired Shōfū
to visit Shanghai. "Shanghai has everything," Akutagawa effused. "Can you
imagine what a triangular room looks like? You can't, can you? In Shanghai
triangular rooms are nothing special. That's what Shanghai is like." For Shōfū,
the triangular room held out promises of experiences impossible within the
four bland corners of a Japanese interior. Shōfū's instincts proved correct, for
he found bliss in Chinese establishments, triangular and otherwise, that he
never matched in Tokyo. Shōfū's attachment to Shanghai—encompassing his
love affairs, his nightlife expertise, his steamy writings about his experiences—
came to far exceed that of Akutagawa or any other ordinary visitor.

Shōfū says that he met Yoshiko after hurrying to Shanghai in early 1932, just as the Japanese launched an assault on the city. This became known as the Shanghai Incident, which was a battle between Japanese and Chinese troops that would result in a great loss of lives on both sides. It was preliminary to the outbreak of the full-scale war between the two countries in 1937.

"Why on earth did I go rushing off all the way from Tokyo to land smack in the middle of this war in Shanghai?" Shōfū wrote later, defending this decision.

Of course, I had not been sent by the military. I just went on my own. People of today would probably find this strange, but those who knew me in those days would not have found anything strange about it. Since around 1923, when I started to take an interest in China, and in the ten years that followed, I've made trips to China often. In one year, I've even gone two or three times, and so I've gone to China sixteen or seventeen times. But in all those many visits I've never been north of the Yangtze River. . . . My trips to China have been limited to the area around Shanghai, or rather you'd have to say that they've been limited to Shanghai itself.

I've come to love Shanghai so much that I can hardly stand it. . . . For me, Shanghai is my second home.

In my beloved Shanghai, a war broke out between the Chinese and Japanese armies. I just couldn't sit still, and that's why I took off for Shanghai the day after I heard about the military attack.

Once in Shanghai, Shōfū found himself involved in a situation quite unlike the romantic hullabaloos that were his usual fare. Suddenly thrust into the middle of a major international conflict, he explains, he was called upon to arrange for an end to the fighting single-handedly. One senses that, from the start, he knew himself unworthy of this task.

What follows is Shōfū's description of his first encounter with Yoshiko, a tale that is probably more or less accurate. Shōfū's factual accounts of his activities can veer off into fiction, since his professional habits allow him to chuck the truth any time the narrative drags. According to Shōfū, a Chinese acquaintance asked him to intercede with the Japanese military on behalf of the Chinese army, which sought a cease-fire. Its request had not been heeded by Japanese officials. Eager to save Shanghai from further bombardment, Shōfū immediately phoned Japanese military headquarters.

"It's a very important matter and can't be discussed on the phone. I want to see you right away."

Japanese major Tanaka Ryūkichi agreed to meet him and, as a further favor, volunteered to send a car and driver to pick him up. Shōfū reports that both arrived within the promised thirty minutes. It was then that he first encountered Yoshiko, who was already known for her masculine style of dressing.

> The driver was a handsome, stylishly dressed youth wearing a banded standing collar and a blue woolen cap, similar to the kind students wear, with a splendid gold-braided insignia. He had deep-black eyes, a well-shaped nose, and charming mouth, and his face was the color of a white peony petal. I had sometimes seen such good-looking, aristocratic young men in China, but this lad was incomparably beautiful. . . .
>
> When I got inside the car, the good-looking fellow turned to look at me from behind the steering wheel. "Muramatsu-san, I'm Kawashima."
>
> "Oh—is that so?" I was more than a little surprised since I had not dreamed that I would now meet this famous person.

This boyish Kawashima Yoshiko drove Shōfū to his meeting with Major Tanaka, her current lover. At the time Shōfū did not know that Tanaka and Kawashima would be held responsible for fomenting the battle in progress on Shanghai's streets.

Shōfū presented his case to Tanaka regarding a cessation of the fighting, but Tanaka mocked the entire scheme and immediately turned him down.

"You're a writer, so you're for peace," Tanaka told him. "I indulge you because of your literary interests. But you don't understand Sino-Japanese relations. Military force is all we have to get control of this continent. Unless China is unified by us Japanese, Japan's very existence will be endangered. People like you go around making noises about Sino-Japanese friendship or about how Chinese and Japanese are brothers because we share the same culture and come from the same racial stock, but let me tell you, you're dreaming. Around here only brute force accomplishes anything. . . . This is between us, but look at what's happening around here now. You have no idea how much I have worked to bring things to the point where a war is about to start. I've been in Shanghai for two years, and all I've done is plan for a war."

Having dismissed Shōfū's diplomatic efforts, Major Tanaka came up with a suggestion that would make better use of his guest's talents. Shifting the topic to Yoshiko, Tanaka said, "Why don't you stop running around with this ridiculous plan of yours and instead write a novel based on her life? I've got all kinds of good material for you."

Shōfū soon went back to Tokyo, but the next year, after the fighting had ended, he returned to Shanghai to follow up on this offer. He was soon living in Yoshiko's Shanghai residence to observe her at close hand.

As many say, the novel that came out of this research trip led to her execution.

*

Muramatsu Shōfū's novel, *The Beauty in Men's Clothing*, has had incalculable influence on Yoshiko's life, death, and posthumous reputation. Despite Shōfū's repeated disclaimers that he made up certain episodes, the fictional heroine and the real thing have been so closely intertwined that separating one from the other has proven impossible: by now this fiction has settled firmly into factual accounts.

Shōfū says that Yoshiko urged him to tell the truth about her, to dig below the surface. "I don't want you to write something that makes me look good. It's perfectly all right if you portray me as the bad woman that the world says I am. The important thing is to figure out what this bad woman is thinking." Having said this, she kept crucial information to herself, and he complained that he was getting nowhere. Shōfū could not have been encouraged when Yoshiko confessed that she did not know how to help him since, "As you know, I'm schizophrenic."

Much later, of course, Shōfū would keep insisting that the novel was fiction, not to be equated with real persons or events. "The author lived with the woman who was the model for the heroine for two months," Shōfū wrote afterward in another of his protestations, "and so could learn about her in detail. Thus the novel cannot be called untruthful, but there are exaggerations about the ever-changing activities of the heroine. . . . Militarism was all-powerful then, so there was no choice but to shroud the real beauty in men's clothes in mystery."

This was at odds with the view of the editors of *Fujin kōron*, the Japanese women's magazine that first serialized the novel. Accompanying an early magazine installment was a photo of the real Yoshiko, who is described as the "model for the novel's heroine." Yoshiko confirmed her connection to her fictional self when she embarked on her own kind of promotional tour after the novel's publication. And Shōfū also did his job well, for his fictional heroine, Mariko, is a credible replica, speaking with the same savvy bitterness that marked the adult Yoshiko's manner of speech. At times Shōfū's heroine seems beyond his control, uttering remarks that he considers dead wrong or foolish. He then dashes in to offer arguments in rebuttal, not at all the novelist holding all the strings on a fictional character.

Certainly Shōfū was sorry for any problems the novel may have caused Yoshiko, in particular her execution in China, but he saw no need to make excuses for his skill in getting around the restrictions facing every Japanese author during the war. Unlike others, Shōfū did not write a propaganda novel glorifying Japan's aggressions. Instead he entertained readers with his spirited, fearless heroine. "She got her second bullet wound," he wrote in a wholly made-up episode,

> after she had accompanied her husband, Kan, to his home in Mongolia . . . and had lived there for half a year. She and Kan were returning to Manchuria when they were attacked by one of Zhang Zuolin's bandit gangs. She fought them off herself with her gun, but an enemy bullet hit her in the lower left shoulder. Five or six of the men from her side sustained fatal wounds. Gradually they beat off the enemy and reached their destination. She was close to death but miraculously survived.

This passage turned a burgeoning war into a historical fantasy, a genre Shōfū had mastered long back, and much welcomed by readers and censors.

★

The Beauty in Men's Clothing first appeared in *Fujin kōron* in September 1932, about six months after the truce in Shanghai gave the Japanese their victory, and came out as a book in April 1933. While the novel has been influential in shaping views about every period in Yoshiko's life, it would be fair to say that Shōfū's evocation of her youthful environment has had the most lasting impact.

Shōfū touches upon his heroine, Mariko's, resentments regarding her early youth but steers clear of the fury that could come out of the real Yoshiko. Shōfū is more inclined to look for melodrama when describing his heroine as a young girl, and, with fanfare, he describes her sudden removal from her family home in China and her adoption in Japan:

> Thus, before Mariko knew what was happening, her fate underwent a great change. Just as one may write of the peony bud that has been planted in a pot and taken far away, Mariko's surroundings completely changed. Flowers and trees, and human beings, too, endure the same vicissitudes of fate. The peony that has been moved to a different place may mature with vigor and send forth flowers more beautiful than any on the parent tree. On the other hand, some flowers shrivel up and produce pitiable blooms. In that same way, no one knew how Mariko would turn out.

Although Shōfū kept well away from sensationalism in such passages, he could not stop himself from embracing it in another episode, which may or may not be true. And since fact cannot be separated from fiction in

Yoshiko at seventeen in Matsumoto *Courtesy Hokari Kashio*

this novel, the episode, once down on paper, gained much acceptance—an acceptance that continues to grow.

The language in this section of the novel does not go into all the details, but Shōfū did convey the gist: his heroine, Mariko's, adoptive father repeatedly forced her to have sex with him. Shōfū gives his most explicit description in the version published in *Fujin kōron* magazine:

One day Mariko went with her adoptive father to Naruko hot springs in Tōhoku. . . .

"We'll stop in Sendai on the way back," her father told Mariko. "I'll take you sightseeing in Matsushima."

It was evening by the time they reached Naruko hot springs. They were received by many of her father's disciples from the area and by locals who shared his political beliefs. Immediately, they were escorted to the inn. That night there was a welcome party for her father in a large room at the inn, and he drank a lot and was in unusually high spirits.

Mariko slept in a futon just beside her father. When she was young she had often slept in the same futon with him, but recently of course this had stopped.

That night, for the first time in her life, Mariko experienced something terrible.

The following morning, her father looked as if nothing had happened. He treated Mariko as he always did, with absolutely no change. Mariko was somewhat relieved at this, deciding that it had just been some drunken prank and really didn't have any deep meaning.

Here's Mariko mulling over her experience as she listens to her father giving a speech the following day:

The lecture was in a school's auditorium. The turnout was big, with an overflow crowd. . . . Her father went to the podium. His speech was titled "The Future of East Asia and the Government of a Virtuous Ruler." He did not need any notes at all and just spoke in a rush of words, thoroughly covering the topic. . . .

Mariko was just to the side of the lectern, and as she listened to the speech, she remembered what had happened the night before. For the first time, she started to have doubts about this human being who was her adoptive father. (That won't happen again. He surely regretted what had happened.)

But things did not turn out at all as she expected. That night they also stayed at Naruko hot springs, and her father was even bolder and more persistent than before. This situation continued without pause after they returned to Matsumoto.

Her father had removed the mask he had been wearing for ten years. His attitude toward Mariko completely changed. When she did not submit, he got angry, shouting insults, hitting her, and kicking her.

"You ingrate!"

Or he'd abuse her, calling her a "whore."

The section apparently caused problems upon publication in the magazine and so only broad hints were included in the published book. Yet there it was, lust, assault, not exactly incest but close enough to keep people talking. Yoshiko herself never came out and said that this is what had really happened, but she dropped enough suggestions in that direction to give the account credence. As a result, the rape of the fictional Mariko by her adoptive father has become part of Kawashima Yoshiko's biography, repeated countless times in the movies, plays, novels that keep on coming. Yoshiko can still be seen being ravished in Chinese documentaries, which trace her later perverse betrayal of China back to this perverse experience in her youth. In their dramatizations, the Japanese too feature this event, but only to mourn, yet again, Yoshiko's suffering.

Responses to this episode have been diverse and adamant, but as is usually true in such accusations, neither side has been able to provide the eye-witness evidence needed to clinch its case. Yoshiko's older brother Xianli gave new life to the charge in a 1956 article he wrote for a Japanese magazine. Xianli recalled a conversation he had with Naniwa just after Prince Su's death, when Naniwa obliquely but clearly floated the idea that he and Yoshiko make a perfect baby together. They would thereby combine Prince Su's "virtue" and Naniwa's "courage."

"In other words," Xianli writes, "Kawashima Naniwa wanted to get his hands on Yoshiko. He was in love with Yoshiko, who was forty years younger. I'd heard from Yoshiko that Kawashima had really been after her. She had cried and complained to me about this."

Naniwa's partisans debunk this testimony, pointing to Xianli's personal history as proof of his untrustworthiness. Among other unsavory endeavors, Xianli has been accused of a swindle involving a fake diamond that he passed off as "Prince Su's treasure" and repeated sexual misconduct of his own. He was well aware of the money to be made from a juicy version of his family history, and so when Kamisaka Fuyuko, one of Yoshiko's Japanese biographers, asked about how much he would charge for an interview, Xianli told her to "add a zero to whatever amount you have in mind."

To counter Xianli, there's the dissenting view of Naniwa's relative Harada Tomohiko, who, as we've seen, was no blind admirer of Naniwa or his politics—"It is said that heroes are fond of women, but Naniwa was no hero." Nonetheless Harada is saddened to find the old man associated with such a tawdry story.

> It is not impossible that Naniwa at fifty-eight or fifty-nine was driven wild by his passion for Yoshiko, who was forty years younger. Yoshiko was his "precious jewel" whom he treated with affection, but at the same time he did not want her taken from him by someone else. Perhaps subconsciously he wished to make Yoshiko his. But the idea that he actually tried to turn Yoshiko into a sexual partner amounts to incest—even though they were not related by blood—and is just too out of the question to be believed.

As if sensing the weakness of this defense, Harada goes on to accuse Yoshiko's Chinese family of promoting this story to smear Naniwa, to top off the old accusations about his pocketing of their inheritance. "When Yoshiko's brother Xianli says that he smelled something like this going on," Harada reflects,

> didn't he have another purpose in mind? Naniwa was in charge of managing Prince Su's estate, principally the income from the Dalian market. Prince Su's family—and there were too many of them to count—was dissatisfied with how he had handled this. . . . In a strange, subtle way, I sense the family's scorn for Naniwa lurking in these accusations. He was for them some no-account Japanese *rōnin*, while they took pride in their noble blood as members of the elite Aisin Gioro royal family.

By comparison with the tentative Harada, biographer Kamisaka Fuyuko is more definite, refusing to seriously entertain these rape accusations, which she considers more of the younger generation's incomprehension of history and the human heart. In researching her well-regarded 1984 biography of Yoshiko, Kamisaka traveled extensively to conduct interviews; no location was too remote when it came to ferreting out documents. The thoroughness and precision of her investigations are impressive

Though her research was wide-ranging, Kamisaka of course failed to come up with any document containing conclusive proof about the rape. Stymied without such evidence, Kamisaka turns obstinate: she declares that Naniwa could not have assaulted such a young woman, and that is the end of the discussion. "There's simply no truth to it," she writes in her categorical mode. "Most important, there was a forty-two-year age difference between the adoptive father Naniwa and Yoshiko."

*

For a more compelling analysis of Naniwa and Yoshiko's relationship, we must go to Muramatsu Shōfū's grandson Tomomi, who bursts into Yoshiko's life story in an agitated state. Like his grandfather, Tomomi became a writer, but the older man seems like a cold tuna slab beside his grandson, who brings to mind shrimp tempura sizzling in the oil. Tomomi's opinions heat up in his book about Shōfū and Yoshiko—also called *The Beauty in Men's Clothing*—which was published in 2002 to provide more background information about the original novel. Shōfū has been accused of various things over the years, the murder of Yoshiko among them, and Tomomi takes this opportunity to present his grandfather from the sympathetic point of view of a close relative. Although Tomomi doesn't say so, his defense of Shōfū feels like an act of filial piety, intended to tidy up a certain amount of mess.

Filial piety, at least in Tomomi's modernized version, comes with jokes and gossip; an absence of reverence pervades. With a gift for anecdote, he aims for—and often gets—a reader's big chuckle. While everyone's still laughing, however, he can go off in another direction and mood, suddenly infuriated by the treatment Yoshiko received.

In his writings, Tomomi has stayed away from the topics favored by his grandfather, the pleasure quarters in particular, which Shōfū made his personal and literary home. Instead, Tomomi has found writing material in another kind of literary underworld. *I'm a Friend of Pro Wrestling*, which became a best seller in 1980, suits Tomomi's ironic tone, put to use here to rescue wrestling from its sneering detractors. Tomomi is particularly hard on the false fans of professional wrestling, who pretend enthusiasm but are in fact just slumming. "These people," he writes,

> pride themselves on going against current trends. They like to spout off about how only circuses and light comedies convey drama's true spirit, how only cheap soup off a food cart or stewed pork possesses the quintessence of flavor. They can find absolute beauty even in someone who has leprosy, and likewise they claim that pro wrestling is the only true sport.

Wrestling aside, it is Tomomi's early life that qualifies him as commentator on Yoshiko's story. In autobiographical works, he has expressed dismay about his own background, which has left him feeling duped and unsettled. This all started in 1938, when his grandfather Shōfū saw fit to foist his great love for Shanghai upon the next generation. He convinced his oldest son, a journalist then in his twenties, to work there at the start of his career. Far from matching his father's fascination, the son felt lonely and overworked in China. He eventually came down with typhoid fever and died at age twenty-seven in his father's beloved city.

Shōfū claimed to take little interest in his children, and the only exception was this son, whom he cherished. When the son died, the grief-stricken Shōfū rushed to Shanghai. Later he readied the next twist in the plot. His son's widow was pregnant, and Shōfū wanted to adopt the child as his own. Here's where his talents for moving characters around in fiction helped him in real life. After a decent interval, he got the widow married off to someone else and gained custody of her baby boy, who was Tomomi. "No doubt he clearly mapped all this out in his head," Tomomi comments, aware that his novelist grandfather did not turn off his creative machine just because the characters were flesh and blood human beings.

In the all-important official family register, Shōfū did not enter Tomomi as his grandson but as his son, thereby giving the fatherless boy a more advantageous status. Having completed all these arrangements, Shōfū headed off for new adventures and new women, leaving Tomomi to be raised by his long-suffering wife.

The grandson/son Tomomi lived out his youth inscribing the names of the people he called grandfather and grandmother as his mother and father in official documents. "I spent my youth juggling truth and lies with my two hands without the slightest problem." More important, he did not discover that his real mother was still alive until he was in middle school. "My grandmother and the other relatives could not tell me the truth, and so, as a smoke screen, they used to tell me sometimes about the wild life . . . [my grandfather] was leading in Shanghai." The realization that his mother had been alive all those years left Tomomi with a profound discomfort about his place in the world that he does not appear to have shaken off.

*

That's why Tomomi feels such a tie with Kawashima Yoshiko in her confusion about precisely who she was. As he puts himself in Yoshiko's place, Tomomi finds himself breathing in again the fumes of his own youth. Yoshiko's life story has drawn in other biographers who have seen echoes of their own early misery in hers, but Tomomi is the most intrepid of these chroniclers. Like Yoshiko, Tomomi grew up with relatives who did not make their primary concern the creation of a blissful home for their children. This has made him an expert on the anxiety of those who must depend upon the whims of selfish, incompetent adults. Boosted by such credentials, Tomomi conjures up a persuasive vision of Yoshiko's childhood.

At first Tomomi tries to take an indulgent view, excusing Naniwa's quirks as a run-of-the-mill China *rōnin's* unconventional behavior. Of course, Tomomi acknowledges, Naniwa did have a number of mistresses, whom he sometimes installed in his residence. And certainly, this kind of sexual looseness caused his wife to leave him. But such habits are surely to be expected of a man who used to go off to organize warrior bands in Mongolia.

After a while, Tomomi's tolerance dissipates, and China *rōnin* or not, Yoshiko's adoptive father starts looking as despicable as any ordinary cad, one who has never traveled further than the corner noodle shop. Tomomi's disdain hardens around the time that Yoshiko and Naniwa return from Prince Su's funeral in China. As Tomomi sees it, the trip changed Yoshiko's view of her future. She had visited China again after a long time and could see herself back there someday, taking up her father's fight for the deposed and struggling Manchus in her native land; she would improve the lot of her people and bring the dynasty back to power. Whatever deeds she undertook in the years ahead would not require assistance from Naniwa, whom she now saw as a temporary figure in her life.

From there, Tomomi moves on to inhabit the tensions, sexual and otherwise, that roiled these lives. On the one hand, there is the ageing and deaf Naniwa, his political clout gone with his physical stamina. Unable to follow conversations, he required an assistant and preferred that a young woman serve him in this role. His hearing may have been gone but his eyes had not, and he, along with others, would have seen Yoshiko maturing into a desirable young woman. As Naniwa surely understood, old and deaf do not stand a chance against young and sparkling. His only defense was his sourness and domestic authority.

The more appealing Yoshiko became, the more strict were Naniwa's rules, especially in regard to her contact with the opposite sex. "Don't look at or laugh with men," the adoptive father orders his daughter in Shōfū's novel, repeating the kind of restrictions imposed upon the real Yoshiko. Naniwa may have done his best to ban male admirers, but, in the end, he could not scare them off. After all, his home teemed with young men also eager to become China *rōnin*—criminals and other social menaces among them—and they too saw that Yoshiko was growing up.

When he writes about this period in Yoshiko's life, Tomomi compounds the impression of sensual and political brutishness in Naniwa's home by turning to the passages from his grandfather Shōfū's novel that described the adoptive father's rape of his adopted daughter. Tomomi dares to referee among the differing opinions about what Naniwa did or did not actually do, and he gets his readers to join him. Tomomi makes us take a hard look at Naniwa, a China *rōnin* living mostly without his wife in the company of a beautiful adopted daughter who has been given to him as a "toy." Here Tomomi relies on his own view of human nature, which he has developed through exposure to his family's complicated and frequently shady activities, as he makes the sexual assault seem quite possible. "Isn't the section from Shōfū's novel [about the rape] actually the truth, as related by Yoshiko?"

Tomomi's views are similar to those of recent biographers of Yoshiko, who are not inclined to honor Naniwa's memory. Naniwa's toils on behalf of Japan, which used to be extolled as patriotic feats, have lost their righteous sheen to all but die-hard partisans, and this has put his personal traits under unfriendly scrutiny as well. The plunge of Naniwa's reputation has elevated Yoshiko and given her a thoroughly new aspect. As biographers like Tomomi study Yoshiko in these different times, she becomes more than the caricature of legend and gains the psychological nuances denied her up to now.

9

EXTREME MEASURES

Moriyama is really a disgusting person. When he was in Matsumoto he used to come into my room. I'd strongly object, telling him that I have a maid to take care of my needs. Then he'd eat my leftover meals and fruits, saying it was a waste to throw these away. Sometimes he tried to get me interested in him by talking about the revival of China's imperial system.

"I leave my life with you," Moriyama told me.

"I have no use for anyone's life," I replied, brushing him off.

—KAWASHIMA YOSHIKO

N aniwa was perhaps correct in trying to keep the boys at bay, since the youths roaming about his house repeatedly proved themselves inadequate candidates for any kind of association with Yoshiko. While Naniwa attempted to exert control, stories about the turbulence that these hooligans stirred up in his residence made their way outside. The gossips were delighted. On the streets, conversations touched upon China, Japan, boyfriends, suicide attempts, and hair, but it's safe to assume that no one commended Naniwa's skills as a parent. All could see the conclusive proof of his colossal incompetence in raising his daughter, a child-rearing failure stemming from the same flaws that had doomed Naniwa's other projects— explosive emotions and faulty assessments of events taking place around him.

First came the young man Moriyama Eiji, better known by his sobriquet Yamatomaru. He was a member of a violent gang of fanatic nationalists, League for the Prevention of Communism, which saw Communism as a grave threat to Japan and vowed to eradicate all traces. Dissatisfied with the Japanese government's mass roundups of Communists, Moriyama's group disposed of these enemies in their own way, along with other proponents of "dangerous, foreign ideologies."

Already well-known to the police, Moriyama took part in an assault on prominent statesman Gotō Shimpei, who had come out in support of a conciliatory policy toward the Soviet Union. Moriyama was imprisoned for a time but begged Naniwa to take him in after his release. Naniwa agreed, saying that he "could see a pure side" to Moriyama, who soon proved the folly of this assessment. A dangerous presence in love as well as in politics, Moriyama eventually decided to whisk Yoshiko off, to rescue her from Naniwa's bullying. He saw her being roughly treated and bragged about his challenge to Naniwa: "I said to him, 'If you want to hit a lovely young woman, especially one from a foreign land, I suggest you hit me instead.'"

A brawl ensued with an incensed Naniwa, who finally understood the peril of letting this "pure" disciple anywhere near his residence. Yoshiko, for her part, heard about Moriyama's intentions and took to her bed with a high fever. Far from reciprocating Moriyama's affection, she rejected him as her savior. "He only has to look at a woman to do something bad," she told one of the ever-present reporters. In case Moriyama had not understood her drift, she went on to elaborate. "I don't care what kind of violence he's planning in order to take me away, but I'll die before leaving with him. I have obligations to my father here and definitely won't be going anywhere."

Moriyama, rebuffed but still ardent, went public with his love story, which the newspapers accorded extensive coverage for some days. He claimed that Yoshiko had become so upset by this episode that she attempted to kill herself with an overdose of morphine. According to Moriyama, he came to her rescue by sucking the drug from her lips.

Next was Yoshiko's entanglement with Iwata Ainosuke, another of Naniwa's thuggish acolytes. Also a violent and fanatical ultranationalist, Iwata was the chief of the Patriotic Society and had just served a twelve-year jail term for aiding the assassin of a high-ranking Foreign Ministry official. This official had come out against the establishment of a separate state, under Japanese control, in Manchuria and Mongolia, and he thereby enraged those Japanese in favor of aggressive moves in China. The official "was murdered in a spectacular gesture of protest by a young man who then seated himself on a map of China and committed hara-kiri so skillfully that his blood poured out over Manchuria and Mongolia."

Fresh from jail, Iwata sought to marry Yoshiko, but she became so agitated at the prospect of another imbroglio that she again declared that she would end her life. Once she expressed a wish to die, Iwata obliged by giving her a pistol. She shot herself in her chest, but survived.

"I didn't think she'd really do it," Iwata offered.

Finally there was Lieutenant Yamaga Tōru of the army's Fiftieth Regiment, who was Yoshiko's first decent suitor. He brought Yoshiko another kind of humiliation. Nine years older and fascinated by China, Yamaga regularly visited Naniwa's home to practice his Chinese with Yoshiko's brother, who also lived there for a time. Yamaga stayed at nearby Tsuta Hot Springs, and Yoshiko would stop off to see him when she went to bathe there. Everyone at Tsuta Hot Springs thought that the two might marry, and her brother also took note of their intimate chats.

Rumors about this friendship began to circulate and eventually reached Naniwa, who, predictably, became furious. Since nothing in Yoshiko's life then or afterward got settled without a public exposé, the local newspaper invaded her privacy again on November 21, 1925, by running a story about her engagement:

Chinese the Catalyst for Yoshiko's Marriage
  Love Develops with Lieutenant from Matsumoto's Fiftieth Regiment

Yamaga, realizing that such newspaper reports would damage both Yoshiko and himself, promptly issued a denial. The next day, November 22, the headline read,

Story About Yoshiko's Marriage Causing Much Trouble, Says Yamaga, Who Denies Account
  Kawashima Also Cites a Misunderstanding

In the accompanying article Yamaga made his refutation more emphatic: "This has no basis in fact. I've only met her once."

Naniwa, who was also interviewed, indicated that he lacked essential information, and, in an effort to push his daughter's reputation in another direction, he told the reporter that Yoshiko was off at knitting class. "If she were interested in a certain Mr. Yamaga, Yoshiko would have told me. And, of course, if the person in question were someone outstanding, I would not be against her marrying." With this vague, cool comment, which mustered up the flavor of a vigilant father concerned about his daughter's friendships, the message was clear: Naniwa was not going to allow this relationship to proceed. Another remark from Naniwa takes on significance because of what happens next: "Yoshiko has an interest in matters like the problems in China and Asia and aspires to be like that mannish Western Joan of Arc. So she has characteristics that make her unsuited to the life of an ordinary woman."

Even a more emotionally hardy young woman would have been crushed at being publicly brushed off by Yamaga and despondent about Naniwa's rejection of her beau. In addition, Yoshiko had been demoralized by constant gossip about her, an especially galling development to someone who did indeed have dreams of matching the dedication of Joan of Arc. Then there are the rumors about her being raped by Naniwa, which would have taken place around this time if in fact it did occur.

No wonder Yoshiko declared around this time, "I've had all this trouble because I'm a woman."

★

Yoshiko soon had most of her hair cut off.

"I don't want to talk now or in the future about what went on in Kawashima Naniwa's house," Yoshiko declared later, issuing what may be a veiled allusion to a sexual assault. "Therefore I also don't want to write too honestly about what happened to me when I was sixteen. But even today I cannot forget the night . . . when I decided to cease being a woman forever."

It was in the November 27, 1925, edition of the *Asahi* that Yoshiko made her first appearance in a severe buzz cut, wearing a boy's university uniform that presumably belonged to her brother. The transformation is stunning, for the photo shows what now looks like a young man with too much in the way of jaw and ears—and very short hair.

The stir caused by this haircut was far-reaching, wrecking any illusion of the Sino-Japanese bonding between Yoshiko and Naniwa that he had boasted about. In the future, her male hairstyle would mark her, merely a catchy trademark to many, but perhaps also a serious reflection of her true identity. Later, Naniwa's side complained that too much of a fuss had been made about Yoshiko's hair since it was merely the result of her going to get a haircut but ending up scalped by mistake. Anyone who's had a bad time at the hairdresser's will find this explanation insufficient for a haircut gone so wrong. No, Yoshiko wanted to become a man, and the photo proves that she succeeded.

She later wrote that she went off to have her hair cut on the evening of October 10, 1924. That morning, she claimed, she had dressed herself up as a typical Japanese young woman, in a kimono and with her hair in a traditional female style. Then she posed for a photo in a field of blooming cosmos flowers, to commemorate "my farewell to my life as a woman." At forty-five minutes past nine that night, she writes, she went to a barbershop for the haircut. "I'll leave it to you to imagine how angry and surprised my adoptive mother and father were."

Biographers have scoured the record for verification of the date and photograph, even going so far as to determine when cosmos bloomed in Matsumoto that year. Recent researchers have concluded that Yoshiko was off by thirteen months and actually went to the barbershop on November 22, 1925, the day the newspaper published Yamaga's repudiation of their romance.

Five days later, that startling photo of her with her crew cut appeared in the *Asahi*, and the headline covered a lot of territory:

Kawashima Yoshiko's Beautiful Black Hair Completely Cut Off
    Because of Unfounded "Rumors," Makes Firm Decision to Become a Man
    Touching Secret Tale of Her Shooting Herself

Not only had she cut her hair and borrowed her brother's clothes, she had also adopted a man's rough style of speaking Japanese. "On the evening of the twenty-fifth . . . ," the *Asahi* article begins,

a handsome youth with a shaved head was found standing in a Chinese restaurant in Matsumoto wearing a Waseda University uniform and high geta clogs.
    "Hey, waitress, get me a drink," the youth demanded in a stern voice, going on to get the old man beside to share some rounds.
    "You better eat more," the old man said, "and put on some muscle, or you'll shame those sturdy geta you're wearing."
    "I don't like Chinese food," the uncouth youth replied, laughing.

Although Naniwa could not get himself to issue a public statement about Yoshiko's haircut, this did not stop the journalists from clamoring for answers. Instead of Naniwa, Yoshiko came forward with a sad explanation about why she'd suddenly changed herself into a man and taken the man's name Ryōsuke. In this explanation, Yoshiko's confusion about her own emotions is evident; after all, she is trying to fathom what she herself does not yet understand. Yoshiko struggles to be honest but at the same time she does not want to reveal too much. She struggles also to express her feelings in a manner that will be acceptable to the newspaper's many readers. The result is obfuscation in one sentence, followed by truth in the next, and back again.

"Please forgive me for causing all of you only worry," begins her statement, which was published two days later in the *Asahi*. "I now realize that all this has come about because of my tomboyish ways, my wish to fool around all the time. I promise to behave in a circumspect manner from now on, so please forgive me." Such an analysis would have been palatable to her Japanese public, who appreciated such polite regrets, and Yoshiko goes on to recount what was already common knowledge: her womanliness had caused her no end of trouble. She says that men fell for her without being encouraged in the slightest. She's been misunderstood, her playfulness taken in the wrong way. She knows that these uproars will continue in the years to come if she doesn't change. And since she doesn't want to get married, she's chosen to become a man.

Up to this point, she is cautious, her motives restricted to keeping the boys away, but as Yoshiko continues, more seems to be at stake. Her next statements, surprising for their clarity and boldness, surely were included because they expressed her true state of mind. "I was born with what the doctors call a tendency toward the third sex, and so I cannot pursue an ordinary woman's goals in life. People criticize me and say that I am perverted, and maybe they're right. I just can't behave like an ordinary feminine woman." Here Yoshiko seems to express a wish not only to protect herself from male admiration by cutting off her hair but also to actually be a boy, a man, male.

Read today, the statement would be considered a sincere expression of the discomfort she felt living as a woman, to be taken very seriously. But Yoshiko found herself in Japan in 1925 and could not hope to make the kind of biological and legal changes that are now possible. And so, after seeming to move in one direction, Yoshiko retreats. Back to soothing the Japanese public, she says that she wants to take on a man's role for strictly practical reasons, to accomplish the things men can achieve, like improving the lot of her people. "Since I was young I've been dying to do the things that boys do.

Naniwa and Yoshiko at Osaka Station just after her
haircut, December 1925

The Asahi Shimbun/Getty Images

My impossible dream is to work hard like a man for China, for Asia. I want
nothing more in this world than to throw my whole life into working for
the nation."

In years to come, Yoshiko's actions would continue to be marked by
such contradictions and distress. Sometimes she flaunted her love affairs
with men, and at other times, dressed in severe male attire, she introduced
a female member of her household as her wife. But whatever she did, she
took care to keep her behavior within a range that was then socially and
politically permissible in Japan: she switched back to a woman's role when
necessary and repeatedly invoked the image of Joan of Arc.

For the most part, Yoshiko's Japanese biographers have not attached great
significance to her proclamation about becoming a man. After all, she was a

flamboyant character, not given to shying away from provocative acts, and the biographers view her fondness for men's clothing and language as just another performance. They point to the fact that the Japanese were already familiar with women dressing as men, having been exposed to so-called modern girls, who cut their hair short and wore Western-style clothing to demonstrate their liberation from ancient rules about female behavior. Then there was the all-female troupe Takarazuka, with certain actresses specializing in men's roles and thrilling their many fans.

Still, it appears clear that there was more to Yoshiko's assumption of a male identity than just a desire to playact or be the center of attention. Her public remarks can be seen as her wish to tell of something deep within her, a need to show what was real. She had endured a miserable childhood, cut off from her family in China, and was left alone much of the time or in the company of Naniwa and his male disciples. Since her early years, she had made certain choices plain: she had shown a strong tomboyish nature and an inclination to use male language. From this time forward, she would use this masculine-style Japanese regularly and often appear in public in her male clothing, which for those times was an extraordinary decision.

10

REPERCUSSIONS

I felt that I had to bow and endure the censure of people from the lower end of society, but it was terrible when my own children criticized me, saying that they didn't want to look at my face.

—KAWASHIMA RENKO

"Our family members all have very thin eyebrows," Yoshiko's grand-niece Kawashima Shōko said in Matsumoto recently. "Yoshiko used to thicken my mother's eyebrows, using a chopstick with charcoal on the tip. This shows you how feminine Yoshiko really was. She also knit a sweater for my mother."

There is no question that Yoshiko's haircut was a momentous event, transforming her life from that day forward. It is also clear that the haircut and its ramifications transformed the lives of some of her Chinese relatives—an effect that persists to this day.

"I never met Yoshiko," Shōko told me, speaking her Chinese-accented Japanese. "But my mother used to say that while she may have worked with the Japanese military, there's no proof that she was a traitor to China. There's no proof about any of those charges made against Yoshiko. My mother always wanted to tell this to the world."

I met Shōko for the first time in Matsumoto, at the gathering held each year to commemorate Yoshiko's death. There is also a Kawashima Yoshiko Memorial Room in the town, with a collection of memorabilia, all part of attempts to rehabilitate the reputation of Matsumoto's famed resident. I have seen Shōko address the audience at the annual memorial, somberly speaking out, as the family representative, against inaccurate biographies of Yoshiko. I have also accompanied Shōko to Yoshiko's grave inside the grounds of Shōrinji, a nearby temple, where the marker avoids inflammatory comment and simply applauds Yoshiko for help in establishing the Japanese state in Manchuria.

Standing amid the temple's gravestones, with their stern calligraphy, Shōko once spoke without drama of her own dramatic life. Though she thinks nothing of it, Shōko's presence in Matsumoto now seems a matter of wonder, reflecting nothing less than the entire history of China and Japan in the twentieth century. Shōko told me about her Chinese husband, whose mind was shattered by the Cultural Revolution; turning to the Japanese side of her story, she spoke of her family's long connection to Kawashima Naniwa and how she never sees his descendants, who live nearby.

In Matsumoto, Shōko can usually put Yoshiko out of her mind as she goes about her daily tasks, but then a news report surfaces about the latest twist in Yoshiko's saga—she's dead, no, she's alive and taught Japanese for thirty years in a secret location—and Shōko is called upon to comment, as a member of Yoshiko's Chinese family in Japan. Shōko seems resigned to this role, well aware that Yoshiko's legacy will always rattle her life.

"My mother felt that it was impossible for Yoshiko to have done all they claimed she had done," Shōko said, persistent in her defense. "They blame her for too many things."

Shōko emigrated from China to Japan in 1983, when she was thirty-eight years old. Her saga is the familiar but still horrifying kind of tale told by many of her generation in China. In her case, an aristocratic family with a traitor in its ranks compounded her tribulations. Shōko has never forgiven herself for taking part in the madness of the Cultural Revolution; she was repeatedly refused membership in the Red Guards because of a background that includes Qing-dynasty nobles, Kawashima Yoshiko, and other strong ties to Japan. "It is hard for me to find the words to describe my feelings at that time," she has written. "Just like countless others who threw themselves into the Cultural Revolution, I threw myself into wild rebellion like someone with Saint Vitus' dance."

Now a Japanese citizen, Shōko is not reluctant to bring back memories of Yoshiko by borrowing bits of her style. Shōko's black hair is cropped exceedingly short around a ruddy face, and her no-nonsense outfits, often black trousers and shirts, shun any kind of female frills. The athletic build recalls her time as a volleyball player in China. An injury ended Shōko's career, as did the Cultural Revolution. The competitive drive has not gone, however, and she remains a forceful and forthright woman.

"History is based on facts," Shōko declared in firm defense of her great-aunt. "They called Yoshiko a prostitute. They called her Mata Hari, but there are no facts to back up these accusations. I worry about how history will judge her. I hope that during my lifetime Yoshiko will be cleared of charges that she betrayed China."

Shōko's present life in Japan is not only tied to Yoshiko but also to the destiny of her mother, Renko (these are their Japanese names), who was Yoshiko's niece.

"Yoshiko, as well as my mother, were victims of the long history of interactions between Japan and China. Those two didn't choose to be part of it. They were just thrown about by fate."

*

Yoshiko's haircut in 1925 gets their story started; soon after that, Naniwa moved his household from Matsumoto to the Chinese city of Dalian. He hoped to escape from those curious about the uproar in his home and also planned to manage the Dalian market that had proven so lucrative to himself and Prince Su's family.

But he could not escape reporters even in China, and eventually his family life inspired another headline: "The Troubled Kawashima Yoshiko Starts a New Life Again," announcing that Yoshiko was leaving Naniwa's Dalian home. According to the article, Yoshiko was breaking her ties with him and sailing off to live with her original Chinese family in Beijing, where she would become "a pure Chinese woman."

"I'm going to have surgery at the Rockefeller Hospital in Beijing to remove the three bullets that are still in my body from my recent suicide attempt," Yoshiko told the newspaper, trying to keep attention focused on her medical problems.

Naniwa presented his side of the story in an interview three weeks later, upon his surprising return to Japan. At the dock, he also delivered some harsh assessments of Yoshiko's character. "There have been various unexpected rumors about how I have returned Yoshiko to her family and even stories about how I have cut my ties with her. I brought her up for these thirteen years with the expectation that I would find her a husband among the Japanese nobility." This expectation has been destroyed, he conceded, by her adoption of a male persona. "I wouldn't say that Yoshiko is asexual, but rather blessed by nature with both male and female aspects."

He didn't believe she would be able to return to her former, more conventional self since she was already set in her ways. That's why he decided to send her back to her family in China, where it would be easier to find her a husband among the Chinese aristocracy.

"Yoshiko is abnormal." Naniwa shared this more brutal observation with another reporter who also caught up with him just as he reached Japan.

These slurs were not the only startling words Naniwa uttered that day in 1927, and here's where Shōko's mother enters the story, for she was standing by Naniwa's side as he spoke and receiving his affectionate pats on the head. Because of Yoshiko's outrageous behavior, Naniwa had escorted Renko over from China as a substitute somewhat earlier. Then fourteen years old, Renko was apparently making her first public appearance as Naniwa's latest Chinese daughter.

A reporter speculated that Naniwa had brought in Renko because he "could not bear his loneliness" after Yoshiko departed. "Renko is different from Yoshiko," Naniwa declared. "Renko is a feminine, graceful woman. In addition she is extremely attached to me." He describes how he will bring her up in pure Japanese style, taking her to the mountains to improve her health.

Naniwa's assessments proved correct, for he had indeed found a more agreeable Chinese daughter in Renko, a sickly young woman with no thirst for rebellion who took to Japan quickly.

"She really became extremely knowledgeable about Japan," Shōko has written about her mother. "But it was not just that she knew things; the Japanese temperament was burned deeply in her entire spirit. This deeply ingrained Japanese temperament stuck fast to her being, and that did not change as time passed."

Shōko makes this observation ruefully, for, later on, Renko's ineradicable "Japaneseness" brought on endless harassment of the family in China.

Unlike Yoshiko, Renko would go on to become indispensable to the deaf Naniwa, serving as his secretary and link to the hearing world. "She accompanied him like his shadow. . . . Almost always the old Naniwa had the young Renko by his side." Appreciative of Renko's services, Naniwa would officially acknowledge her as his daughter by entering her name in his family register. This gave her rights to Japanese citizenship—a favor denied Yoshiko.

As a result of being chosen to take over for Yoshiko, Renko would know tranquil days, especially at Naniwa's country retreat: "They rowed and swam on Lake Nojiri. After that they'd grill the sweetfish that Naniwa had just caught and eat them. She never forgot their delicious taste." Renko, like many others, warmed to Japan's allures—fresh country air, fresh fish, conviviality, the seasons.

But she faced difficulties too in those days of her youth, such as when she had to spend some months as Yoshiko's roommate "Yoshiko's selfish character still had not changed," Shōko writes, transmitting her mother's recollection of that brief period in 1934.

> One night when Yoshiko was about to go out she could find only one of her geta. "You're a fool," she said, immediately getting angry and berating the maid. From the entranceway, she threw the single geta into the room.
>
> Renko saw this, frightened, and her face turned pale.
>
> But the next morning, Yoshiko behaved as if nothing had happened when she greeted the maid with, "Good morning."
>
> The others who lived there were confused, wondering about how to get along with Yoshiko.

*

Standing beside Naniwa on the dock that day in 1927, Renko would not have known about her future participation in such a small-scale domestic scuffle, nor would she have known about her future involvement in full-blown conflicts in China. After living in Japan for some years, Renko would return to China and, in 1940, marry a Chinese, settle down in Beijing, and eventually have six children. Once the war was over, Renko would be refused employment and shunned by neighbors because of her Japanese sympathies and noble blood; she would forage for discarded scraps of food in Beijing's dustbins. During the Cultural Revolution, with her daughter Shōko scrambling to join the Red Guards, Renko would be denounced in public and feel fortunate to have escaped with her life. Her own children would revile her for her past associations. Decades would pass before she, along with some of her children, would be able to return to live in Japan.

Though much of her grief could be traced back to Yoshiko, Renko never sought to play the heroine in a revenge saga, lashing out at those who had brought her so much misfortune. Instead Renko took up the milder role of a woman who had made numerous mistakes and seen her share of woe. She was willing to look with pity upon Aunt Yoshiko, who had done the same: "She made sure she got noticed in everything she did, but she was truly a good big sister to me. She associated with the Japanese army and with the Chinese, protecting and helping many."

11

ON HER OWN

To put it briefly, she was a pretty princess from a foreign country,
very frank and easy to get close to. . . . I thought of her as a somewhat
eccentric woman. . . . She was quite beautiful, and I think that her
beauty became the source of her misfortune.

—HARADA TOMOHIKO

After Yoshiko's break with Naniwa in 1927, she was left on her own in China, alien territory after her years in Japan. She had a large family there, certainly, but she could not always count on a warm welcome. On previous visits, she had been made to feel like an outsider because of her Japanese ways and faulty spoken Chinese. "I came to understand why the word 'foreigner' was considered a synonym for loneliness. (Ah, I thought, such an emotional rift develops if you can't make yourself understood?) I had returned to my own home, but I felt I was staying at an inn in a distant land."

In addition, Yoshiko had to settle down there at a time when her financial situation was shaky. While some regular income was due her from the Dalian market, this would not have been enough to support her in the style she preferred. A spendthrift by nature, Yoshiko did not find it easy to curtail her way of life. Princesses, she seemed to feel, had standards, and deposed or not, she intended to maintain them. On bad terms with Naniwa and dependent on the Chinese family she hardly knew, she had to consider her new and straitened economic prospects. Her solution was not so different from that of women who had no royal blood.

In November 1927, Yoshiko was in the newspapers again, and this time it was an announcement of her imminent marriage in Lushun.

With her longer chic hairstyle and high heels, she had apparently put aside her vow to become a man for the time being. She was to marry Ganjurjab, the son of Babujab, a Mongol military leader who had been killed in a battle for Manchu-Mongol "independence" financed by Prince Su. Naniwa had also been behind this uprising, and so he was well acquainted with the family. In fact, Ganjurjab had lived for a while in Naniwa's home in Tokyo. Ganjurjab had just graduated from Japan's Army Academy at the time of the marriage, and in the wedding photograph, he maintains his reserve, not revealing whether he is the man to carry on the martial exploits that had distinguished his father. A very young twenty-four, Ganjurjab wears Mongol wedding silks, while his bride, Yoshiko, sits beside him in her own flowing silk gown. She had herself arranged the long veil that extends from her head to the floor, and in heavy makeup, she seems ready to take part in ancient marriage traditions that require, above all, submissiveness in brides. Nothing on her face shows any embarrassment about her very feminine appearance, nor are there traces of her habits of defiance and pride, enemies of the wifely role.

Marriage of Yoshiko and Ganjurjab, 1927

Courtesy Hokari Kashio

Years later, Yoshiko claimed to have been forced into this marriage: "I was recovering from an illness . . . when I was told that I was to be married the next day. Surprised and furious, I sometimes walked out during the ceremony. When my groom tried to put the wedding ring on my finger, I brushed his hand aside, and the ring fell to the ground. It's odd, but to this day I don't know where that ring went."

Yoshiko wrote this after she had transformed herself into a military heroine who led warriors on horseback across the Manchurian plains. A commander on horseback would prefer to forget that she was once fitted out in a Mongol bridal gown, on her way to becoming a docile wife. Also Yoshiko clearly wears her ring in the official wedding photograph, casting doubt on her entire recollection.

Family members, disputing other facts, insist that Yoshiko had been fond of Ganjurjab since the time he had lived in Naniwa's Tokyo home. Yoshiko's brother Xianli, for example, has no doubt that Yoshiko entered into this marriage of her own volition: "She told me, 'Ganjurjab keeps sending me letters, and also I don't dislike him, so I am thinking that I'll marry him.' I thought that if she felt that way, then I would give permission. . . . After my father died, I was the oldest son [of Prince Su's fourth consort], and so it was my responsibility to grant permission in such matters. He and Yoshiko had lived together in Kawashima's Akabane [Tokyo] house as children, so objectively speaking, it was a good match."

Jin Moyu, Yoshiko's younger sister, who was nine years old at the time, attended the wedding ceremony in Lushun and sang school songs during the reception. She also did not see any sign that Yoshiko was pushed into this marriage against her will. "Yoshiko really looked like a bride at the wedding, and the guests were impressed." In other crucial matters, however, Jin Moyu acknowledges deficiencies. "Ganjurjab was extremely handsome and manly, and though he loved Yoshiko, she wasn't the domestic type."

Jin reports that the guests at the small wedding were mostly Japanese, which seems surprising at a Manchu-Mongol wedding. Even more significant, the chief of the General Staff of the Kwantung Army played a prominent role in the ceremony, and also on the guest list was Colonel Kōmoto Daisaku, who would, about six months afterward, pull off the cunning assassination of the Chinese warlord Zhang Zuolin, a feat for which Yoshiko is still blamed on Chinese television.

These Japanese military officials were busy men and would not have attended if they did not attach importance to the alliance between the Manchu princess and the Mongol independence leader's son. This marriage fit in nicely with the Japanese army's campaign to prove that Manchuria and Mongolia were not—historically, racially, culturally—part of China, in preparation for their takeover of the region. "If they could plant the idea that 'Manchuria and Mongolia Are One' in the minds of the public, ordinary people would go along with the military's goal of establishing an independent state . . . and give it their support." What better way to drive such a point home than to promote the marriage of this young, attractive pair—who were not, strictly speaking, Manchu-Mongol royalty but pleasing enough in their own way to serve as the kind of symbol the Kwantung Army sought.

No matter what inspired the marriage, Yoshiko had to live with Ganjurjab's family after the ceremony. Now the daughter-in-law in an old-fashioned household, Yoshiko encountered the usual problems as well as others unique to her. With even Yoshiko's spoken Chinese below par, it is certain that she could not communicate easily in the native language of her in-laws. She claims to have worked hard in the kitchen, trying to please her husband's family, and while her relations with her mother-in-law were satisfactory, others in the family did not take long to find her unacceptable.

"My daily life was unbearably oppressive. If I wanted to go out even to the garden, someone would immediately accompany me. I had almost no time by myself."

Rumor has it that Yoshiko refused to go along with the custom of showing the bloodstained cushion from her marriage bed, and there has been speculation that she objected because she opposed this feudal custom or because she was not a virgin. Since there is no proof behind either of these theories and no information at all about the couple's private life, one could just as wildly guess that the cushion was not displayed because they never had sexual relations. Whatever the reason, such behavior would have gotten her off to a bad start, and nothing in her character would have impelled her to improve.

Yoshiko further irritated her in-laws when she left the house alone one night and walked out into the moonlit desert, "as bright as the noontime sea," to have a brief encounter with nearby villagers. Thrilled, they later made up tales about how this princess had come to them from a distant land in the east. "These Mongols liked to make up stories, and they made up a drama about me that even surpassed those created by the author of *Arabian Nights*. It spread by word of mouth." Her adventure, however, did not similarly thrill her husband's family, who objected to her associating with coarse farmers.

Ganjurjab had joined the so-called Mongolian independence army, which was trained and supported by the Japanese. He may have told himself that he was following in his father's footsteps, fighting for the Mongols' independence from the Han Chinese. But times had changed since his father's heyday, and though Ganjurjab may have seen himself as a freedom fighter, he was now under Japanese supervision. His education in Japan would have made him more amenable to cooperation with the Japanese, and he was in agreement with the Japanese military in wanting to suppress the power of the Han Chinese in the region. In this, he had much in common with his wife, who had similar dreams of "liberating" Manchus in Manchuria. No matter how Ganjurjab justified his activities to himself, he was in fact assigned to "maintaining law and order" in Mongolia, and this, as the conflicts intensified, amounted to eradicating the local populace's opposition to merciless Japanese incursions.

In his postwar "confession" of his crimes, written after the Japanese defeat and his imprisonment as a war criminal, Ganjurjab gives an idea of what he eventually did:

My troops spent a half year in Jidong and Rehe fighting against the anti-Japanese forces that were headed by General Deng Hua and Commander Li. Altogether there were forty battles, not counting the small ones. . . . In total, more than three thousand members of the anti-Japanese forces were killed or wounded. We seized sixteen hundred weapons—rifles, carbines, and pistols. A truck was also part of our booty. More than ten members of the anti-Japanese forces were captured (I can't remember how they were dealt with). My troops also seized more than two hundred of the civilians' work animals—horses, donkeys, and mules. Although some of them were returned to their owners before we withdrew from the region, we still kept more than thirty for ourselves. Later, I received four mules from the Fifth Regiment without feeling any shame.

In the summer of 1933, under orders from the council of the puppet state Manchukuo, we started to confiscate the weapons scattered among the local population in the southern part of Xing'an Province. I divided my officers in the police bureau into three groups (each group was headed by a Japanese) and sent them to work in the different districts. We confiscated any weapons we could find, rifles, guns, as well as cannons. The three groups had various troubles when they were collecting the weapons. The Mongols lived on hunting and grazing and found it hard to survive without weapons. In a fight between the Japanese and the Mongols, a Japanese stabbed a Mongol with his Japanese sword. After a long time, we finally confiscated seventeen thousand weapons in the area we controlled. We made the lives of the people there worse, especially the people who depended on hunting and grazing. We caused much suffering among the people, whose livestock was wounded or killed by wolves during that time. According to the statistics of Xing'an Province, there were ten to twenty thousand head of livestock lost per year after we confiscated their guns.

Yoshiko accompanied her husband to a posting but very soon was back in Dalian. Freezing in Mongolia was not for her. Ganjurjab's brother, who is not inclined to sympathize with Yoshiko's adjustment problems, provides his family's assessment of their new daughter-in-law.

Almost immediately after her marriage, she just abandoned all her domestic responsibilities. She went out and enjoyed herself all over town every day. The dance halls and coffee shops became like home to her. The Japanese were extremely curious about her and would clamor around her whenever they spotted her. They asked her to dance or got her autograph or escorted her to restaurants. She stopped spending any time in our house. Afterward Ganjurjab took her away with him to Tushiyetu and tried to lead a quiet life there. But how could you expect her to have the patience to live on those bleak, lonely plains? . . . Then she just disappeared. We had no idea where she was. My brother felt that she was already sunk into depravity by then, and nothing could save her. So he didn't go looking for her.

Others disagree and say that Ganjurjab, disconsolate at losing her, was a sad sight as he awaited his wife's return. Their life together was over, but in Yoshiko's mind at least, the connection continued in another form. Ganjurjab eventually married again, and Yoshiko made a show of turning up at the wedding ceremony, where she gave a congratulatory speech. Since they had not gone through the process of legalizing the marriage or its termination, Yoshiko could continue to see herself as the "official" wife and the new one a secondary consort. Delighting in this role, Yoshiko arrived with a gift each time Ganjurjab's wife had a child. Ganjurjab, however, never again spoke to Yoshiko in public.

Ganjurjab's setbacks were only beginning, for after the Japanese defeat, he was imprisoned by the Chinese Communists and forced to undergo "rehabilitation," along with other collaborators. Amnestied in 1960, Ganjurjab returned to Mongolia only to have his life upended still more by the Cultural Revolution. Other members of his family were denounced as well, and when his younger brother committed suicide in 1967, Ganjurjab was left to collect his effects, which had been scattered over a snowy plain in Mongolia.

★

The marriage over, Yoshiko returned to Japan and paid a visit to her brother Xianli, who was living there at the time. He was surprised when she suddenly appeared at his Tokyo home, since he believed he had seen her safely married off and established in Mongolia, far away from where she could cause him any trouble. But suddenly she was back, complaining about married life, a discontented, idle sister in need of money.

Almost as soon as she had announced her return to Japan, she was gone once more, and the next communication Xianli received was from Shanghai. She explained that she had gone to see a friend off on a boat but got to talking so much that she didn't realize that the ship had set sail. Next thing Yoshiko knew, the boat had docked in Shanghai. Her brother speculates that she feared the arrival of Ganjurjab, coming to search for her in Tokyo. After she had gone, Xianli realized that she had relieved him of two thousand yen, a significant sum at the time.

There are other reports about Yoshiko in Tokyo, scavenging around for cash. In a 1932 magazine article, Morita Hisako remembers visiting a Tokyo novelist's home, where she met a woman who claimed to be Yoshiko's younger sister. "She was a small woman, about twenty-two or twenty-three, wearing yellow Chinese clothes," Morita writes. "She was beautiful and looked perfect with no makeup. She had thick eyebrows and a short, casual hairstyle free of any permanent wave. There was an air of refinement about her."

This sister of Yoshiko's pitched a proposal to the Japanese novelist: for two thousand yen, no more, no less, she would sell him the rights to create a novel based on her sister Yoshiko's fantastic life story. Later the sister got Morita alone and continued her sales campaign, in the hope of influencing the novelist.

"What she told me," Morita writes, "was pretty much the same as what has been written about Kawashima Yoshiko in the newspapers and magazines. But she told the story well and with embellishments, so I was thoroughly drawn in."

The sister narrated the tale of Yoshiko's doomed romance with the army officer Yamaga, her parting from this first love, their reunions, their partings again, his descent into alcoholism after losing her.

"Many who have felt the sorrow of a failed, lost love," Yoshiko's sister informed Morita, "turn to alcohol for consolation, and Yamaga was only one of those who followed this same path." He'd also accrued enormous debts along the way, and Yoshiko was threatening to kill herself if she could not get the money for him. That's why the sister needed to sell the story to the novelist.

"Please ask him to do it," the sister pleaded with Morita. "If you will do that for us, my sister's life will be saved."

With this, the two women parted, and Morita declares, "I felt as if I had just seen a movie."

Morita's movie came to an end later on when she saw a photo of the real Kawashima Yoshiko, who, to her astonishment, looked just like the "sister" she had met at the novelist's home. Only then did Morita start to believe that it had been Yoshiko herself seeking the money from the novelist.

"She said to me, 'My sister is suffering a lot,'" Morita mused afterward, convinced that she had been duped. "Was the person who had spoken to me so confidentially in fact the same person doing the suffering? I believe that to this day."

12

POISONOUS DEVIL'S BREW

To appeal to the Chinese mind I was sure that I had to have something different. They would not be satisfied, I believed, with just good danceable music. I had to have something bizarre with plenty of novelties. Some of the things I tried in that beautiful gold-plated, marble pillared ballroom bordered on heresy. They resembled the Disney fantasies. I had a miniature train built to run around, over and through the band stand and Mama Schmidt's son, Whitey, stood out in front of the band swinging a red lantern calling out the names of Chinese stations while my musicians rendered choo-choo effects in the background.

—WHITEY SMITH

For a woman in China with insufficient funds, insufficient skills, and excessive ambitions, Shanghai was an obvious next stop. In 1930, when Yoshiko arrived, the city was still trying to catch up with Roaring Twenties Paris but, in fact, never closed the gap. Publicity touted Shanghai as the "Paris of the East," but there was much to separate the spirits of the two cities. Paris of the 1920s exulted in the peace it enjoyed after a long war, and artists from all over the world flocked there, to glory in the freedom and camaraderie offered on every boulevard. Those artists came in search of liberation from oppressive political regimes and families, and found just that, as well as a rather orderly society that allowed them to do their work.

Shanghai, by contrast, had long been a prize in conflicts among imperialist powers. Torn into pieces, law and order a dream, it offered a different kind of pleasure, one that endured despite bloody conflicts in the present and the certainty of more to come. There was music and dance and Art Deco, but there was also crime and civil war, giving a special fillip to moments of abandon. Beginning in the nineteenth century, Shanghai had been divided up by foreigners seeking to grab pieces of China. While contending with these outside plunderers, China also had to contend with the chaos created by homegrown groups; unification under the Republic had proven impossible, and eventually warlords, Nationalists, and Communists battled for their share of turf.

For those inclined to live for the moment, the justifications were everywhere, and even those of a more ascetic bent were moved to join the party. Chinese caroused in their own way, while the foreign residents could match their resolute jolliness.

By then jazz had made its way to Shanghai, fueling the festivities. Bands were brought in from the United States and elsewhere, with sounds of "Somebody Loves Me" getting guests into the right state of mind at Shanghai's many dance clubs. One Shanghai cabaret owner heard Whitey Smith playing the drums at a jazz club in San Francisco, and over ham and egg sandwiches discussed the possibility of Smith taking off for Shanghai for an extended engagement at the Carlton Café on Ningbo Road. On August 24, 1922, Smith and his wife sailed away on the *Nile*, arriving in Shanghai three weeks later. "My great adventure was opening out before me," he writes, and this was putting it mildly. After that he would only make sporadic visits to the United States, soon heading back to continue his music career in the East, which survived the Second World War and several years in a Japanese internment camp

But when he first went to Shanghai, Smith merely contended with the technical problems facing an American jazz musician transplanted to China. He was able to collect enough Americans to play in his dance band but discovered that his clientele was limited to the foreigners: they were the only ones who would dance in public. Confucian morals forbade such intimate contact between men and women, keeping down the number of Chinese couples on the dance floor. "Competition for the foreign trade was heavy. I believe there were more night clubs in the International Settlement of Shanghai at that period and subsequently than in any other city of comparable size in the world."

Smith felt pressure to expand his market because the club owners, who would not be reined in, built extravagant pleasure palaces that foreign customers alone could not support. One of Smith's employers constructed the fabulous Majestic, which had a ballroom of gold leaf and marble, with carpets two inches thick in the dining area, and Italian and French murals on the walls and ceilings. "Off to one side of the ballroom was the Empire

Room where only royalty could enter. For cocktails before dinner they had the Winter Garden, with running waterfalls, artificial stars in the 'sky' which sported a traveling moon."

To attract Chinese patrons, Smith subjected Chinese folk song melodies to American band treatment and "calmed down the Charleston." Quickly catching on, his approach brought in the Chinese crowds. "They liked Singing in the Rain, Parade of the Wooden Soldiers, and the Doll Dance." Pearl Buck herself acknowledged Smith's achievement when she said that he had "brought more good will to China than many an ambassador. He had taught China to dance." When Generalissimo Chiang Kai-shek married Wellesley-educated Song Meiling in 1927, the new couple held their wedding reception in the Majestic ballroom and headed off for their honeymoon to the tune of "A Love Nest for Two," played by Smith's band.

Another foreigner who hated to tear himself away from Shanghai in those days was of course Muramatsu Shōfū, the author of *The Beauty in Men's Clothing*. Among his other pursuits, he had established himself as an expert on the dance halls.

> I can't even go through the motions of dance, and so I would camp on the second floor and drink while looking at what was going on. I am to an unpleasant degree pretty much formed from Asian tastes, and so effete entertainments like dance, which those barbaric foreigners so enjoy, do not suit me. But when I see men and women embracing as they dance so skillfully to the music of the lively fox-trot or the quiet waltz, even a contrary person like myself starts to get carried away and wants to dance.

Shōfū knew that Shanghai meant danger and debauchery as well, but bewitched as he was by the city, he fell for those allures also. "Before I had even the slightest inkling, I was attracted, as if drawn in by the aromas of a poisonous devil's brew, to the powerful charm of just knowing that such sins and secrets existed."

Yoshiko fit in well with this daring lot, who looked to make themselves anew in Shanghai. She shared Whitey Smith's adaptability, having been forced to adjust to changing circumstances since her childhood, and along with Shōfū, she was partial to pleasure. Also, she liked to dance.

Yoshiko, however, faced a more frightening situation than these others in Shanghai, for she was a single woman who had left behind a messy private life that she would never be able to tidy up. Added to her bad relations with her adoptive father, she had discarded a husband and so again earned the disapproval of proper society. She often walked about in male attire. There was no longer any chance that she would find herself an ordinary home life, a peaceful domesticity that she intermittently professed to desire.

"From the bottom of my heart," she once said, "I feel jealous of those ordinary, gentle housewives who see their husbands off to work in the morning and are eager to receive them home in the evening. So if I just get the right opportunity, I'll really make a complete return to being a woman."

In a more despondent mood, she wrote to a much older, sympathetic Japanese army officer about her travails: "Grandfather . . . I've been chased out of my native country, my parents have both died, and I've broken with my adoptive father and mother. Why do the gods torment only me? . . . I've become a weird creature because of the hardships I've endured throughout my life. You have been so very kind to this weird creature."

Yoshiko's celebrity, which grew each time she mocked convention, got in her way too. It guaranteed her special treatment but also made an anonymous future impossible. Not that anonymity seemed to be on her mind when Yoshiko was out in public. On the contrary, she gradually came to take her life force from newspaper coverage and from the strangers who recognized her on the street. The journalists, grateful for the bonanza of so much racy material, were not averse to using their imaginations when facts did not suffice. "That problem daughter of Prince Su, Kawashima Yoshiko," goes one Japanese report from Shanghai in 1931,

> is now staying here in a Chinese lodging, the Zhonghua Hotel. She meets with important people in the Nationalist government and seems to be in the process of planning something. When night falls, she goes around to the dance halls and seems to be soaking in eroticism. At the same time she puts on a show of saying that she's Joan of Arc and is going to bring about a revival of the Qing dynasty. She is trying to meet with Hu Hanmin, who's at the center of the anti–Chiang Kai-shek movement. . . . Her activities have been carefully noted by those important Chinese people with a taste for the bizarre. She is the very incarnation of eroticism and the grotesque and gives off such a strong taste of a whore that her mental stability has been questioned. On top of that she seems to be in financial trouble and has a large unpaid bill at the hotel.

Such unflattering coverage appeared to be pushing Yoshiko toward a hedonistic life that would be ignored by history. Badly in need of rehabilitation at about age twenty-four, she had to be careful about whom she approached for assistance. In the public's mind, she veered between being the potential savior of her people and a blue-blood prostitute, leaving an unsavory range in the middle. Only solid backing would boost her standing.

13
ADVANCE INTO MANCHURIA

The Pacific War began with the invasion of China in 1931.

—IENAGA SABURŌ

C onveniently, at just that moment, the Japanese military required
Yoshiko's services.

Yoshiko had become well acquainted with various military officials during her childhood; some paid visits to Naniwa, who did their bidding in secret. As an adult, she called certain top officers "Uncle," unnerving
their underlings when she swanned in and out of their headquarters unan-
nounced as if she were visiting a relative. Even without her husband to complete the picture, she was still striking and bold, a member of a royal family,
and thus a powerful public relations symbol for the Japanese, who liked to
show that they had this genuine Qing princess on their side.

By 1931, junior officers of Japan's Kwantung Army in China had lost
patience with the Tokyo government's indecisiveness regarding Manchuria
and made secret plans for a full-scale invasion of this northeastern territory.
The officers' insubordination was not so secret as it appeared, however, since
they received support behind the scenes from certain officials back in Japan.
The army felt a takeover of Manchuria imperative for reasons that made
perfect sense if you agreed that Japan had an undeniable right to control
China's Northeast. In the minds of many Japanese, of course, Manchuria
had been "purchased with the blood of Japanese men," who had died on its
soil during the Russo-Japanese War.

By the treaty ending that war, Japan had gained control of the important ports of Dalian and Lushun and had also acquired rights to territory in
other parts of Manchuria. Fast action in Manchuria was said to be necessary because rising anti-Japanese activity by the Chinese there imperiled

Japanese investments and the large Japanese expatriate community seeking to make their fortunes; along with this, there were fears that Chinese nationalism, spurred in large part by outrage at Japan, grew more united and more fierce by the day, threatening to overwhelm the entire Japanese enterprise. And then, as had long been the case, there was the need for that bulwark against the Soviet Union.

Army ideologues stormed forward with the similarly accepted idea that Japan also required Manchuria's natural resources to relieve economic hardship in their own country. "Manchuria and Mongolia are not territories of China," declared Lieutenant Colonel Ishiwara Kanji, one of the architects of the invasion. "They belong to the people of Manchuria and Mongolia. It is a publicly acknowledged fact that our national situation has reached an impasse, that there is no way of solving the food, population, and other important problems, and that the only path left open to us is the development of Manchuria and Mongolia."

Having heard rumors about the Kwantung Army's plot to seize Manchuria, the Tokyo government sent over General Tatekawa Yoshitsugu and charged him with putting a stop to this. This general, however, was on the plotters' side and, upon arrival, allowed himself to be locked inside a geisha house in Shenyang, where he spent the night. By the time he awoke, the invasion had already begun, putting an end to his mission.

"The gunfire so frightened the geishas that they trembled," a Japanese officer later reported, "but Tatekawa told them not to worry while they were with him. He slept soundly until morning, and then it was too late to stop the incident."

The Manchurian Incident of September 18, 1931, began with the bombing of a railway line controlled by the Japanese outside Shenyang. Although the Kwantung Army was behind this explosion, they claimed it was the work of Chinese saboteurs. Using that as an excuse, Japanese soldiers were dispatched to fight against Chinese troops stationed in the city and next fanned out through China's Northeast. They eventually took the rest of Manchuria and, despite international protests, would not withdraw.

The bare facts about this invasion do little to convey the true nature of the Japanese occupation of Manchuria. Slogans tried to convince the public that this was a triumph for Asians, for now this part of China had been "liberated" from the Chinese warlords and imperialist Western powers that had carved up China. In their place would rise *ōdō rakudo*, "a paradise of benevolent government" created by the Japanese. There was, too, the promise of solidarity and prosperity for the five Asian races (Mongol, Manchu, Chinese, Korean, Japanese), who would live and work together in this new heaven.

In reality this was the commencement of a cold-blooded regime that would force Chinese farmers off their own property to make way for new settlers from Japan; the Japanese would acquire great swaths of Chinese land—about fifty million acres by 1941—by "price manipulations, coerced sales, and forced evictions." By the end of the war, more than two million Japanese—military and civilians—were living in Manchuria. Some Chinese would become tenant farmers on land they had owned for generations; others would face starvation when crops were taken to feed the Japanese. Atrocities committed by the Japanese were widespread. The "pacification programs," which were instituted to rid the countryside of opponents, would send whole villages into collective hamlets, little different from concentration camps, and even a Japanese official wrote that the program was "forced through mercilessly, inhumanely, without emotion, as if driving a horse."

Two months after the Manchurian Incident, Kawashima Yoshiko's departure for Manchuria was announced in the *Asahi*. "Miss Kawashima Yoshiko Plunges into the Turbulence," was the headline. "Dressed as a Man in a Suit and Cap, She Goes to Manchuria, the Land of Her Ancestors."

Departing for Dairen [Dalian] on the ship *Dairen Maru* in the drizzling rain was a youth who wore an elegant suit and a gray raincoat with a hunting cap pulled down low over the eyes and was surrounded by many Chinese people. . . . This youth is actually the orphan of Prince Su, who has changed herself into a man and cuts a manly figure. She is seizing the opportunities offered by the upheaval in Manchuria and Mongolia and is now hurrying away to be a part of the new land that must be developed in the home of her ancestors, a region rich in history. . . .

As usual she had been spending every night at the best dance halls in Shanghai, sporting her new haircut and Western clothes in the style of a "modern girl." Sometimes she came and went disguised as a man, always in the company of all sorts of people.

Along with her strange behavior and deluxe lifestyle, she brings with her the air of someone with inside information, whose true persona is impossible to pin down. In the past there have been various rumors about her in Shanghai, but during that time Yoshiko continued her behind-the-scenes doings.

Now, in the wake of the Manchurian Incident, there is the chance that a new era will dawn in the birthplace of her ancestors. and so she is rushing off to the north. She says that from now on she will increasingly go about her activities as a man. Will she go to Dairen or Hōten? For a while, the answers to these questions will be wrapped in mystery.

Kawashima Yoshiko had found herself a new job.

14

AN EMPEROR IN FLUX

I thought that the talks with the Kwantung Army would present no problem and that soon the secrecy would be over and it would be announced that I, the Great Ching Emperor, had returned to the throne in the palace of my ancestors in Shenyang. The thought made me so excited that I paid no attention to the worried expressions of Cheng Hsiao-hsu and Cheng Chui. I happily ate an exotic Japanese supper and gazed out of the window at the beautiful sunset then went to bed, at peace with the world.

—PUYI

Yoshiko's first major assignment for the Japanese army involved the marital problems of her distant relative, the deposed Qing emperor Puyi, whose dislike for her throughout his life was one of his few consistent positions. Yet Puyi could not argue when Yoshiko was called in to do him a favor: his situation had deteriorated, drastically, due to his own miscalculations, and he could not be picky about his saviors.

After his 1912 abdication, Puyi had been allowed to stay in the Forbidden City under conditions very favorable to an unemployed emperor. At last one warlord tired of this generosity, and in 1924 Puyi was evicted from his palace. Immediately the Japanese came to his aid, first taking him into the Japanese legation in Beijing and then affording him refuge in Tianjin, where he lived in the Japanese concession.

All along Puyi wanted his throne back wherever he could get it, and the Kwantung Army obliged by coming up with a new spot for him. Puyi understood that the place on offer in Changchun, Manchuria, was no patch on the Forbidden City, Beijing, but he was willing to settle.

What had happened was that the "rampageous" Kwantung Army, having taken over Manchuria, had to tone down its ambitions because of opposition from the central government in Tokyo. Instead of an outright occupation of the area, the army told the world that they were going to establish an independent state. Chinese would, in fact, take up important posts in the new regime, but they would serve in what would become a Japanese puppet state and be trotted out only to give the enterprise the appearance of authenticity. Behind the curtains would be the Japanese ordering those locals around. Bureaucrats were one matter, but the Japanese were also eager for a royal figurehead, to decorate the tableau and unify the population. This is where Yoshiko and, more important, Puyi came in.

Yoshiko and Puyi would later state that they had been deceived and mistakenly believed that the Japanese were truly doing their people a favor by creating a Manchu state and restoring the Qing dynasty. Their realization that the Japanese had other motives, unrelated to improving the fortunes of the Qing, was slow in coming. Puyi would later say that he had, innocently, stuck his head into "the tiger's mouth."

In his autobiography, Puyi wrote about how he and his whole court in Tianjin were greatly stirred by the news of the Japanese attack in Shenyang during the Manchurian Incident and the rout of Chinese troops. "As soon as I heard the news, I longed to go to the Northeast, but I knew that this was impossible without the consent of the Japanese." The former emperor was then languishing in what was for him toned-down splendor, occupying a Spanish-style mansion on Tianjin's Anshan Road.

Serenity, however, only blessed the exterior of the estate, with its soothing Moorish arches, fountain, and red-tiled roof. Inside, Puyi found it hard to relax. A former emperor without a genuine palace to call his own, Puyi was being pummeled by domestic strife. His wife had become an opium addict, his consort had taken off in a fury, and he felt himself too old to uproot himself and start again. Political unrest took startling turns by the day and threatened Puyi's physical safety. His enemies had reasons to wish him eliminated, and in addition, Chiang Kai-shek, his power on the rise at the time, was no friend of the Qing dynasty. By that time Chiang's troops had fought their way past Communists and warlords, enabling him to emerge as China's strongest leader. A monarch in exile with his own band of supporters, Puyi posed a threat to Chiang, and there were reports among the exiled courtiers about murder plots and attempted poisonings.

While Bertolucci's film *The Last Emperor* has fixed Puyi's character in the public's mind, Puyi's 1964 autobiography, *From Emperor to Citizen*, goes further, deepening the impression of a vain and thick exile, unequipped to face the challenges of life outside the palace and not inclined to change. Puyi's autobiography takes him beyond the film's broad strokes, the Western clothing, and Chinese-flapper milieu to show exactly how he won himself a second turn as emperor in Japanese-controlled Manchuria, a second try that brought so much agony to his people.

From Emperor to Citizen began as Puyi's postwar confessions to his Chinese Communist jailers. Apparently in that first draft, he had flogged himself so thoroughly for his defects that it was deemed unsuitable for a mass readership. Revisions toned down Puyi's self-criticisms, and he did not seem so much the eager penitent, doing everything he could to avoid execution by the new Chinese state. In the 1964 version, there emerges instead a hedonist down on his luck in prison and scrambling to adapt. Puyi endeavors to flail himself for his flaws, but at the same time he caresses the memory of his luxurious former life, which had been so blessedly distant from the suffering masses.

About the Jingyuan Garden, his quarters in Tianjin's Japanese concession in 1925, Puyi recalls the positive features of the new place: "I found a foreign-style house with flush lavatories and central heating far more comfortable than the Mind Nurture Palace [in the Forbidden City]. . . . I was still addressed in exactly the same way as before. . . . All this seemed to me both natural and essential." He remembers how he had made provisions for his cash needs: "The economics of the Jingyuan Garden were naturally on a far smaller scale than those of the Forbidden City, but I still had a considerable fortune. Of the large quantities of valuables I had brought with me from the Forbidden City, some had been converted into money which was now earning interest in foreign banks and some had been turned into real estate to bring in rent."

Nonetheless, Puyi confesses that he was strapped: "After I moved to Tianjin there were many places to which money had to be sent every month and a number of offices were set up for this purpose. . . . There were also officials appointed to look after the imperial tombs of the Qing house. . . . The biggest item on the budget was the money spent on trying to buy over or influence warlords. . . . Purchases, excluding such items as cars or diamonds, probably accounted for two-thirds of an average month's expenses. I spent far more money on buying things when in Tianjin than I had done in Beijing, and the amount increased every month. I never tired of buying pianos, watches, clocks, radios, Western clothes, leather shoes and spectacles." His shopping tours convinced him that foreign goods were superior to Chinese products. "A stick of Spearmint chewing-gum or a Bayer aspirin would be enough to make me sigh at the utter doltishness of the Chinese, though I did not include myself as I saw myself superior of all my subjects. . . . My body would be fragrant with the combined odors of Max Factor lotions, eau-de-Cologne and mothballs, and I would be accompanied by two or three Alsatian dogs and a strangely dressed wife and consort." Though Puyi was trying to prove his remorse after the fact, the brand-name precision shows him warming to these memories.

Enjoyment of Spearmint and Max Factor products was imperiled by the threats to Puyi's safety, some real and others cooked up by the Japanese, who were eager to transport him out of Tianjin and up north to Manchuria. Impatient with their vacillating would-be emperor, the Japanese army sought to propel him toward a speedy departure. A gift of fruit arrived at the former emperor's residence, and bombs were discovered hidden in the basket; the Japanese orchestrated a riot by Chinese in Tianjin that also threatened Puyi's personal safety. Next a waiter from the Victoria Café called to say that it was dangerous for him to eat there, since armed and suspicious characters had been seen lurking around the premises. "I do not know who that waiter was, if he ever existed," Puyi later recalled with bitterness.

Puyi at last agreed to leave at once for Manchuria, where, the Japanese assured him, he would be safe and restored to power. Some of his advisers objected to this plan, fearing that he would have no recourse once under the control of the Japanese. Family members also were opposed to his alliance with the Japanese, and, fearing that he might submit to the enemy, urged him not to "acknowledge a bandit as my father." Yet Puyi, already airing out his regal dragon robes, allowed himself to be won over by Japanese promises. "I was too far carried away by my dream of restoration to heed any warnings."

With his Japanese handlers on board, Puyi left by boat for Manchuria in November 1931, answering a fellow Manchu's plea for his presence in the "land where our ancestors arose." He believed that one day he would be proclaimed emperor there and rule a unified China again. Instead, as had been predicted, he found himself sequestered in Lushun—in the same red hilltop house where Prince Su and his family had lived after fleeing Beijing—and immediately diminished, subject to Japanese orders.

Puyi describes himself as both dumbfounded by Japanese lies and help-less before their demands. He would allow the humiliations to continue, participating in court ceremonies aimed at giving legitimacy to a murder-ous regime that lasted until 1945.

"Thus it was that both trembling with fear and dreaming of my future restoration," he writes, turning on the contrition, "I shamelessly became a leading traitor, and the cover for a sanguinary regime which turned a large part of my country into a colony and inflicted great sufferings on thirty million of my compatriots."

15

THE RELUCTANT EMPRESS

Twenty autumns later,
again the garden,
the archery field silent,
broken pavilions, dance halls abandoned,
a sea of shards,
new birth perhaps from rubble . . .

—YIHUAN, PUYI'S GRANDFATHER

Back in Tianjin, Puyi's wife, Wanrong, had not gone along on his journey north; she had no interest in joining him and refused to budge. Her stubbornness exasperated the Kwantung Army, which wished to present a harmonious royal family to the citizens of its new state: Puyi without his wife would not do. Furthermore, Wanrong's capricious moods, fed by opium, were also worrisome since she might one day declare her allegiance to a Chinese leader unfriendly to the Japanese, providing opponents with a great propaganda boon.

When the army could not persuade Wanrong to join her husband, they requested assistance from Yoshiko, another woman of the imperial Manchu clan. As Yoshiko's brother Xianli remembers, she did not hesitate to do the bidding of the Japanese military. "All Staff Officer Itagaki [Seishirō] had to say was, 'I'd like Yoshiko-san to go to Tianjin to meet her.'" Yoshiko was soon off to Tianjin to effect the empress's removal to Manchuria.

When Wanrong married Puyi in 1922, he had already abdicated as the ruler of China but was still living in the Forbidden City. Thus Puyi was sixteen years old and already an anxious former emperor when his advisers decided that he should take a wife. Without giving the matter too much thought, Puyi chose a bride from photos presented to him. "Their faces were very small in the pictures so that I could not see whether they were beauties or not. . . . It did not occur to me at the time that this was one of the great events of my life."

Things didn't work out. Wanrong, who was from a prominent, noble Manchu family, had received a Western-style education in the French concession of Tianjin. She had mastered English, tennis, and the two-step, preparing her for contact with an international social set. Once Puyi chose her, all possibilities narrowed, with little hope that her life would extend beyond the palace. As it turned out, she did get to move about more than anticipated, but mostly in haste and in extremis, as an empress on the run. After Puyi was at last expelled from the Forbidden City, she took her first hasty flight to Tianjin along with the rest of the court.

When most chroniclers catch up with Wanrong, she has given up her English studies and become a full-fledged opium addict. The downsized life of the court in exile in Tianjin wore on her, as did her husband, whose homosexuality was widely rumored. There were also the rituals she was expected to observe, though the return of the Qing dynasty seemed ever more implausible. Never-ending were the conflicts with Puyi's consort, who competed for his attention and also spat in the garden to emphasize her disrespect when Wanrong was nearby.

Wanrong sought and got the opium that alleviated these tensions. "Few of the royal family members took opium except the empress, . . ." a court eunuch recalled. "It was a hard job to serve her when she smoked. One had to kneel on the ground and move quickly with the smoking set as she turned from one side to another. The empress usually took four smokes at each side."

Here again Xianli supplies a charged tidbit about the empress's state of mind in Tianjin: "Puyi's homosexuality was an open secret. The empress wended her way toward her husband but I don't think you can say that she'd joyously rushed off to be with him." Xianli thus confirms the gossip about Puyi's sexual preferences, and, significantly, he's the one who also confirms that Yoshiko, at the Kwantung Army's request, sped off to Tianjin to haul Wanrong to Japanese-occupied Manchuria. The facts surrounding this event, and many other events in Yoshiko's life, are often substantiated by the likes of Xianli and Yoshiko, who, as is clear, have their own ways with the truth. With no hard proof at hand, we can only look with admiration upon their swashbuckling, confident testimony.

The successful transport of the empress from Tianjin to Manchuria is one of the most enduring of Yoshiko's myths, the boldness of her actions growing with each retelling. In his fiction, nonfiction, and also works that belong somewhere in between, Muramatsu Shōfū told of this deed, and the versions he popularized gained wide acceptance. In her 1940 autobiography, Yoshiko took Shōfū's account for her own, boasting about flawlessly carrying out this assignment, and more. "I wore a black suit with a hunting cap pulled down low over my eyes and gripped the steering wheel firmly," she wrote about the transport of her charge, exulting in her ingenuity and guts.

As Shōfū tells it, the outbreak of anti-Japanese violence in Tianjin delayed the start of Yoshiko's gallant mission. This was the Chinese uprising orchestrated by the Japanese army, to impress upon Puyi the wisdom of an immediate getaway before those mobs succeeded in tearing him to pieces. As we've seen, he took their advice. "At 11 o'clock last night bands of Chinese ruffians began firing at the police near the Japanese concession," the *New York Times* reported, "and at two o'clock this morning larger groups attacked the police."

Getting the same message about the perils of Tianjin, the empress at last agreed to leave for Manchuria. With bullets whizzing by on the streets, Yoshiko believed that only she possessed the courage to bring Wanrong to safety. She drove a Cuban-make automobile herself—Yoshiko had actually learned to drive in Shanghai—and planned to keep her headlights off as she made her way to the boat that would take the empress north. Wanrong, hurried out of her residence, was ready to stash herself in the car trunk when she realized that she had left her beloved dog behind.

"Get the dog," she ordered Yoshiko, whose responsibilities extended to these matters.

Yoshiko, in Shōfū's portrayal, is as ever the cool-headed operative, headlights out, dog and Qing empress in the Cuban car trunk. With no streetlights and no Tianjin residents outside, she drives through the darkness, making her way toward a light atop a pillar, which is her only landmark. Finally they reach the dock, and the empress boards a crude cargo ship headed for Dalian. The empress, who left Tianjin with only her dog and the clothes on her back, expresses gratitude to Yoshiko with the gift of a jade ornament that had belonged to her mother.

In real life, this was how Yoshiko liked to see herself—audacious in the dark, shrewd, impeccably well connected; it is no wonder that she embraced

Puyi and Wanrong en route to Changchun, capital
of the new state of Manchukuo, March 1932

Alinari Archives/Getty Images

Shōfū's version of the adventure. By the time a member of Wanrong's entourage ventured to cast doubt on this triumph, stating that Yoshiko had played
only a minor role in the empress's flight to Manchuria, no one was listening.
Yoshiko had done a good job of living up to Shōfū's account—until she had
to turn around and deny everything when she was arrested after the war.

Since this was the first notable favor that Yoshiko is said to have done for
the Kwantung Army—and one of the reasons the Chinese sought her execution later—it is a good place to explore why she would have been willing
to help the Japanese. At her trial, Yoshiko was at pains to state that all her

actions, including this one (which by then she had disavowed), were not in any way aimed at helping the Japanese achieve their goal of domination of China. On the contrary, she insisted upon her resolve to come to the aid of China in general and the Manchus in particular.

Yoshiko's sense of herself as a Manchu had, of course, been fostered since childhood, and this potent Manchu identity impelled her forward. After the fall of the Qing, many Manchus had lost their government stipends, and all had lost their prestige in the land they had ruled for centuries. Accustomed to government support, the newly downtrodden lacked the skills and the grit necessary to reconstruct their lives. In addition, the Han majority disparaged them as ignorant, foreign barbarians who had brought ruin to the country; Chiang Kai-shek's troops pillaged the Qing imperial tombs with impunity. Having seen her fellow Manchus struggling against poverty and ostracism, Yoshiko was drawn to the idea of Japan's new Manchu "homeland."

And about the accusations that she had betrayed China with such actions as the rescue of the empress, the justification is somewhat murky. The central government of China, which she was later accused of betraying, was a shaky, elusive entity in those days; identifying exactly who or what truly represented China could be a matter of opinion. Amid this chaos, she had convinced herself that a Manchu government was the best choice for China. Carrying on her father's dreams, she seemed to picture herself striving to rid China of warring factions and finally achieving unity once more under Qing rule. Establishing a Qing regime in Manchuria would be a start on these larger goals.

"I didn't know anything about what kind of political setup China would have in the future," she wrote in her confession to her Chinese jailers after the war. "I hated myself for being so useless. I wanted to restore the Qing dynasty and bring our emperor back to the Forbidden City so that he would control Beijing and Chiang Kai-shek would control the south. Both of them would work together to develop much industry and commerce in China. From then on, no one would dare to invade China. This has been my dream since I was a teenager."

Undercutting these claims about longing to save China and about not assisting the Japanese were her complicated feelings about Japan itself. Since her youth, Yoshiko had fumed at the racial slurs that came her way in Japan. Disparaged as a "Chink" repeatedly, she was discriminated against in other ways because of her Chinese origins. As an adult, too, she complained about the racism of the Japanese, and so she never became a starry-eyed Japanese loyalist.

But she could not get away from the natural attachment she felt to Japan, the place where she had grown up, and the comfort she felt in those familiar surroundings. She found reasons to rail against Japan, but she returned time and again, and was taken in. Once there, she had access to important people, who flattered her and made sure she appeared on the front pages of newspapers.

She certainly had hopes of aiding the Manchus and did not consider herself an ally of Japan. But she just as certainly needed sympathy, the spotlight, and lots of cash and so could not resist taking what the Japanese army offered.

*

To find out more about what happened to Empress Wanrong after she settled down in Manchuria, we must turn to Saga Hiro. We last encountered Hiro just before her 1937 marriage to Puyi's brother Pujie. After that Hiro had lived peacefully by the coast outside of Tokyo while her husband completed his military studies. In October 1937, several months after Japan's full-scale invasion of China, Hiro left Japan for Manchuria.

Hiro's residence there, in Changchun, illustrates the imperfect conditions facing this new, cobbled-up royal family. Her expectations had been raised by a grand photo of her prospective home that had appeared in a Japanese newspaper before her departure, but she and her husband were given a home elsewhere. Hastily put together, their house lacked certain walls, phone, and a protective fence. Since the building sat on what had once been the untamed pasture of a Mongol king, roe deer and wild rabbits roamed through the thick grasses. The overall security situation was not comforting either since bandits infested the neighborhood, and sensible citizens avoided those streets.

Having been told by no less than the mother of the Japanese emperor that serving Emperor Puyi in Manchuria was the same as serving the emperor of Japan, Hiro was still determined to uphold royal standards. Her resolve was tested the day she first met Puyi, who got the encounter off to a good start by presenting her with a watch studded with diamonds, sapphires, and emeralds.

Hiro remembers being taken aback by Empress Wanrong, her sister-in-law. "She was a little over thirty, about five feet seven inches tall, and well built. In her high heels she was so tall that I had to look up at her. She had flowers and jewels all over her hair. Her big eyes really were striking, and she possessed a refined beauty. Of course I performed my formal kowtow before her, kneeling three times and touching my forehead to the floor nine times."

Stoical where Wanrong was awash in gloom, preternaturally disciplined where Wanrong was limp, Hiro could not have been more different. She was shocked to observe the damaged empress at the Western-style dinner that followed. "The empress was seated to my right, and while I was watching, she kept on taking more and more turkey for herself. I was surprised at her good appetite. Perhaps to make sure that I didn't catch on to what was happening, her younger brother Runqi went so far as to rudely grab the chocolate from the person next to him. He kept on eating in a comical way to turn everyone's attention toward him. Afterward I found out that the empress was an opium addict and often suffered from bouts of mental instability. She just wasn't aware of how much she was eating."

16

POWERFUL CONNECTIONS

YOSHIKO: What will you do?

TANAKA: I'll survive of course.

—KISHIDA RISEI, FROM THE PLAY *FINAL NEST, TEMPORARY LODGING*

I n testifying at the Tokyo War Crimes Trial after the Second World War, Tanaka Ryūkichi always insisted upon the purity of his motives. Of course there was much speculation about why he decided to appear at this trial: Tanaka, a major general in the Imperial Japanese Army, cooperated with U.S. Occupation authorities and testified, with enthusiasm, against his military colleagues. Defense lawyers questioned why he had chosen to present wide-ranging evidence, bolstered by his breathtaking memory for detail, that would surely doom his former associates. Accused of turning against his fellow officers in retaliation for being denied a wartime post or to escape indictment himself, Tanaka rejected any suggestions of base intent.

"My expressions in the tribunal," he explained in his high-minded fashion, "are for the purpose of giving expression, giving voice to the cause why Japan has met her present fate and . . . [to] let the truth be known to the people in order to set this country aright and also to let . . . these truths [be known] to our posterity." Much later he claimed that he'd testified only to absolve the emperor of Japan of any responsibility for the war and thereby prevent the emperor's prosecution for war crimes.

Seeking to undercut the devastating impact of Tanaka's insider accounts, defense lawyers raised doubts about this star witness's sanity. Was it not true, one lawyer inquired, that when Tanaka was a staff officer in the Kwantung Army, he was hospitalized for emotional collapse? Tanaka hastened to assure the court that he had not lost his wits at that time but instead suffered from mere "gas intoxication." Then what about the two months he had spent in the hospital after his resignation from the army? That, Tanaka reported, was only a forty-six day stay in the hospital, where he was treated for insomnia. He conceded that hospital officials would not let him out as quickly as he had wished, and so he resorted to bribery.

"Yes, I spent quite a bit of money, because I wanted to get out of the hospital as soon as possible—by giving away theater tickets and buying fruits." In between these remarks, he managed to work in a declaration on a loftier subject: "However, the other disease with which I was afflicted—that is, serious anxiety over the state of affairs of my country—that disease was not cured."

Tanaka appeared before the tribunal a number of times, sometimes for the defense and sometimes for the prosecution. He strove to implicate his former rivals and clear the names of those fortunate defendants he still considered friends. His smooth delivery, complete with all those very specific names and places, left him open to charges that he was a "professional witness." "He testified glibly and often on a great variety of matters," one lawyer complained.

> He acknowledged good friends sitting in the dock, and then proceeded, with what seemed eagerness, to do his best to convict them. He appeared as a "happy and smiling warrior," but the key to all of Tanaka's testimony is that he is an exceedingly unhappy warrior—a man of intelligence, but of jealousy and consuming ambition, who had natural aspirations for promotion and recognition, who left the Army because of illness, and who could not bear the fact that another man was appointed to the position he aspired to.

Perhaps nothing so undercut the witness's testimony as a defense lawyer's allusion to Major General Tanaka's activities during the war. At the trial, Tanaka was called upon to swear that Tōjō Hideki—a wartime prime minister and Tanaka adversary—had attended the meeting that resulted in forcing prisoners of war to work in labor camps. Without any hesitation, Tanaka corroborated his old boss's leadership role at this gathering, thus making Tōjō responsible, indisputably, for the brutal treatment of POWs—one of the crimes for which Tōjō was later hanged.

After Tanaka finished incriminating Tōjō, the defense would not let him step down from the witness stand so fast.

"General, aren't you known by the people in Japan as 'The Monster'?"

When objections were raised about the relevance of this line of questioning, the lawyer responded, "I think it is very relevant. . . . Here's a man that has come and testified here, that has admitted he is the head of the *kempeitai* and isn't even indicted. I think the Tribunal should know the type of man that is testifying for the prosecution."

Tanaka was at pains to distance himself from any Japanese military group responsible for countless evil acts. Though he conceded his role as head of the Military Service Bureau, he denied that he had anything to do with the day-to-day doings of the *kempeitai*, the savage military police. "We handled affairs pertaining to the gendarmerie, or *kempeitai*, but not to supervise or control that organization. . . . The gendarmerie was under the control and supervision of the war minister and the war vice minister." By preening here as nothing more than a military clerk, he strove to exonerate himself while simultaneously heading back for another go at Tōjō, who had also been the war minister.

Tanaka's "sybaritic and unsavory character," as well as his manner of speaking—he shouted each time he spoke in court—contributed to an impression that he had most likely participated in the same kind of vile acts that would eventually get his comrades executed by the Allies' court. He had made his way up through the officer ranks in the Japanese army, serving for long periods in China. He was noted early on for his skill in strategy, honed by his vicious instincts.

"To put it bluntly," Tanaka once told a Japanese journalist, "you and I have basic differences in the way we view the Chinese. You seem to treat them like human beings. I think of them as pigs."

*

Tanaka Ryūkichi was doubtless a ruthless army officer who turned against his colleagues after the war. He was also an important figure in Yoshiko's life; he was her lover, her mentor, her source of cash, and the person who made her most vulnerable to execution. It was an involvement that stemmed from Tanaka's personal weaknesses, which, along with his professional skills, brought him attention. Women sent the violent and unstable general into childish mood swings. Unhinged by passion, he abased himself and wept. Kawashima Yoshiko would possess his spirit for years, and later, in order to exorcise her, he pushed for her assassination.

As of New Year's Day 1931, when Tanaka became involved with Yoshiko, he had already demonstrated the rash side of his character. He'd become involved with a married woman, and the lovers attempted double suicide by throwing themselves into a lake. The woman died but Tanaka lived on, making his superiors aware—not for the last time—of his unsteadiness. Ordinarily such behavior meant automatic expulsion from the army, but an exception was made this time since Tanaka had shown so much promise in military matters. The army ordered the newspapers not to publish a word about the double suicide attempt, and Tanaka continued his rise in the army.

In a later essay about Tanaka's relationship with Yoshiko—written by Tanaka's son but with facts straight from the father—the couple's Shanghai courtship is recalled by Tanaka in a mood of calm reflection. While contemporaries have described Tanaka as driven crazy by his sick, fierce passion for Yoshiko, he sees himself as a restrained and chivalrous suitor. Early in their acquaintance he rejected this Qing princess when she made lewd advances in his Shanghai office, and he urged her to act in the chaste manner that befitted her royal status. After she tricked him out of some money, badgered him into finding her a place to live, and besieged him with sexual importunings that he turned down, he happened to run into her at a dance hall. As they took a turn on the floor, she chided him for his coldness, saying she had never been treated so badly by a man. Despite this, she could not forget him.

Worn down, Tanaka escorted her to the room she had reserved in the Kasei Hotel. Here the essay confirms the well-documented obsession that haunted Tanaka from that day forward: "After that, while he was working in Shanghai, her existence was always essential to him, both publicly and privately. During this period in his life, she became very important to him, a woman he could not get out of his mind."

This account, though bowing to certain facts, does not own up to the true nature of their alliance. Muramatsu Shōfū, no stranger to bizarre romance in the China of those days, found himself not only aghast when he witnessed the couple's exchanges but also fearful for his own safety in associating with them. In one of his accounts, perhaps embellished, Shōfū sized up Tanaka and Yoshiko's domestic interactions in Shanghai: "When I met him, he struck me as different from what I'd imagined. Based on what other people had told me, I had formed an impression in my mind of a gifted military man, but in person he was the exact opposite. He had a wide forehead, puffy cheeks, pug nose, and more of a certain solidity than you would expect of a man of his age. In his arrogance, he seemed to fear nothing."

This impression changed minutes later, when Yoshiko came into the room. "Kawashima was imperious and rude to Tanaka," Shōfū writes, "like a master to her servant.... He just kept saying yes, yes to whatever this female master told him." In spite of the army's high opinion of Tanaka's professional abilities, "he had something big missing inside his head," Shōfū concluded.

More startling to Shōfū was another occasion when Yoshiko became infuriated at Tanaka for boasting in public about how he supported her, how she did nothing for the army, and how, without his money, she'd be out on the streets tomorrow. "Her voice was shocking," Shōfū says. "It was such a roar of anger that you had to wonder about what part of the woman's throat that sound came from.... Her face became as red as a peony."

Yoshiko ordered Tanaka to apologize for insulting her, and he immediately obeyed. He got down on his knees and begged forgiveness. An incredulous Shōfū could only attribute this to Tanaka's "well-known perversion."

★

After she had successfully transported the empress, Yoshiko could declare herself launched on a new career. The job description was hazy, however, and so employee and employer had different views about her responsibilities. Yoshiko of course always insisted that she was a liberator—Manchus returned to power and prosperity, peasants uplifted, all of China saved—but the Japanese army saw her more as royal window dressing, a captivating distraction from awful goings-on and proof that they had the Manchus on their side.

Tanaka's son recorded his father's reminiscences years after Yoshiko had been executed—as had a number of Tanaka's former military associates, thanks in part to the elder Tanaka's testimony at the Tokyo War Crimes Trial. Excoriated afterward as a turncoat and a lunatic, Tanaka had not been able to endure the strain of this notoriety in postwar Japan. There were mental crises and a suicide attempt. His son says that he had a miserable twenty years after the trial and, forgotten by the world, he died a "tragic" figure.

Tanaka likely did suffer in the aftermath of his appearances at the trial, and hounding by journalists and critics could have easily wrecked his emotional balance. Sympathy for Tanaka comes hard, however, and this is especially true after reading his account of his time with Yoshiko. Although Tanaka had failed to win Yoshiko's affection in life, he has reason for the triumphant tone in these reminiscences. In particular, he allows himself to gloat over the difference in their circumstances at that moment, for he has come out the winner in a big battle: he has managed to stay alive, and she is dead. Smug in victory, he reviews his former lover's bad luck.

Tanaka's reminiscence is our only detailed source of information about Yoshiko's involvement in the Shanghai Incident of 1932. The self-serving words of a person prone to betrayal and nervous breakdown must be read with skepticism. It should also be remembered that this is the view of the only surviving participant in a love affair that ended badly.

Still, Tanaka's basic facts about the Shanghai Incident have more or less been accepted, with even Yoshiko's sympathizers finding them hard to refute. Biographer Kamisaka Fuyuko, who always looks for ways to defend Yoshiko's doings, is pained by her subject's involvement in this bloody conflict. "She was manipulated and chased into a corner before she understood the whole situation, and this was doubtless due to her own stupidity." Softening, Kamisaka reverts to her view of Yoshiko as a helpless female who cannot be held accountable for her own decisions: "But if we take a closer look and try to find the guilty party, doesn't the real blame for this crime fall on those who engineered this woman's participation in this grand plot?"

Tanaka's son reports that his father "bought a house for Yoshiko and made a love nest for him and her." But Tanaka was then the assistant military attaché for the Japanese legation in Shanghai and "did not forget about his basic duties." In short, Tanaka saw that Yoshiko could be helpful to the Japanese military. "While he was living with her, he understood her personality and made use of her for his work, realizing that she would be good at gathering information." He enrolled her in a Chinese school to study English, and because she already knew some Chinese, he wanted her to put the two languages to work in spying on prominent figures. "In other words he poured all his effort into making her a full-fledged spy, and his plans succeeded beautifully. She became his invaluable assistant and followed his instructions."

Of course the work also went along nicely with her personal philosophy. "She never for a moment forsook her pride at being part of the old Qing royal family," Tanaka's son reports. "She often mourned their decline. She had made the firm decision to bring about the return of the Qing with the backing of Japan. She said she would not regret sacrificing her life for this cause." Tanaka sent her north to Manchuria, where she took orders from Colonel Itagaki Seishirō, who had been one of the planners of the Kwantung Army's invasion of Manchuria. Tanaka again gloats about his superb judgment: "Her talents as a spy were extraordinary."

Yoshiko also kept up her appearances at the dance halls of Shanghai, where, the gossips charged, she joined the taxi dancers, whose services were purchased with a ticket at the door. Yoshiko always rejected the idea that she ever had danced for pay, though she did win renown for dancing in the man's role and a first prize in a Shanghai waltz competition. Shōfū, who always enjoys emphasizing Yoshiko's male clothes and habits, wrote that she had become "expert at dancing the man's role" and praises the "very distinctive, inimitable style, good sense of rhythm, and good form." In such passages, Shōfū views Yoshiko's male ways as nothing more than a gimmick, a way for her to get publicity; he never thinks there was anything deeper involved in her assumption of a male persona. Later on in Tokyo, when Shōfū saw Yoshiko taking the woman's dancing role dressed in feminine clothes, he was scornful of her performance, saying that she looked as if she'd "swallowed an iron rod, very stiff."

Afterward, Yoshiko also denied using her charms and her dancing skills to wheedle intelligence out of the prominent Chinese officials who liked to dance with her. Yet biographer Kamisaka points to a passage from *The Beauty in Men's Clothing* that, in Kamisaka's view at least, expresses the "basic beliefs" of the real-life Yoshiko. Defending herself against criticism that a Qing princess should not degrade herself by toiling in dance halls, this fictional heroine sounds like a woman who danced with a purpose and did not take to the floor just to polish her technique:

> Talk about being a member of the Qing imperial family had some meaning when there was a Qing court. But now people like us are shunned by society and pressured by those in power more than ordinary people. We are rushing every which way in order to escape. Don't you think it would be really pathetic if the only thing we carted around was our pride at being

part of the imperial family? You can only laugh at an attitude like that. I am a mere insignificant woman, but to help the restoration movement, I will offer what little support I can at any time.

★

After the war, Tanaka proudly admitted that he was entirely responsible for the Shanghai Incident, showing no remorse for the thousands who died as a result of his ingenuity. He explained that the plot to foment violence in Shanghai had been hatched as a distraction from bigger doings in Manchuria. The Kwantung Army was getting ready to expand its hold by taking Harbin and then wanted to officially organize its occupied land into the independent state that would be known as Manchukuo. Fearing an international outcry once this was achieved, the army ordered Tanaka to start an uprising in Shanghai to divert the world's attention.

On January 10, 1932, Tanaka received a long telegram from Itagaki and was sent twenty thousand yen, for use in exacerbating the already volatile relations between the Chinese and Japanese in Shanghai. "At that time," a Japanese eyewitness in Shanghai recalled, "you have to think of the impact of the Manchurian Incident. All of China was in an uproar because of the Manchurian Incident, and the waves of anti-Japanese sentiment were on the rise. Their country's territory had been usurped. The country had been humiliated." There were protests against Japanese imperialism by Chinese students and workers as well as boycotts of Japanese goods. "Even so, the Japanese living there were not in direct danger."

Aiming for an explosion of violence, Tanaka set to work immediately. He says that he gave half the money to Yoshiko, and she then contacted Chinese workers from the Sanyou Towel Company, with instructions to cause trouble.

On January 18, a group of Japanese Buddhist priests strode down the street near the factory, intoning sutras and beating their drums. "The important thing to remember," says the Japanese eyewitness, "is that at that time, the Chinese in Shanghai were very riled up. Anti-Japanese feeling was getting more and more fierce. Then you have Japanese priests walking down a Chinese street and creating a warlike atmosphere by beating their drums. Such things didn't happen in China. Chinese monks are very gentle. . . . I thought at the time that the Chinese would take this as provocation."

As Yoshiko had supposedly arranged, Chinese workers from the factory set upon the Japanese monks. One monk was killed in this attack, and two were wounded. "That incident occurred so suddenly. Now we had a direct confrontation between Chinese and Japanese."

This was followed by the predictable accusations on both sides and revenge attacks. Next, Japanese youths, again commissioned by Yoshiko, burned down the storage area of the Chinese towel factory. The Japanese residents of Shanghai had already presented objections to Chinese officials regarding anti-Japanese activities in the city. Not only did the Japanese protest against boycotts of their goods and efforts to get them out of China, they also demanded severe punishment for the Chinese who had attacked the Japanese monks. Soon enough, Japanese warships appeared in the Shanghai harbor to bolster troops already in the area.

Likewise, the calls for action from the Chinese side intensified. "The Chinese government in Shanghai didn't have the military strength to get into a war with Japan," remembers the eyewitness. "What students were saying [against the Japanese presence] was absolutely correct, so it was no use trying to get them to back off. The Chinese government was really in a bind."

Although the Chinese mayor eventually had to accede to Japanese demands, the Japanese military nonetheless commenced its huge assault on the Chinese sections of the city by land and air. The military cited provocation by the Chinese and the need to defend Japanese residents of Shanghai as the reasons for its massive onslaught. "The Chinese refugees," one journalist wrote, "report that vast numbers of the 200,000 population of Chabei [the Chinese district] have been slain, and that the dead and dying number thousands." In spite of this gory fight, the Chinese troops fought with surprising effectiveness, and it was not until the Japanese brought in additional divisions, bringing the total to ninety thousand Japanese troops, that they were able to prevail.

Tanaka had nothing but praise for Yoshiko's contribution to this hard-won Japanese victory. "While this fierce battle was going on, she followed his directions," Tanaka's son reports, "and acted with remarkable bravery. Tanaka also was astonished by her abilities. . . . These deeds of hers would never appear in the newspapers but were rather schemes carried out behind the scenes." Implicating her in every aspect of the operation, Tanaka says that Yoshiko was indispensable in ferreting out information from the Chinese side, at a time when up-to-the-minute intelligence about the enemy's next moves was desperately needed. On her own, he says, Yoshiko infiltrated her way into a Chinese military installation and informed Japanese officials about its inventory of armaments. She was in constant contact with Sun Fo, the son of Sun Yat-sen, who was a high-ranking official in the Nationalist government at the time; Sun Fo is said to have provided her with valuable information that she conveyed to Japanese military headquarters.

Once the truce had been declared and the fighting over, Tanaka rejoiced in all that he had achieved. As his son writes,

> With Staff Officer Itagaki as the driving force, the Kwantung Army in Manchuria took advantage of the fact that the eyes of the world powers were all focused on Shanghai and made good progress toward the establishment of the independent state of Manchukuo. A proclamation establishing the independent state of Manchukuo was issued. . . . And so Tanaka's mission had been accomplished. Also that heroic woman Kawashima Yoshiko, who had been indispensable to him in this work, of course came to be known to posterity as "Mata Hari of the East" as a result of activities like this and achieved fame among the Japanese military and around the world.

Again, such reports about Yoshiko's service to the Japanese army are all impossible to confirm. Tanaka has reason to give an exaggerated appraisal of her contributions and thereby emphasize the strictly business side of a bond that consumed him. Postwar, he also did not mind taking credit for being the force behind a fascinating, famous woman.

Those who doubt Tanaka wonder about how a woman so instantly recognizable from many newspaper articles about her could have been involved in any clandestine operations in the first place. There are questions, too, about Yoshiko's Chinese language skills, since a number of the feats Tanaka attributes to her required a fluency she did not possess.

Still, Yoshiko's cocky behavior and her extravagance after the Shanghai Incident indicate that her circumstances had suddenly and greatly improved, suggesting reward for services rendered to the Japanese army. The newspapers treated her with more respect and stopped focusing on her sexual excesses.

In fact, of all the charges brought against Yoshiko at her trial, her incitement of the violence during the Shanghai Incident seems most believable. The assignment required basic but not perfect Chinese language skills, good connections, instant recognizability among the workers she had to recruit, commitment, the gift of gab, energy—all qualifications within her capacity. And finally, Yoshiko's brother Xianli has been found credible by some when he offers evidence pointing to her culpability in the Shanghai Incident and the deaths of so many.

"Afterward Xianli remembered that Yoshiko had introduced him to workers from the Sanyou Towel Company, proving that Yoshiko played a large role in the swirling machinations of the plot. There seems to be no room for excuses here."

17
WOMAN OF INFLUENCE

As we sucked the luscious grapes, bit into fresh dates, and peeled juicy oranges, the Princess gave me an introduction to the many strange tales of her adventurous life. Aided in her English now and again by various members around the table, the Princess told me her story, a true story which turned out to be stranger than fiction.

—WILLA LOU WOODS

Muramatsu Shōfū has left a report about the state of Yoshiko's personal life around this time, when the fighting was winding down in Shanghai, in the spring of 1932. It was then that he went to Shanghai to do research for *The Beauty in Men's Clothing*. Shōfū spent two months collecting background information about the woman he would turn into his novel's heroine, and while he was at it, he took a close look at Yoshiko's daily routine.

Shōfū is especially qualified when it comes to providing an intimate description of Yoshiko's household during this period because she not only insisted that he stay with her but also had him sleep in her bedroom. "There were two beds on either side," Shōfū recalled. "One was a big luxurious bed with a thoroughly Western-style table by the pillow. The other was a small, ordinary bed. From the day of my arrival I slept in the splendid big bed, and Kawashima took the small one." Elaborating further, Shōfū refers to Yoshiko as "he," to again bring attention to her male persona.

I imagined that he usually slept in the splendid bed and one of his maids in the other. The servants seemed to sleep on the second floor. There were about six feet between the two beds. Since there was no one else in the room, we slept with our beds side by side.

I was surprised by Kawashima's wildness and daring, but at the same time, I was perplexed about what to do. Kawashima's relationship with Lieutenant Colonel T (he had been promoted) was well-known around town. . . . I wouldn't call him brilliant, but I would say that he was somewhat crazy. If this became a love triangle, I'd really be in danger. . . . I well understood how terrifying this powerful woman could be. My struggle for self-control was absurd, but just this once in my life, I restrained myself.

Shōfū believed that Yoshiko never forgot this rejection of sexual involvement and sought revenge several years later by trying to poison him. But when they lived in the same room in Shanghai, Shōfū was determined to keep things as businesslike as possible, always fearing the jealous wrath of "Colonel T," Tanaka Ryūkichi.

When he tagged along on Yoshiko's nightly visits to Shanghai dance halls, Shōfū was worn-out by her pace and shocked by the quantities of money she spent. "After a late dinner every night Kawashima and I, accompanied by a servant, went to the cabarets. Kawashima always had a wad of ten-yuan bills about an inch thick. He wouldn't count the money but instead would decide how much to tip the manager, waiter, and dancers by the thickness of the wad. I never saw anyone spend money like that. He started a big commotion wherever he went." Always, Shōfū wondered about the exact source of these abundant funds and decided that her cash must have come from the Japanese military, all channeled through Tanaka.

Yoshiko stayed out until one or two in the morning, and then woke up around noon to the sound of "Moonlight Sonata" and jazz. "Once I got dressed, I'd be smoking a cigarette when Kawashima would get up and come toward me in pajamas after a good night's sleep, face glowing like a flower petal."

During the day, Yoshiko received many visitors in the reception area of her home. Why these hordes of people came to visit her or what advice she dispensed was never clear to Shōfū, since at that time there were no official statements about her doings. Nor was Yoshiko inclined to explain, preferring to tease Shōfū with her enigmas. As far as Shōfū could make out, she had set herself up as something between a social worker and political fixer, all this sanctified by her status as a member of the former royal family and her alleged political clout. Since Yoshiko had earned a reputation on rumored activities so important that they could not be divulged, her allies and enemies were forced to put up with her whims.

Shōfū became convinced that Yoshiko carried out espionage assignments for the Japanese, and this conviction was reinforced by Tanaka, who produced evidence. "Why did T show me these secret documents?" Shōfū wondered. "Included were those called 'Kawashima's Reports.' These reports, akin to newspaper scoops, were on file everywhere. He showed these documents to me to prove the extent of Kawashima's activities."

Despite this, Shōfū had a low regard for the quality of her secret information. "At that time those top-billed telegrams containing 'Kawashima's Reports' would fly into the [Japanese army's] General Staff Office in Miyakezaka, but they really contained many fishy accounts. Simple-minded soldiers got fooled." More ominously, Shōfū goes on to observe that she "gave the military what they wanted." No matter how trivial her reports may have been, in this period just after the Shanghai Incident, Yoshiko was still valuable to the Japanese army, which was planning further conquests in China. The military continued to view her as its public relations treasure, whom it sought to flaunt whenever possible.

In *The Beauty in Men's Clothing*, Shōfū included among the heroine's larger-than-life adventures an ordinary episode—or as ordinary an episode as is possible in a novel about a former Qing princess who talks like a man and likes to wear a tuxedo. Shōfū told of his heroine's servant Shulian, and he wrote later that at least this part of the novel was completely true, based on an episode he witnessed while he was living in Yoshiko's home. Taken from real life, the sections about Shulian are not Shōfū's kind of inventions, since they lack the bluster that usually bucks up his heroine in the novel. Shōfū considered Shulian's tragedy the "clever gift of providence," since it gave him insight into his heroine's true character. Genuinely moved, she at last seems human.

Shulian—Shōfū uses her real name in the novel—is a Chinese teenager whose family had served the heroine's royal clan for many years. When Shulian's stepmother sells her to a geisha house, Shōfū's heroine rescues her and brings her to work in her own Shanghai home. But Shulian, who becomes utterly devoted to her mistress, is eventually raped, and soon after that she kills herself.

Grieving over Shulian's death, the novel's heroine takes responsibility for her young servant's suicide. "I am the one who killed Shulian," the heroine wails in the days that follow. Shulian had lived in her mistress's home for more than a year, but no attempt had been made to teach her to read or write. Instead, the heroine devoted all her energies to one subject: she taught Shulian to value her virginity above all else.

"A woman must protect the purity of her virginity," Shōfū's heroine announces. "If a woman loses her chastity before marriage, she is worthless. She's worth less than a rag or a scrap of wastepaper. She is a piece of filth on the garbage heap. It is a woman's responsibility to protect her virginity with chastity and consecrate her immaculate body and spirit to the man she truly loves."

With such teachings in mind, Shulian believed that, after being deflowered, she could only swallow opium and die.

Biographer Terao Saho attaches much importance to these proclamations about the need to maintain female chastity, issued by the heroine of Shōfū's novel and by the real-life Yoshiko. Terao believes that this horror of physical violation is additional evidence of Yoshiko's own violation in Kawashima Naniwa's home. "Kawashima Yoshiko put too much emphasis on female purity," Terao believes. "This can only reflect what Naniwa did to her."

*

Several years later, Yoshiko entertained another houseguest, this time her first American visitor, Willa Lou Woods, who was a college student from Wenatchee, Washington, on an exchange program in China. Woods was just twenty at the time of the visit, and although she understood virtually nothing about China, she was an adventurous sort, who into old age would launch herself off ski jumps and scale mountains back home in Washington. While visiting China, Woods happened to strike up a friendship with a stranger on a boat and went along with this new acquaintance to pay a call on Yoshiko. One thing led to another and Woods found herself invited to extend her visit.

"Our hostess suggested that I stay at her home a few days," Woods writes. "Rather overcome by such spontaneous hospitality, yet eager to learn the story of this strange royal personage and her household, I accepted."

Over the next few days, Yoshiko regaled her new American friend with her life story, which Woods later summarized in *Princess Jin, the Joan of Arc of the*

Orient. This starstruck remembrance must bring despair to the heart of any biographer. In talking to Woods, Yoshiko shows a stupendous disregard for the facts, calling into question every word she ever uttered about her personal history. Gall unremitting, falsehoods pouring forth, Yoshiko told Woods that she was the daughter of the last emperor of China and had been "disguised as a boy to save her from Chinese revolutionists who went to Japan to seek her life." She was shot three times in the Shanghai Incident and "was carried away as dead, but miraculously recovered." Her parents were killed in the Chinese revolution of 1911, and her brothers drowned or were poisoned or stabbed. She told Woods that she pilots airplanes, is an ace with a pistol and rifle, can write magazine articles, play musical instruments, sew, paint, and compose Japanese poetry. Also, she is ready to assume leadership of China, if summoned.

"The present Nanking government has been disorganized. If a change comes, someone must be ready to step into the hole. Who else can do it but I?"

The dazzled Woods may not have been qualified to distinguish truth from fantasy, but she could at least describe accurately what she saw with her own eyes; like Muramatsu, she was struck by the constant stream of visitors. Perhaps Yoshiko's crowded reception hall should not have come as a surprise since there were those many factions battling in China at that time. In such an environment, power brokers were in demand, whether they were self-styled or truly influential.

Woods also met Chizuko, "a little Japanese girl," who introduced herself in English and went on to explain the reason for their modest meals: "Our food here is all Chinese. . . . You see, we are trying to save money for our soldiers . . . so we have only three food items with each meal." This strikes Woods as quite perplexing: "A Chinese Princess who has Japanese attendants, a luxurious household, and is saving money for 'her' soldiers!"

Yoshiko is little help in clearing up the mystery when she offers more information: "Chizuko, who brought you to the dining room, is my 'sister.' She left her well-known parents in Kyoto to be my companion."

In fact, Chizuko had joined Yoshiko's household in 1931 and was alternately called Yoshiko's sister, secretary, and companion. Her devotion to Yoshiko was unflagging, and Yoshiko certainly returned these feelings.

"I am always lonely. I have no home to call my own, no parents," Yoshiko once declared in a cautious statement about her private life. "In my present

Naniwa, Renko, Yoshiko, and Chizuko   *Courtesy Hokari Kashio*

loneliness Chizuko shows me much sympathy and is my only ally." But
in another mood, she once went so far as to call Chizuko "my beautiful
wife" and posed with her for what looks like a wedding photograph, with
Chizuko in a woman's kimono and Yoshiko as the groom in a Japanese
man's formal robe.

For her part, Chizuko worries like a doting wife about Yoshiko's taxing
schedule and poor eating habits: "When she went to Rehe, she ate millet
and corn for her meals and then went about her many activities. Finally, her
health gave out, and when she returned to Shinkyō [Changchun], she had to
stay in bed for a month and half."

In such remarks, the two make no secret of the affection they felt for each
other, and though this sounds like more than just a deep friendship between
two women, no one knows the extent of their intimacy.

"What could be more chaotic than the dilemma in which Princess Jin
found herself at the outbreak of the Sino-Japanese War in 1931? [*sic*]," Woods
asks, concerned about the conflicts plaguing her hostess. "Her adopted people, the Japanese, were at war with her own native country. 'And I wanted to
help both,' she said."

Yoshiko goes on to provide more detail about her loyalties, and in talking publicly about such dangerous topics, she is far too forthright, a bad habit that would later get her executed. "She thought of the way in which her parents had been treated and her brothers killed," Woods reports, alluding to Yoshiko's fabricated tales about the deaths of relatives, "and decided to stay with her Japanese friends."

Yoshiko seems to have had second thoughts about such a wholehearted endorsement of the Japanese and later told Woods, "As for the Japanese, they have been very kind to me. But I do not like what they do in Manchukuo. I tell them so. But they will not shoot me yet, I think."

★

Getting shot by the Japanese was not out of the question, and although Yoshiko liked to think that the threat was a result of her valorous role in China's turmoil, her physical safety was more imperiled by events closer to home. The deviant passion had always been on Tanaka's side, but Yoshiko also enjoyed her power over him and of course liked to spend his money. Their relationship was no secret to the public and to his superiors since Tanaka boasted of the connection. Yet even he eventually recognized her menace.

"She became intoxicated by her success and fame," Tanaka's biographer son reports. "She'd always had the kind of personality that made her act on whatever came into her head and that came into play here too. Her intolerable attitude became worse than before. Her relationship with Tanaka Ryūkichi gradually became more distant. Putting the matter of their personal relationship aside, he warned her many times that she had built a record of many achievements but if she continued this wild life of hers, she would throw away her future. She wouldn't listen to a word of this, and instead she abused him with her foul tongue."

Though Tanaka knew that he had to be rid of Yoshiko, it was not an attachment he could abandon with ease. "From the start, she didn't love Tanaka," one of his army colleagues wrote years later. "She just stayed with him for sex, to satisfy her curiosity, and to take his money, and so getting even slightly involved with her was a mistake. . . . On the surface Tanaka talked tough and seemed composed, but inside he was extremely timid and cautious, driven by jealousy and his strong sex drive."

Tanaka, his eyes swollen with tears, at last told this associate, "I have definitely broken with Kawashima. I'll never see her again. That one's a devil, a she-devil." Furthermore, Tanaka confessed that he could not go on if Yoshiko remained alive: he asked the associate to kill her.

The associate, mulling over the request, realized that he didn't have any particular grudge against Yoshiko and faulted her only for her promiscuity. Still he agreed to murder her, as a favor to Tanaka and others who might come under her spell. The plans were hatched, and the would-be assassin tried to keep up his resolve despite growing sympathy for his intended victim. In the end, Tanaka changed his mind and canceled the assignment.

Soon the moment came when Tanaka really had enough; he felt impelled to get Yoshiko out of his life by other means since she'd taken to smearing his reputation in military circles. If he did not break with her, he'd be the one killed. She had told a Japanese navy commander that Tanaka, an army man, constantly disparaged the navy's performance in the recent Shanghai Incident and at the same time glorified the army's contribution. Enraged, the navy commander wanted Tanaka murdered.

Soon a band of navy men armed with swords and guns appeared before Tanaka: "Give us your life!"

They relented only when Tanaka agreed to sign a document stating, "Since the beginning of the recent situation, I have had only respect for the navy's performance."

After that, Tanaka shipped Yoshiko out of Shanghai. He arranged to have her sent to Manchukuo, where she was to serve as the chief of the women's quarters in Puyi's court. Although the empress welcomed her, Puyi absolutely refused to abide her presence, and so she was back in Shanghai in less than a month. Confounded by this, Tanaka says that he next arranged for her to be carted off to her family in Lushun, putting an end to their relationship.

Her brother, who'd been summoned to escort her to Lushun, disputes Tanaka's account, saying that after Yoshiko reached Lushun, Tanaka sent her a coded telegram: "I cannot live without you. I've decided that we should live together and die together. Come back to me."

The relationship with Tanaka did end at last, and this sent Yoshiko back to her old disarray. At this time, she does not seem alarmed by the political and personal ramifications of her close connections to the Japanese military. Also, Yoshiko shows little comprehension of the grief the Japanese were bringing to China: this comprehension came to her too late, when she was unable to extricate herself from involvement. No wonder that the judges at her trial excoriated her for remaining oblivious for so long.

Too unsettled to consider anything else, Yoshiko was principally concerned with her loss of access to Tanaka's "money tree." She could not last long as an independent operative who had lost her most important backer.

18

A GROWING AWARENESS

One day a field officer suddenly barged in with a friend to inspect Puyi's reception room. They even rubbed their hands around the chair reserved only for Puyi's use as they walked around. They did this without informing Puyi in advance and without following proper procedures. They just demanded that Puyi's servant Wu Changming hand over the key and Wu, also without informing Puyi, just opened the door for them. At that time, Puyi could not say anything to the Japanese "guests" even though he was angry. When the "guests" left, he was beside himself with fury and lashed out at Wu.

I looked on at all this from the side, thinking that there was no comparison between Puyi's life as a puppet ruler and his life back in the Forbidden City.

—PUJIE

Yoshiko was not the only one who took time to understand the truth about Japan's operations in Manchukuo. Saga Hiro, too, shows a staggering inattention at first as she keeps her distance from the lives of the Chinese people around her. Once she moved into her leaky residence in Changchun, Hiro was cloistered and obedient as always, and kept to her regal duties.

It must be said that Hiro sensed trouble at her wedding in Tokyo, when the military wouldn't allow more than five hundred guests—way too few in her opinion—and, apart from a few close relatives, forbade imperial family members who wished to attend. "When I heard about this, I had some dark thoughts," writes Hiro. "If this is supposed to be a marriage that shows the goodwill between Japan and Manchukuo, wouldn't the very act of inviting other members of the imperial family bolster Japanese-Manchukuo harmony? And if they ignore our wishes and exclude the people closest to us, then tell me, who is this wedding for?"

After her marriage, Hiro expected the courtesy due a member of Manchukuo's royal family, but the Japanese army saw no need to treat her with respect once they had her married off. She was unprepared for the insults and disdain she suddenly faced. When she went to the Changchun airport to receive a visiting member of the Japanese royal family, a Kwantung Army officer rudely shouted at her, scorning her husband's rank in the Manchukuo army. "What did you come here for? This is no place for some captain's wife. Go home! Go home!"

Still, she steeled herself to forge on despite these affronts. "Hiro, don't think about yourself," her father had told her. "No matter what happens to you, just endure it."

There was also the implacable weather, which did not spur Hiro to get out more to establish contact with her subjects. "During my first winter in Manchuria, the cold seeped into my bones. The temperature outside was many degrees below zero, a temperature I had never experienced before. Except for those events I couldn't avoid, I stayed inside our home, which was heated."

Her first daughter was born shortly after, but a Japanese army officer, reflecting the feelings of his military colleagues, was furious that she had given birth to a girl. He tossed away his baby gift and stormed out of the hospital. The Japanese army had banked on her producing a male heir to Manchukuo's throne; with an aristocratic Japanese mother and royal Manchu father, this male heir would represent a blending of the two nations, increasing Japan's psychological and political hold. Since Puyi either would not or could not—because of his rumored homosexuality—cooperate in this project, the army had put its hopes in his younger brother, Pujie, and Hiro.

On the other hand, the birth made Emperor Puyi, the baby's uncle, ecstatic, since this baby girl could never become a rival for his throne. "The emperor sent over a congratulatory message, and in addition, every day a large portion of a different kind of nutritious Chinese soup arrived," Hiro wrote.

Hiro's troubles increased by the day, and so did the contempt of the Japanese military. When a growing family meant that Hiro and her husband required more living space, the Japanese army refused their request for an addition to their residence. Here the sneers of the Japanese army shook her domestic arrangements: "How can a mere captain request all that luxury?"

Her pride hurt, but her dignity intact, Hiro collected herself. "After that we decided not to depend at all on the Kwantung Army and the like." With their own funds, the couple bought property just beside their home, where they cultivated vegetables and apricots.

Echoing Yoshiko's accounts, Hiro tells of having known nothing about Japan's true intentions in China and of being caught up in the prospect of the "paradise of benevolent government" that the Japanese said they were creating there. In her autobiography, she consistently presents herself as uninformed and dutiful, loyal and strong, a made-in-Manchukuo version of the virtuous samurai wife, whom her Japanese readers would readily adore. Her descriptions about her ignorance of Japanese activities in China also won over ordinary Japanese readers, who would defend their own wartime behavior in the same way.

In particular, Japanese expatriates in Manchukuo in this period describe sequestered communities, where, they maintain, they had no idea about the carnage not so far away. "My contact with non-Japanese was mostly with Russians," one longtime Japanese resident of Harbin recalled. "Even my servants were Russian. I had contact with the Chinese only when I went to eat Chinese food. But even then, I didn't go alone but with friends. We Japanese feared being kidnapped by the Chinese and disappearing forever. The Chinese houses were complex, one built inside another, and the Japanese police wouldn't enter their territory. So we feared the Chinese section of town."

When spring came, Hiro was at last willing to venture outside with her baby, and only then did her observations take in a wider world, including two Chinese children who came over to peek at her daughter. "The children were open in their innocent way, and so they gave me invaluable information." They told Hiro about how prices had gone up because of the Japanese occupation, how the Japanese soldiers and police refused to pay their bills at the family restaurant. "They don't pay, act like big shots, and walk out."

Though these are trifling complaints compared with widespread Japanese cruelty in China, Hiro is astounded at even these little transgressions. "These were all stories unimaginable to me up to then. Once I learned these facts, I was seized with dark thoughts about what would happen to the Manchukuo slogan about 'the harmony of the five races'—Japanese, Manchu, Mongolian, Han, Korean—if such behavior continued."

Hiro's husband, Pujie, tells a different story in his autobiography, which was written under different circumstances and for a different audience. Hiro's autobiography was published in Japan in 1959, when memories of the war were fresh and readers welcomed her tale of a Japanese woman who had behaved well during a period that brought no honor to the Japanese. Pujie's account came out in China in 1994, after his years as a lackey for the Japanese occupiers; their defeat; the fall of Manchukuo; his arrest by the Soviets and then by the Chinese Communists, who held him as a war criminal; the complete refashioning of his ideas while in a Chinese prison for eleven years; his "rehabilitation" into Communist Chinese society; the death of Hiro.

Also, Pujie's story was meant for Chinese readers, who would not have been charmed if he, a former high-ranking royal official of Manchukuo, kept insisting that he had been ignorant of conditions in China during the war. Pujie writes as a newly minted admirer of the Chinese Communists, who had been so kind as to not execute him when they took power. To return the favor, Pujie extols the Communists' humanity, their acumen, even their concern for his teeth. While not exactly a searing act of self-flagellation, his book is an apology for the man he used to be.

Throughout, a contrite Pujie acknowledges that he had wholeheartedly backed the Japanese. He shows himself as more astute than his brother Puyi, whose wits were not keen to start with and whose understanding of the world had not been improved by a sequestered palace existence since his birth. Pujie clearly got out more and could assess people and places in ordinary settings. His commitment to the Japanese, therefore, is harder to accept than his brother's, since Pujie at least had the ability if not the will to make reasonable judgments.

Pujie seeks forgiveness as he provides examples of his wickedness. He tells of the time he served as company commander of Manchukuo's Military Academy, a Japanese-backed institution. Only after the war did he comprehend that the Chinese students there were trained to develop a "slave mentality," bombarded with slogans about "Japan and Manchukuo—United in Virtue and Spirit" or "The Inevitable Victory of Imperial Forces." At the time, he gave wholehearted backing to the academy and put his prestige behind Japanese policies. When the Japanese military police tracked down students considered "anti-Manchukuo and anti-Japan," Pujie agreed that such odious elements would have a terrible effect on the reputation of the academy and the other students. Asked for his opinion about what should be done, Pujie recommended that the anti-Japanese students be "severely punished." So it was with his consent that the rebellious students were sentenced to six months imprisonment with hard labor, and upon release found themselves without homes and no hope of finding employment. He heard later that one student threw himself under a train in despair.

In the manner of repentant autobiographies, Pujie gets to return to this shameful episode in 1950, when he again encounters one of those rebellious students. Now Pujie is the prisoner, on the train going from his Soviet prison to the prison in China where he would remain for a decade. He recognizes the former student, who is part of the Chinese Communist cadre charged with escorting Pujie and other prisoners to their Chinese jail. Fearful of retribution from this man whose life he had destroyed, Pujie instead is treated by the former student with the consideration and wisdom he finds so typical of Communist officials.

"Your tenure as company commander of Manchukuo's Military Academy is a fact that cannot be denied," the former student tells him with astonishing sagacity. "But if you study and seriously change your ideas, your future will be bright."

In fact Pujie's loyalty to the Japanese regime had not stopped with military education, and as he took up various posts in the Manchukuo government, he always wanted to affirm his devotion. While Pujie was military attaché at the Manchukuo legation in Tokyo, a Chinese secretary was suddenly arrested by the Japanese military police and taken to places unknown. Thinking that Pujie would come to the aid of a fellow Chinese, the secretary managed to smuggle out a secret plea for help several years later. Far from rushing off to rescue his former aide, Pujie became furious at being put in a potentially damaging position. He burned up the message, destroying all traces, and sent word that he wanted no part in such doings. When Pujie learned that the secretary had been executed, his remorse, overdue, is profuse: "This episode preyed on me afterward and sometimes I couldn't sleep. Not only had I refused to help him out, I may have actually speeded up his execution. What a terrible sin I'd committed!"

At last Pujie perceived the truth about his role in Japan's China enterprise. By then he was in too deep, because, like his brother, Pujie was not the man to give up royal trappings and turn on the occupiers of his country. He describes a visit to Beijing to see his father, Prince Chun, a nostalgic journey from Manchukuo to the city where he had spent his childhood. Each morning he took a walk around the garden in the Northern Mansion, his father's residence, and remembered times long past. "With much emotion I wondered whether we would ever be able to return to the quiet life of the old days."

But he is back to reality soon enough when he is invited to dinner by Yin Rugeng, also a collaborator with the Japanese, who headed the East Hebei Anti-Communist Autonomous Government, another puppet regime in China. Yin Rugeng—whom Pujie has the temerity to label a "traitor"— urges Pujie to remain in Beijing and work with him. With a sense that his life had complications enough, Pujie hurries back to Manchukuo.

"I understood why the Kwantung Army did not want us to go to Beijing. The army saw that we'd run into problems likes these. Everyone wanted to use my brother and me as their puppets."

19
COMMANDER JIN

[Rehe] is all mountainous, a magnificent country that becomes more
rugged and splendid with lonely panoramic beauty as one penetrates
inward. Its traffic arteries, old caravan trails, are steep and narrow,
and only three or four main highways are wide enough for motor traffic.
As you come into it from Manchuria every road winds through numerous
narrow defiles. Held by determined men, they are formidable barriers
to conquest. A few hundred soldiers with machine-guns and dynamite
at any one of them could, it was thought, stem the advance of all kinds
of vehicular war machines, and for days inflict severe casualties against
Japanese infantrymen.

—EDGAR SNOW

The photo would be reprinted countless times, summing up all that
needed to be said about Kawashima Yoshiko's life. It is easy to imagine Yoshiko's delight as she sat before the camera in the stirring pose,
and how she later regretted being linked to the damning image. Approximately twenty-six years old, Kawashima Yoshiko is pictured in the evening
edition of the February 22, 1933, *Asahi*, dressed in a Japanese military uniform, from her soldier's cap down to her long boots. She sits unsmiling on
a chair and rests her hands on a sword, definitely ready for combat. (See
cover photo.) "The Beauty in Men's Clothing Kawashima Yoshiko," blares
the headline, "Is Backed to Be Commander of a Vigilance Corps in Rehe.
With Heroism She Will Lead Troops in the Suppression of Bandits."

The article goes on to explain why this female soldier has come to the
fore with new and daunting responsibilities. She has left frivolous pursuits
behind as she readies herself to serve in her first official military post.
Up to now, the former Manchu princess carried out her activities behind

the scenes, "but at last the time has come for her to ride out into public view." Her responsibilities will be enormous, of this there is no doubt, since she will head a large band of Chinese soldiers. Together they will assist the suffering masses of Rehe, who have "cried under the warlord Tang Yulin's despotism but at last have emerged from the darkness of tyranny and begun to see the light of a new life." To emphasize her new role as commander, she will assume the name Jin Bihui—"Jin" the surname used by her Chinese relatives and "Bihui" meaning "Radiant Jade."

Apparently, some Japanese were skeptical about Radiant Jade's selection for this position. "When it comes to this important job, critics acknowledge the lack of a qualified person in Manchukuo but feel that sending her is a mistake." The article begs for patience: "You have to let her try and then see what she can do. Much expectation rides on her activities."

Readers of this account cannot be blamed if they are stunned by the sudden upgrade in Yoshiko's status: she has been granted skills enough to subdue "bandit" gangs in Manchuria. What the newspaper does not say is that Yoshiko has been brought forward because of Japan's further aggressions into China. Having established itself in Manchukuo, the Japanese army has decided to expand into neighboring Chinese lands. The "bandits" Yoshiko is going off to vanquish are, among others, Chinese fomenting rebellion against the Japanese advance.

*

The newspaper declares Yoshiko ready for a leading role in such undertakings and reminds readers, who may have missed intervening events, that she has already proven herself. After leaving Tanaka Ryūkichi, she sought out new challenges, as well as new sources of cash. She found both. "At the time of the Hulunbuir Incident last September," the *Asahi* explains, "this elegant young officer accompanied the generals serving as advisers of Manchukuo and braved danger, joining the difficult fight to save the Japanese hostages held by the tyrannous rebel Su Bingwen, who made his stand in the severe cold of Qiqihar."

The article is touting Yoshiko's heroism of the year before, when the warlord Su Bingwen seized a railway line in Manchukuo. Although he was supposed to be one of the local Manchu warlords allied with the Japanese, he was not the first of their "allies" to switch sides without notice. He had been charged with guarding the railway line on behalf of his Japanese patrons but turned around and took it over, next establishing his own state independent of Japanese control. He also took Japanese hostages, the unconfirmed number as high as 284. "Gen. Su," reads a vivid newspaper account, "has had these captives for several weeks but as he has released all the women and children only the men remain and these Gen. Su has steadfastly refused to release as he finds them useful for parading in the streets when Japanese aeroplanes bomb the towns under his control." The Japanese eventually sent in troops to put down this uprising, part of their widening "pacification campaign" in hostile areas, and Su Bingwen was forced to flee to the Soviet Union.

But the story came out too damaging to the Japanese in China when told that way—warlord's insurrection, hostages, Japanese troops—and so the Japanese military created a more winning account by making a star out of Yoshiko. Here she was again, an appealing protagonist in the military's efforts to win over support for its onslaughts. On a 1933 radio program, a Japanese army officer spoke with much enthusiasm about her contributions at Hulunbuir, and these remarks were repeated in the newspaper, the headline proclaiming her the "Glittering Joan of Arc in the Bandit Suppression Army." According to the army officer, "She took a plane to northern Manchuria, where she played an active role everywhere and with such deeds truly risked her life for the sake of Manchukuo, much like the maid of Orléans, Joan of Arc."

It was not hard to go from there to other concocted stories that gave Yoshiko credit for convincing Su Bingwen to give up his rebellion and those hostages. Eventually the tale gained swagger and had her floating down to Su Bingwen's camp in a parachute. To emphasize this idea of airborne action, a newspaper photograph taken around the time of this incident shows her with a radiant smile as she arrives in Qiqihar, wearing aviator glasses.

Even Yoshiko, however, could not let this fable go uncorrected, and in her autobiography, she admits that her plans for an act of mercy during that crisis came to nothing in the end. According to her, she sought to help the Japanese during this episode because she longed to protect the security of Manchukuo, the new Manchu homeland, which was imperiled by Su Bingwen's revolt. She did want to parachute down to begin negotiations with this fellow Manchu and so asked army officials for permission to perform such a stunt, to do her bit for the hostages and Manchukuo's well-being:

"I don't mind dying," she told them, "or care about what the world thinks of me. I just want to do my utmost to urge Su Bingwen to change his position and do not wish to disturb the dawn of Manchukuo."

Yoshiko says that she practiced parachuting in the wind and cold several times, but the recurrence of an old "nervous ailment" and the escalation of the conflict beyond the possibility of negotiation compelled her to give up this idea. That did not stop the military from extolling her crucial role in ending Su Bingwen's rebellion in China's north, a triumph that would have meant facing temperatures forty degrees below zero.

★

And that is how she came to be photographed in a military uniform for the 1933 newspaper article announcing her next exploit, this time in the region then known as Rehe, southwest of Manchukuo. "The public's attention," declares the *Asahi*, "has been focused on whether this lone weak woman can in the end carry out this job." Yoshiko insisted that she was again providing crucial aid to Manchukuo, ensuring the country's continued existence by beating down foes. Such a belief makes sense if you believe that Manchukuo was a genuine Manchu homeland, nothing else, and under assault. But the Japanese army, which was in control of Manchukuo, was of course not principally concerned with the safety of the Manchus. Rather, it wished to extend the border of its puppet state, increase its hold on China, and along the way quell Chinese "bandits" bent on sabotaging the army's advances

The Rehe region was a prize for the Japanese not only because it bordered Manchukuo: there was also the lure of the rich opium production in the region, a prime source of income for the Japanese occupiers. Major General Tada Hayao, Yoshiko's latest military patron and lover, is sometimes cited as the force behind her new assignment in Rehe. "He was her supervisor, her leader, her favorite uncle." At that time Tada was also Japan's chief military adviser to Manchukuo.

"I must go forward now in accordance with my convictions," Yoshiko informed her brother, who objected to her intimate relationship with Tada. "I confess that I made use of Tada. Please, I ask you to avert your eyes from our secret connection." Yoshiko claimed to be the one in control, merely using Tada for her own aims. "Tada adopted me," she bragged. "That makes it easier to snatch his money."

But others had no doubt that Tada, unlike Tanaka, had a good grip on his sanity and all aspects of their alliance. "When she caused him trouble, he threw her out like old shoes and didn't think anything of it." Tada later joined the list of ex-lovers who plotted her assassination.

In her autobiography, Yoshiko says that she was implored to take on the assignment in Rehe. "I was living in a second-floor apartment above a furniture store on a side street in Shinkyō with two of my sisters and Chizuko, who had been deeply attached to me since my days in Shanghai. Also there was a Chinese servant, and others. . . . One day Fang Yongchang came to visit out of the blue. He said that he'd been leaderless since the murder of his chief, Zhang Zongchang, and asked me to become his commander."

Yoshiko says that there were both military and spiritual considerations behind Fang Yongchang's appeal that compelled her to participate. He wanted to take advantage of her stellar leadership abilities and also sought to erase the bad karma accrued by his assassinated warlord boss, who had "accidentally" slain Yoshiko's brother—reportedly over a woman. Now that the warlord was dead, his underlings wanted to demonstrate their loyalty to Yoshiko, and so "lessen the spiritual debt to my siblings and me that Zhang Zongchang had incurred while he was alive."

Yoshiko says she was won over by the sincerity in Fang Yongchang's eyes and agreed to take command of his troops. She has nothing but praise for Fang's unswerving devotion to her and for the troop's thirty secondary leaders, who were "uncharacteristically quiet and obedient." She describes the loyalty ceremony, when Fang presented his formal request that she take up the post and performed a formal kowtow before her. Though she accepted the vows of fealty and kowtows from him and the others, she could not ignore the condition of her new colleagues, who were unmistakably ragtag bandit chiefs supporting the Japanese. The Japanese army may have wanted to convince the world that Kawashima Yoshiko was a leader in the Rehe campaign, but it would allow her only a bunch of wrecks for her fighting force.

"They were all men who gave no thought to whether they lived or died," Yoshiko wrote anyway, "as they rode on wooden saddles and rushed around the wide plains of Manchuria and Mongolia." Some were missing fingers or had parts of their ears cut off, she writes, some cheeks bore scars from sword slashes. As her army pledged loyalty to her, all vowed to work for peace.

If Yoshiko is vague about exactly what she achieved in Rehe, others also struggle to come up with solid information. What exactly did she do there, if anything? A Japanese reporter who was present at the loyalty ceremony did not come away feeling that she exuded the authority attributed to her later on. "There she was, the female commander Eastern Jewel sternly standing there in her usual khaki-colored imitation military uniform. She was small, pretty, and looked just like a soldier out of a Chinese opera."

After the ceremony also, Yoshiko did not project the gravitas of a general about to steer a militia up frozen mountainsides.

> "Ha ha ha." In the car, she suddenly burst out into uncontrollable laughter.
>
> "What happened?" [the reporter asked]
>
> "They all look like monsters. Some of them have fingers missing. Another one has a big lump on the back of his head. Others have scars on their foreheads. A bunch of monsters, I tell you."
>
> "I also got the creeps looking at them."

She refused to attend the banquet after the loyalty ceremony—"I don't want to spend time with those monsters"—and went off to the Capital Dance Hall.

Although the exact number of men under her command was never clear, she spoke of being shot three times in battle; she definitely took time off afterward to "recuperate," and this has led to speculation that she had some experience under fire. But even granting that she led troops in some way, their role was most likely negligible. Later she said that her men would gather together as necessary, and then disband, leaving the impression of a very helter-skelter, part-time battalion. Emphasizing this notion of the troop's flimsiness, Muramatsu Shōfū considered her army "a bunch of toy soldiers." Most significant is the report that the Japanese army had banned such motley auxiliary forces from their invading army.

"She has no special rank or title," the Japanese journalist wrote. "She sells the jewelry she inherited from her mother and receives some money from various gentlemen in Japan." This, again, brings to the fore the matter of her financial backing, and who exactly those "gentlemen" were. One biographer contends that Yoshiko paid a call on the Japanese army later on, wearing her military uniform and boots, and packing a revolver.

"I created the Ankoku Army to benefit the new Manchukuo. Now we are only three thousand men, but I want to rally all the bandits of

Manchuria together, get them to cooperate in the Rehe operation, and maintain the peace." She next demanded two hundred thousand yen as payment.

Even more illuminating is the recollection of her nephew, who says that she received cash from Doihara Kenji, the Kwantung Army's notorious plotter, whose many dark acts furthered Japanese advances in China.

"In those days you needed money to lead a flashy life," the nephew says. "According to [her half brother] Xianjun's writings, Yoshiko would go to Doihara and pester him for cash. And Doihara would give it to her. But no one knows what she did with that money. Even Doihara didn't know. . . . She'd go there and pester him for half a year's funds, and if he didn't give it to her, she'd lash out at him or get violent or turn on her female wiles. Doihara was on to various secrets. If he gave her the money, for half a year she wouldn't come back. So Doihara gave her money from the Special Service Agency, but after he gave her the money, he didn't know what he'd paid her to do."

Whether or not Kawashima Yoshiko and her army played a part in the battle of Rehe, it is certain that the Japanese army did not need her help. The actual push to take over Rehe was a swift victory for the Japanese army, which gained control within two weeks. Eyewitness Edgar Snow was disgusted about the Chinese military's performance in this long-expected confrontation. "Perhaps not since the Crusades has a great army taken the field with so little intelligent preparation. Given 17 months in which to get ready for the invasion, the Chinese generals conducted their defense as if against a surprise attack." Even Boy Scouts with some dynamite, Snow wrote, could have held off the attacking Japanese on Rehe's numerous mountain passes, snow and wind making them even more impregnable. But the disciplined and well-equipped Japanese army seized the region with ease. "[Rehe] was a debacle for the Chinese. Probably it ranks as one of the worst debacles in Chinese military history."

Before the Japanese invasion, a *Time* correspondent journeyed to the "chill, bleak, mountainous" region to interview the Chinese warlord in control of the area. This reporter too was flabbergasted by the spotty preparations. "The Master of Jehol [another name for Rehe], whose warm opium-growing oases have made him vastly rich, is sturdy, walrus-mustached War Lord Tang Yulin." Before the battle, Tang expressed confidence in his forces, boasting that "Japan and Manchukuo cannot control Jehol without taking my Capital and we are certain we can hold out here for at least six months."

But his capital was captured in eleven days, by speedy Japanese units, which covered more than fifty miles on the last three days, "about as fast as any modern army can climb mountain passes in the teeth of blizzards."

Just before his flight from the approaching enemy, Tang Yulin "seemed to be in a befuddled stupor—possibly from opium, . . . 'I am in a difficult position,' mused Governor Tang. 'I don't even know where my troops are.'"

20

STARTING OVER IN MANCHUKUO

I'm going, so you go too
I've had enough of living in cramped Japan
Across the sea there is China
Four hundred million people are waiting for us in China

—"SONG OF A BANDIT ON HORSEBACK"

"**N**o matter how much they urged me, in the end I decided not
to go," the film historian Satō Tadao writes, remembering the
days when the government pressed Japanese to emigrate to
Manchukuo.

While Yoshiko was organizing her troops and the Kwantung Army seizing more territory, Japanese officials were determined to firm up their control of the region in other ways. Government representatives would soon
be out in force, urging Japanese citizens to abandon their lives in Japan and
make a new start in Manchukuo.

Then a student, Satō recalls that the recruiters held out the allures of
Manchuria's abundant land and natural resources, all awaiting Japanese
settlers. Nonetheless, Satō stayed put in Japan. "I had absolutely no confidence that I would make a good farmer since I had been brought up
in the city. . . . I was surprised that one of my teachers, who had enthusiastically urged us to leave, did go to Manchuria himself, as a leader of
the Patriotic Youth Brigade. . . . He was a good person, but he bears a
heavy responsibility for inducing his students to go to Manchuria. . . . In
those days, moving to Manchuria was considered a 'noble cause.' Though
you might be thinking that you didn't want to go, everyone was afraid to
express such feelings out loud since it would be taken as proof of insufficient patriotism."

For strategic reasons, the Kwantung Army pressed the settlers in Manchuria to make their homes close to the border with the Soviet Union. "Of course," Satō writes, "the settlers were going to do more than just cultivate the land, since they would also serve as sort of farmer-soldiers, prepared to do battle against the Soviets if necessary. They were made aware of the danger of bandit attacks but were assured that they would have the protection of the Kwantung Army, which even within the indomitable Japanese army was considered an elite force."

Satō's reminiscence appears in the introductory notes to the 2008 documentary *A Story of Manchurian Settler Communities*, a harrowing film from start to finish. The film's focus is on those Japanese families who did leave their lives in Japan behind, swayed by the promises of fertile soil and riches in Manchuria. As the film shows, the Japanese government's aggressive campaign was launched in the late 1930s, aimed at populating Manchukuo with plenty of Japanese settlers; the government planned to send five million farmers there over the course of twenty years. This would alleviate overpopulation in farm communities and the poverty of dismal economic times. Recruitment efforts were intense in areas hard hit by financial disaster, with quotas and coercive government officials badgering families and sending them on their way. It is estimated that more than three hundred thousand Japanese set out to make a fresh start in Manchuria.

In the film, the dreadful fates of these settlers are remembered by now-elderly survivors, those who managed a safe return to Japan after the war. This was no small achievement. Living in "paradise" was one thing, but getting out when the Japanese lost the war was an escape from hell.

"Immigration to Manchuria became the full-scale policy," writes historian Katō Kiyofumi, "but no matter how poor the people might have been, virtually none of them wanted to emigrate of their own free will to a place they had never seen or heard of." But there were the government quotas to be met, and if a region did not round up the required number, names were selected by lottery. "At first, the settlers were given uncultivated land, but very soon there were too many settlers to meet the demand. So the government took the cheapest, simplest way out. It forced the prices down and for a pittance bought land that the native [Chinese] farmers had cultivated with the sweat of their brows, then distributed this land to the settler groups.... The settler groups arriving from Japan were surprised to see such well-prepared land. Many of them had been tenant farmers, and they were able to take possession of land of a size unimaginable in Japan. Conversely, the Chinese farmers who had been chased off their own land became the tenant farmers of the settler groups."

One aged survivor remembers that at age thirteen he was greatly moved by a lecturer who had come to his Japanese hometown to encourage all to pack up and depart right away. "An officer from the military came to give a talk at our school. I think he was an army first lieutenant. I must have heard him speak for around an hour about settling in Manchuria. He said that once we cleared an immense stretch of land, all would belong to us, and then we'd have huge farms to run. The bandits were a danger but the Kwantung Army would protect us, so it would be all right. I remember that he gave a talk like that. In short he was telling us, 'Rather than suffering here in Japan as a farmer on some tiny farm, how would it be to go to Manchuria and have your own big farm to manage?' . . . I remember that I listened to his talk and thought, 'This is amazing. That's the place for me.' That was all it took to get my heart beating with excitement."

Once they got to Manchukuo, many settlers found just the sort of heaven they had been searching for. "I was ten years old when we went over," another survivor recalls. "My father was in the military. He was part of an army unit stationed in a town close to the border with the Soviet Union. So four of us, my mother, brothers, and I, went there as a military family. My father headed a small military unit. We suddenly left our mountain village in Niigata and once over in Manchuria found ourselves living like great lords. I thought it was paradise on earth. That was at the beginning."

Even when it became increasingly apparent that Japan was losing the war, the government continued to send new settlers over. "My father taught students how to sew Japanese kimonos at a school," one woman remembered. "Once the war broke out, as you know, people gradually stopped wearing kimonos. Then my father went to work at a factory. But he was getting old, was about forty-six or forty-seven at the time, and that kind of work was hard on him. There was rationing, and with five of us children, we didn't have much to eat. So they tried to flatter and coax him about going to China, that is, going to Manchuria. A village official often came to the house. He said that if we went to Manchuria, there would be no rationing. We'd have a lot of rice. Crop production was good, anyone could do it. The official came every day, to entice my parents into going. He was a smooth talker and went on about various things. Finally my parents were taken in by his smooth talk. They decided to go."

Her family arrived in Manchuria on May 26, 1945, just months before Japan's defeat. "I'd like someone to ask the government, why didn't they know that Japan was going to lose the war? Why did they send us over? Shouldn't the government have said something? If they had told us, 'Don't go, it's dangerous,' no one would have gone. I'm not sure of the date, but I think it was on August 14 or 15 that the leader of our group sent out an order. He said that Japan had lost the war and that we'd be hunted down by bandits if we stayed. He said, 'It's dangerous, so pack your bags and get out of there.' That day, our belongings from Japan had just arrived. We didn't even open them. We just fled."

I saw *A Story of Manchurian Settler Communities* with the poet Takarabe Toriko, who was born in Japan in 1933 but soon after was taken to Manchuria by her parents. After the defeat, she endured the ordeal of the escape back to Japan, her younger sister and father dying along the way. Takarabe, along with much of the audience, gasped at the testimony by the former settler who'd been sent to Manchuria so late in the war. A restrained woman she may be, but Takarabe knows all about fury.

"Even though the Japanese government knew defeat was imminent," she exclaimed, "it kept on sending people to Manchuria, to make it look as if everything was still going well. Someone should take responsibility for what happened in Manchuria. Why weren't people at the highest levels of the government punished for this?"

Takarabe now lives in a suburb of Tokyo, her dignified ways offering little indication of the violence and tragedy that bludgeoned her youth. Her manner conveys the sense that life can hold nothing more terrible than what she has already experienced, and so she does not get ruffled easily. While she does not favor drama in conversation, death and blood often march through her poetry, leaving their traces along the way in Manchuria.

In "The Death I Always See," Takarabe remembers her sister:

My little sister wears sky-blue clothes
as she shows herself and then hides behind the tall grass.
My little sister carries a peony that looks like a face.
But oh, she falls from the bridge
to the bottom of a deep and distant valley stream.
I lie awake.
I lie awake to embrace my little sister and stop her fall.

A blue gash
runs across my arm.

Takarabe has also written about her father, who was a rowdy, hot-tempered misfit in Japan but perfect for Manchuria. "When he was thirteen years old in Japan, my father was sent to live with his uncle," Takarabe explained one day. "His father felt that the boy was a ruffian and should be beaten into line with lots of hard work." The relatives did not succeed in reining him in, and so her father went to China, where he joined the ranks of the China *rōnin* and so became one of those contributing to the Japanese occupation of China. As this volatile man with no use for the rules settled in, he became an "adviser" on the staff of the warlord Zhang Zuolin. The Japanese army sought the support of Zhang at the time, and Takarabe's father taught Japanese to Zhang's son. When Zhang Zuolin proved to be an unreliable ally and was assassinated by the Japanese, Takarabe's father was implicated in the murder and had to leave Manchuria temporarily for his own safety. He was married in Japan, and when the coast was clear, he and his new family returned to Manchuria.

"He was responsible for rounding up bandits and getting them to join the Japanese side," Takarabe once told me, while she sifted through photos of her father, as a chubby and robust young man aglow in Manchuria. "Or killing them. My father was a violent man, scary. He used to hit my mother when she did not please him. After all, he spent his days murdering people. He didn't think twice about hitting his wife. Once a neighbor's dog attacked my mother, and so my father killed the dog. That's how violent he was. But he must have considered this a way of protecting the family. He was showing the neighbors what he was capable of if they harmed his family while he was away." In a poem, Takarabe wrote, "My father gave off the chilling smell of blood."

Takarabe's autobiographical novel *Fertile Land, Land of the Dead* is based on her family's life in Manchuria before and after the Japanese defeat. In returning to those days of her youth, Takarabe savors the landscape of Manchuria but remembers that murder was as much a part of the scenery as the grand and gently flowing Sungari River.

Through Yamamoto, the fictionalized version of her father, Takarabe describes Manchuria's wonders:

Yamamoto had always deeply loved the roughness of great, sprawling Manchuria. He had chosen to settle at the basin by the entrance to the Lesser

Khingan Range, perhaps because this region was surrounded by a wonderful, thick forest. For the most part, the forests of Manchuria were in their natural state, untouched by human hands, and thickly covered with red pines, lacebark pines, spruce, fir trees, Mongolian oaks, linden trees, poplars, birch, among others.

Few of these trees had been cut down, and so in season hunters came to shoot. For the most part they came for the animal skins. Most of the people who went up into the mountains deep inside this settlement area were Russians. They would throw their freshly skinned animal pelts onto the backs of their horses and ride on top of them as they left the mountain. The Russians looked as if they had been spit out by those beasts' untamed, wild breaths and just awakened from a dream.

Yamamoto was totally enchanted by this view of the Russians, which spoke to him of the mountains' depths and cruelty.

Takarabe tells another kind of story about her fictional mother, Yukie's, first days in Manchuria:

They passed by a horse-drawn cart whose driver was showing off what he had stuck on the end of his bamboo pole. Yukie looked at the driver's smiling face, which was covered with sand. At the end of the pole was a face with the mouth opened in the same way.

"That's the head of a bandit," Yamamoto Yoshirō told her casually.

Yukie drew back in fear when she glanced up and saw that freshly severed heads caked with sand were also hanging from the electric poles. She did not shout out, but, firmly supporting the baby she carried on her back, she just half closed her eyes. She had heard stories about the bandits but didn't think that things would be like this.

The streets were full of freshly severed heads!

She kept herself from crying out, not because she had to maintain her pride as a Japanese woman but rather because she was so stunned that she could not speak. Even so, for the sake of her baby, she would not under any circumstances go back to Japan.

21

IN THE BRIGHT LIGHT

An ordinary person would probably think twice about living in a free way. But Yoshiko was not at all afraid to grab such a life for herself. The public, which likes oddness, turned her into a hot topic, at times laying her down on a cutting board, making a meal of her, and adding decorations. It seems as though she had already been made into a legend during her lifetime.

—WATANABE RYŪSAKU

In April 1933, Muramatsu Shōfū's novel *The Beauty in Men's Clothing*, which had first been serialized in the magazine *Fujin kōron*, came out in book form in Japan. Yoshiko added to the buzz surrounding the publication by returning to Tokyo soon after. With the stories about her heroism in Rehe fresh in the public's mind and the splashy release of a book about her, Yoshiko enjoyed the greatest celebrity of her life. She was a natural in the bright light, delighted and talkative, aware that a properly dignified media star should remain aloof but unable to stop herself from basking in the attention.

Only later would she understand how much damage she did to herself during this period. In fact, her return to Japan and the publication of *The Beauty in Men's Clothing* marked the high point of Yoshiko's fame but also the start of her slide to ruin. She would live for fifteen more years, be a darling of the journalists on numerous occasions, and issue her opinions on the day's major events. But her usefulness to Japanese military officials had peaked, and increasingly she annoyed them.

In addition, the portrait of herself that she fashioned with so much pleasure at this time could not be effaced, and her own exaggerated descriptions of her military triumphs were used as evidence of her betrayal of China at

Yoshiko in a celebrity pose   *The Yomiuri Shimbun*

the postwar trial. "My whole life has been formed by false gossip about me," she complained in the first sentence of a confession she wrote in prison, "and I will die because of false gossip about me. This has been the case throughout my life."

Yet her grand-niece Shōko, who has reviewed Yoshiko's various statements, disagrees. "Perhaps, as these words suggest, unverified reports were used as evidence and led to her death sentence, but perhaps this was simply her own fault."

In one splashy media event during the 1933 trip, a *Fujin kōron* correspondent tracked her down at Tokyo's Manchukuo legation, where she was staying, and obtained "exclusive" rights to her version of recent events. "Up to now," the correspondent noted, "there have been various third-person accounts describing her feelings, but this time she herself has relied upon her own pen and written these words."

In her personal essay "I Love My Homeland," Yoshiko shows that she has returned to Tokyo as a Chinese. Childhood in Japan a memory, she adopts the stance of a thoroughly Chinese citizen whose loyalties are obvious and unshakable. This embrace of her Chinese origins marked another of her transformations, which continued to fascinate her Japanese readers.

Yoshiko's minor or nonexistent achievements in battle had not stopped the shower of accolades that gave her credit for slaying "bandits" who wished to destroy Manchukuo and for "liberating" Rehe. So intense was the coverage that even she felt moved to object. "I led these troops and rode around to every corner of Rehe," she writes, in a rare moment of modesty, "but compared with what I actually did, I got ten times the publicity. This was totally embarrassing." Having acknowledged her small contribution, Yoshiko goes on to boast about her importance. She seeks the tone of a war-weary general, Grant at Appomattox say, satisfied in victory but melancholy about the bloody folly of war.

The photo on the article's first page catches her in shorts and sneakers at the entrance to the Manchukuo legation, where she is relaxing after boxing practice. Another photo further on shows her wearing boxing mitts, working out at a punching bag. Her physical fitness established, Yoshiko shares details about her experiences as a warrior. She wants the magazine's readers to understand that she fought, not for her own glory but to bring "happiness to the thirty million people of Rehe."

She remembers the worshipful crowd that saw her off to battle—there were barbers, dance hall girls, gang members ("the good kind"), public officials, army men, the wives of Manchukuo ministers. Although the women wept as she departed, Yoshiko managed to smile back in return. This cheerfulness was only for her public, as joy was far from her heart. "In leading troops and going off to battle, I was not the slightest bit proud, nor did I rejoice." She could not forget that her mission would end in many deaths. "As a poem from your country states, 'Those who inflict wounds, and those who are wounded, take note! These are all the same human beings from the same country.'"

Yoshiko goes too far—at one point she claims that her troops made it possible for the Japanese army to enter Rehe without facing any opposition—but she sounds believable when at last detailing her reactions to what she has seen in Japanese-occupied China. She has in the past been absorbed in her luminous self, charging across China, without a glance at the devastated landscape. But in this essay Yoshiko shows that she has finally taken in the scenery. She saw all of it—slaughter on the battlefield, as well as the terror of the civilians, their lives crushed in the ongoing bloodbaths.

She tells of her horror—which would deepen as the war progressed—at the ruin the Japanese invasion has brought to China's villages. "They are suffering in hell compared with what your Japan is going through." Far from the dance halls, Yoshiko saw hopeless farmers desperate for food and clothing. In particular, she feared for the orphaned children. "I thought I heard a child crying and couldn't ignore it. I had my soldiers go out to look, and finally they came to me carrying a young child. . . . Even though I was going off to battle, I couldn't leave the child behind."

With these outpourings, Yoshiko throws herself into the middle of China's upheavals and seems to look over at Japan, where she had grown up, from a distance. She presents herself as a wise ambassador, one familiar with both China and Japan, who seeks to inform her Japanese readers about the true situation. Aware that she must be careful, she first expresses gratitude to the magazine's female readership for the Japanese army's help in Manchukuo.

I speak to you intellectual women from the Japan I love. Manchukuo, bolstered by the strength of Japan's properly disciplined, deeply empathetic army, is gradually maturing into a fine country. Together with the people of Manchukuo, they are trying to develop Manchukuo's natural resources and build a paradise beyond what humankind has ever known."

That out of the way, Yoshiko shifts to less agreeable observations.

While there are Japanese whose inherent good nature impels them to make such touching efforts, we cannot deny that mingled among these are also bad Japanese known as "China *rōnin*." They are also Japanese, and for the people of Manchukuo, it is a sorrow to have to think of them as Japanese. I spent my youth growing up in Japan. I understand the intrinsic virtues of Japan. Japan has done me many favors. So I cannot believe that these people are really Japanese.

She was not alone in being repulsed by the *rōnin*, who had come to be seen as a bunch of lawless thugs, roaming about China at will, forming vigilante gangs or tormenting Chinese as they liked.

Yoshiko and Naniwa   *Courtesy Rekishi no Sato*

In this essay, Yoshiko shows some restraint, but as the years passed, her comments about the Japanese in China grew more caustic and outraged. The Japanese army, which had been eager to make her their celebrity collaborator, came to regret the wide following they had helped her build. Her criticisms were a mere nuisance at the beginning, but as she grew more forceful in her denunciations of Japan, she became a louder subversive voice.

It was then that Japanese officers made plans to eliminate her.

*

In her heyday, Yoshiko was not only in Japan trying to spread the word about the war, she also went to China, where she lived it up in Manchukuo.

The Japanese had still not determined whether she was an asset or a threat, though this decision would soon be made. For the time being, Yoshiko could move about Manchukuo freely.

In a magazine article published after Yoshiko's death, the European law-yer Thomas Abe takes up her story in Harbin, where he helped her enjoy her fame and her money. Abe, whose name suggests Japanese ancestry, had just completed his law studies in Paris when he read about the Japanese invasion of Manchuria in 1931. His interest piqued, he soon traveled to Harbin, where he established a law practice among the large Russian community there.

"It was a time when educated Russians could speak French. My office thrived." His reputation soared when he won a case involving a White Rus-sian doctor blamed for the death of a beautiful young Russian Communist patient during a hemorrhoid operation. Abe's legal expertise seems less for-midable, however, when he claims that he did not realize that the Japanese army had ignored the law in creating Manchukuo. "I shamelessly showed off my knowledge of legal theories, but only those that applied to the cultural centers in the heart of Europe."

Abe says that he and Yoshiko were well suited, since his triumph in the hemorrhoid case had brought him a flashy renown that could compete with hers. They became intimates when she came to Harbin on behalf of a Manchu chief's widow who sought compensation for her late husband's property, which had been confiscated by Japanese railway authorities. Yoshiko planned to use her influence to assist the widow and also get a big cash reward for her efforts.

"She stayed at the splendid Modern Hotel," Abe writes, "which was owned by a Russian. She joined two of the best rooms together and had her meals in the middle of the large dining hall. Several tables were joined together, and she would invite dozens of people over as guests. She'd have them play her favorite music and set herself up at the center of the table, which was full of flowers. Really she dined like a queen."

As a token of "respect" for her efforts on behalf of the Manchu chief's widow, Yoshiko received twenty thousand yen from the Japanese branch manager of the South Manchurian Railway, one of Japan's sprawling, per-vasive enterprises in China's Northeast. She next devoted herself to spend-ing this money as quickly as possible, with Abe's help. Abe says that he was not in love with Yoshiko but found her company agreeable; obviously he also found it agreeable to live with her in grand style. The couple also went together to Changchun, where they again stayed in luxurious quarters, the same room Yoshiko had shared with General Tada Hayao. Her need for money constant, Yoshiko sent her assistant, Chizuko, out to get some from Manchukuo's finance minister, but he refused to hand out anything unless Yoshiko turned up in person.

"That kind of money I don't need," she said and obtained cash from the more accommodating hotel.

Yoshiko boldly sat on Abe's lap while riding down the streets in a car whose inside light was on, making them visible to passersby. "You're just a high-class whore! " someone shouted at Yoshiko, but she didn't get flustered. Dressed in gaudy Western clothes with a ribbon in her hair, she made an appearance at the Monte Carlo Dance Hall, and once she started dancing "like a butterfly," she did not stop. The owner put a sign outside announcing "Kawashima Yoshiko is now here," and curious crowds swarmed in to have a look.

Abe tries to show that Yoshiko was no obsequious ally of the Japanese military. In fact, Japanese authorities were as confused as anyone about which side she was on; they considered both Yoshiko and Abe suspicious characters and tailed them everywhere. "She knew too much about the inner workings of the Japanese military and looked upon them with contempt. . . . She was famous, and I also had a very flamboyant existence among the Russians. So of course the army did not look upon us favorably."

Then there was Yoshiko's thoughtful, beguiling personality that so enchanted Abe. "Sometimes when she felt like it, she went out wearing a general's uniform. Her dressing as a man, which was like her trademark, was not at all unpleasant. She was no different from the Takarazuka actresses who, even though they're not on stage during the day, dress like men when they go out. . . . When the two of us were alone together in our room, she was very feminine, very considerate of me. If she thought that I was bored, she'd put on the record of her singing Mongolian songs, whose music and words she had composed herself —'If your long eyelashes are a forest, your moist eyes are a stream . . .' After that she'd recite some poems that she liked. Even today I remember her voice."

Abe also witnessed a more poignant scene when he accompanied Yoshiko on a visit to the Japanese army lieutenant general Tsukushi Kumashichi, with whom she had a close personal relationship.

"To tell you the truth," Yoshiko said to Tsukushi, "I am now thinking of going to France or Germany with this man. So I've come to ask you for some vacation time."

In his response, the general acknowledged the pathos of her precarious existence. "I think that's a good idea. There's nothing to be gained from always being at the beck and call of the army."

A European journey would require a lot of money, for, once she went, she would probably not come back. Unable to collect sufficient funds, Yoshiko instead traveled in style to closer destinations. Abe tells of their departure from Harbin:

> That morning many people came to see us off at the station. Even members of the military and the Special Higher Police, the same ones who had recently viewed us as enemies, came to see her off with flowers, sad to see her go.
>
> By complete coincidence Yoshiko bumped into the branch manager of the South Manchurian Railway, and so she asked him, "Tell me, do you have a special compartment available? I've never ridden in a regular compartment."
>
> She was trying to coax him into giving us a VIP car. The branch manager rushed around to ready a special compartment and then ushered us in. Next she gestured to him from the deck of the compartment, pointing to her pile of luggage close by on the platform.
>
> "Those are my bags. Could you quickly bring them in here?"
>
> There were no redcaps around, and the departure whistle had sounded. Since Harbin was dependent on the railroad, this branch manager was like the lord of the city. But he served as her redcap and brought the luggage into the compartment.
>
> Kawashima Yoshiko employed this same style in coaxing a hefty amount of secret funds out of the commander in chief and the head of the General Staff.

22

WILD CHILD

No, rather than merely saying that her situation was insecure,
we should rather see her as having been thoroughly hounded out
of her former position. Yoshiko, who had a sense of all that had
gone on behind the scenes during the Shanghai Incident, became
a nuisance to the military after the Sino-Japanese War began.

—XIANLI, YOSHIKO'S BROTHER

And then, suddenly, the bad times started and didn't stop.

In August 1933 Yoshiko returned to Matsumoto after eight years away and, despite a fever, agreed to give a speech. Arriving at the packed hall, she discovered that the military police had issued a gag order.

"I complained to my father and to my brothers," Yoshiko told her audience. "'What's wrong with letting me talk?' I anguished over what to do. In any other prefecture, I wouldn't care, but this happened upon my return to Shinshū, my second home, and so I am very upset."

Excusing herself for a little while, she went to negotiate with the authorities and managed to get the order lifted. Once back at the podium, she began to tell her hometown listeners about what she had been doing. Her clothes proclaimed her sympathies, for she was wearing not a Japanese military uniform but a man's black Chinese robe and cap.

"Think of me tonight as that wild child who left town on a work assignment and now has come back in rags to visit her second home for a little while."

No wonder the police tried to keep her quiet, for Yoshiko went on to extol peace, Sino-Japanese amity, the essential unity of all people. This humane approach did not accord with the bellicosity the Japanese military was trying to stir up in the populace as the fighting in China proceeded.

Yoshiko in Chinese clothes   *Courtesy Hokari Kashio*

WILD CHILD

"As commander I have ventured out into the hail of gunfire a number of times, and indeed I have sustained three bullet wounds. But when I think about it, I see that, friend or foe, we are all brothers."

Yoshiko must have made the police even more nervous when she described the hopes of the people of Manchukuo. According to her, they considered the occupying Japanese incarnations of the Buddha and awaited blessings of compassion and mercy. The people of Manchuria had a long wait ahead of them.

In this speech, Yoshiko can again be seen grappling with new perceptions of her world, which had gone thoroughly awry. But she seems to lack the will or capacity to do anything more than express her alarm. Yoshiko has been criticized for not presenting new approaches or policies that would assist those in need of her help. Her focus on the restoration of the Qing dynasty was definitely not sufficient. "She had no ideals and no ideology," writes Harada Tomohiko. "And virtually no sense of what it takes to live in the modern world."

Her brother Xianli issued a harsher critique when he took the measure of Yoshiko's achievements. No matter that he was hardly the one to talk about nobility of vision, his disdain is not easily forgotten: "Yoshiko had no ideals, and also she associated with many vulgar people. If she had been educated so as to construct an intellectual framework in her mind, she might have played some kind of role in history since she was smart, with sure instincts, and had outstanding natural abilities. But she was unfortunate in her family and was born with a peculiar sort of personality. So you can sum up her life by saying that she just went about meaninglessly, always carried away by whatever struck her fancy."

Although the times called for focus, she could not bring clarity to her principles. To the end, her view of current events remained inchoate, shifting, a muddle, and a piece of solid belief in one area did not mean that anything firm was just beside. Frank about her growing confusion and disillusionment, her shock and shame, she was at least able to describe her moods to the public, who kept coming in to listen.

Yoshiko's floundering state was confirmed several weeks later when she was back in the news. She had visited the resort town of Atami with some friends, including the dance instructor who was her new companion. When the inn's owner refused to allow a group photograph out front, Yoshiko and her pals took offense. They stormed into the inn with their dirty shoes on,

Yoshiko in radio studio, around 1933   © *Bungeishunju*

a grave breach of Japanese etiquette, and generally disturbed the peace. "Behaving in a rowdy fashion," a newspaper reported, "Yoshiko used the cushion from the reception area to wipe off her dirty shoes. Things gradually got more out of hand and turned into a big commotion." Eventually apologizing for their rudeness, Yoshiko and her friends made their getaway by car that night.

More than anything, it was her next boyfriend who made clear where she was heading, and the crash, long in coming, should have taken no one by surprise. Itō Hanni was a perfect companion for a woman willing to overlook matters of fraud and absurdity in exchange for media attention and money. Itō had taken the stock market by storm early in his career, explaining that certain investment strategies were guided by his personal astrologer. With a con man's verve, he sold himself as the "genius of speculation" and persuaded investors to put money into his schemes, siphoning off quantities of funds for himself and becoming, intermittently, very rich.

Up, down, rolling in cash and then on the run, Itō had a literary side as well. He wrote books, songs, and at various times ran a newspaper and magazine. The power of words, his own in particular, intoxicated him, and

Itō set out on lecture tours in Japan and China as his publicity proclaimed him a "messiah." Huge crowds came to hear him expound upon his philosophy of "New Asianism." Like Yoshiko, Itō depended upon a hodgepodge of shifting ideas to attract fans; in his case, the thoughts took much from Rudolf Steiner, who was a favorite of his astrologer's. To his Japanese audiences, shaken by hard economic times and hostilities abroad, Itō forecast the triumph of Japan and the decline of the West.

> Rescue all Japanese citizens from the wretched economic hardships of the past decades!
>
> Japan has no connection to the economic hardships of the rest of the world. There is a way toward everlasting economic prosperity. Hanni has discovered this way. And he has discovered the real way that humans should live.
>
> This is Hanni's "New Asianism," which will rescue men and women from debt, poverty, and the sufferings of illness. Both the British Empire, which possesses one-fifth of the world's land and wealth, and the big United States, which holds two-thirds of the world's gold, are agonizing over unemployment and economic depression. This is because their politics are bad. Even though they have money, Britain and the United States are suffering through economic depression.
>
> Isn't this proof that even without money, Japan can achieve economic prosperity?

Eventually Itō's rock star status on the lecture circuit whipped him into such euphoria that he forgot about the police, who also came to listen. When he began to advocate revolution and other rousing concepts during a time of great political turbulence in 1935, he was arrested and charged with swindling.

But before Itō was jailed, Yoshiko joined his entourage, and the journalists agreed that this was an ideal couple. The two made the rounds of dance halls together, and Yoshiko attended Itō's lectures, apparently won over by his teachings. For one public appearance she turned herself out in brash feminine clothes—a crimson Chinese outfit—and fended off reporters, who wondered whether a marriage was in the offing.

"You have returned to being a woman. Is that because marriage is in the cards? What about Mr. Hanni as a prospect?"

Yoshiko had a sassy response to this query, citing the stiff price of taking her on. "I'll be happy to marry anyone who will have me, but for my expenses, I require more than ten thousand yen a month."

The couple lived together in Tokyo, and an acquaintance remembers the bright-red bedcover and green rug, as well as the sign on the bedroom door, which proclaimed this "The Commander's Room."

With Itō's money, Yoshiko returned to Matsumoto, where she hosted a seventieth birthday party for Naniwa, even though the tensions between father and daughter remained. Anyone who had followed their troubled connection could easily imagine the conflicts within Yoshiko as she organized the party; ever back and forth, she seemed to loathe and need her adoptive father.

There were about a hundred guests, with entertainment provided by masters of the traditional arts, who had been brought in from Tokyo along with two truckloads of party supplies. Yoshiko herself sang a ballad of congratulations to samisen accompaniment and again astounded those following her fashions. The impulses of a dutiful daughter may have been behind her birthday party for Naniwa, but she looked more like his geisha escort in her pricey, splashy kimono and elaborate Shimada wig.

Naniwa flanked by Renko and Yoshiko at his seventieth birthday party, 1935

Courtesy Hokari Kashio

Naniwa, resigned to his adopted daughter's outlandishness, was heard to remark, "I never have the foggiest idea about what Yoshiko is doing."

Twenty of Yoshiko's former "soldiers" mingled among the guests, adding an odd touch to the gathering. "You only have to imagine the scene," a reporter observed, "to realize how very amusing it was to see these weird-looking men prostrate themselves and pay their respects to this lovely Japanese woman."

Later on, one of her men assured the journalist that this party was merely a break from Yoshiko's serious endeavors. "The commander's next moves are definitely worth keeping an eye on. Of course at this point we have not been told anything, but she is going to be living in a place called 'The King's Residence' in Tianjin and is formulating some secret policies."

Energized by public attention, Yoshiko is said to have piloted a plane bought with Itō's money. Back in Tokyo, she was spotted at a sumo match in the company of prominent ultranationalists Tōyama Mitsuru and Iwata Ainosuke—he was the acquaintance from her youth who had supplied the gun for her failed suicide attempt. Since that time, Iwata had diversified his activities and, through his "patriotic" organization, become a dogged agitator for his radical ideas. Following his jailing for complicity in the assassination of a Foreign Ministry official, he'd gone on to play a part in the murder of a prime minister who'd compromised on a naval treaty with Western powers.

Yoshiko's chumminess with such extremists was of course brought up at her trial in China, when she would claim that they were not political associates but almost family members whom she had known since her childhood in Naniwa's home. While such assertions were in fact true, the Chinese court could assume that these men also found her useful to their agendas.

Despite the high-powered company, Yoshiko held her own in the sumo hall, no chance of being overlooked in her latest womanly concoction—"a pink Yūzen kimono with silver and gold embroidery on the long red sash, her hair in the high topknot Shimada style, and carrying a fan decorated with a bright-red peony."

After Itō Hanni was arrested in 1935, there were sordid rumors about Yoshiko's moneymaking efforts. Muramatsu Shōfū, who took credit for her fame, was appalled by her increasingly tempestuous behavior. He became more than appalled after she invited him over for a visit and then injected him with a potion she guaranteed would do wonders for his health. He fell violently ill and later suspected that she had tried to murder him with opium, because, in his view, he had refused her sexual advances in Shanghai. Convinced that friendship with Yoshiko was no boon to longevity, he avoided her from then on.

In addition to these unseemly antics, Yoshiko's health worsened, and she sought cures as she shuttled back and forth between Japan and China. Among her ailments was a spinal inflammation, perhaps from an injury involving a plane propeller; she was increasingly dependent on various substances—what have been identified as painkillers, opium, and the like—consumed on a daily basis. At the same time, she became more distraught about Japanese brutality in China, and, probably liberated by the drugs, she was fearless about expressing her opinions in public.

When she was interviewed at a hot springs in Japan, where she was said to be recovering from a bullet wound, the reporter saw her inject herself in the leg with "glucose." Afterward she talked politics, trying out new thoughts: "The establishment of the paradise of Manchukuo is still not easy. The Japanese must learn more about the land and the people of Manchukuo and deepen their understanding. Some surprising misunderstandings and rumors have started to circulate there."

Around the same time, she met up with a Japanese businessman, who later became a prominent politician, and had discussions with him in Matsumoto restaurants. Decades later he remembered the courageous way she spoke out about the Japanese in China.

"At this rate, Japan's policies in China are sure to fail. If they can't put forward policies that encourage more understanding between Japanese and Chinese, then both countries will go to the dogs. When people like Doihara ride horseback on inspection tours through the towns, the Chinese have to get down on their knees before him. I'm telling you—making people do things like that will bring disaster to Japan also. There must be drastic changes in relations between Manchukuo and Japan."

With tears in her eyes, she implored him, "For Japan's sake too, please go to Manchukuo. I'll tell Emperor Puyi that you'll be there."

All of her contradictions slam against each other at such times, and the impact resounds to this day. On the one hand she liked to woo the crowds by wearing silken, feminine Japanese kimonos, topped by fancy wigs. She sat in sports arenas with men linked to assassinations of public figures and dedicated to Japanese supremacy throughout Asia. She knew such people well, even calling them "Uncle." On the other hand, she appeared in unadorned Chinese black for her speeches and railed against Japanese aggression in China that was instigated by those same intimates. She wept at the killing and the cruelty.

★

In March 1937, only months before the Japanese embarked on their full-scale war in China, which would lead to many millions of deaths, she gave another public lecture in Matsumoto before an overflow crowd. Yoshiko foresaw what was to come, and again in her black Chinese cap and robe, she took up her role as spokesperson for China, appealing for mercy beforehand.

Luster and strength diminished, Yoshiko had to be helped to the podium. One observer had no doubt that an opium addiction was behind her sickly appearance, which added impact to a gloomy message.

Yoshiko came to the point straightaway, her embitterment on full display: "All of you who have come here tonight have perhaps been drawn by an interest in me and some measure of kindness as well. If only the Japanese in China bestowed a smidgen of that kindness on our Chinese brothers and sisters, how grateful they would be!"

> The fact of the matter is that many of the Japanese in China and in Manchuria have crossed the waters to make money hand over fist. I'm telling the truth and not exaggerating when I say that they're only a bunch of losers no one would associate with in Japan, the kind of people who can't hold down a job long enough to feed themselves. . . . The Japanese, who should become the leaders of Asia, go over there and all of a sudden make a quick change into un-Japanese Japanese. They bully our Chinese brothers and sisters, make them suffer, and strike terror into the hearts of the Chinese. They are hated. Tell me, is this acceptable behavior? . . .
>
> Japanese from the Foreign Ministry, the military, the privileged, and the capitalists talk about Sino-Japanese friendship every time they open their mouths. But the Sino-Japanese friendship they're talking about is only a Sino-Japanese friendship that profits the Japanese.

This amounted to a blatant denunciation of Japan and would not have been tolerated ordinarily, but Yoshiko, hometown celebrity and nationwide heroine, was not so easily hustled away. At one point she told the crowd that Japanese diplomats in China were utterly incompetent, like doctors who treat a patient with lung disease by administering stomach medicine. Her agitated voice rose when she reminded the crowd of her basic belief in the humanity of all people. With such thoughts in mind, she said, she had led her troops forward only in the cause of peace.

To confirm the authorities' fears, the reporter covering the speech was moved by her words and saw reason to reflect upon her message. "She spoke directly and pointed out the flaws of the Japanese," the journalist wrote. "She offered many suggestions and was truly an 'Eastern Joan of Arc.'" Deep thinking about Japan's China policies was of course just what the government did not want to encourage. Nor did it require a speaker, ailing and tearful, who had the power to move a large audience.

"As you can see," Yoshiko said in a faint voice, "I also have been wounded and am now an invalid who can perform no useful service. But the least I can do is erect a stone memorial for our many dead brothers and sisters and bring solace to their souls. At the same time I will pray for eternal peace in Manchuria and Mongolia. That is absolutely all I can do. Please, I beg of you all, help to make this fervent wish come true."

23

A DAUGHTER LOOKS BACK

After the defeat of Japan, my brother and I were sent to the Soviet Union and kept under detention there as war criminals. In 1950, we were transferred to the Fushun War Criminals Prison in Northeast China. At first, we were much worried that we would be put to death. But gradually we found to our relief that the War Criminals Prison wanted us to repent for our sins and start a new life.

My brother and I were granted special pardons and set free in 1959 and 1960 respectively. We both turned over a new leaf.

—PUJIE

On a chilly spring day, I met Fukunaga Kosei for tea in Tokyo. She, too, knows much about disillusionment and bafflement, shame and remorse, which came to dominate the lives of her parents. As a consequence, Kosei has spent a lot of time deciphering their emotions for the world at large, and for herself as well. Kosei's difficulties, like Yoshiko's, started at the moment of her birth. And just like Yoshiko's, her difficulties seemed never to end. Born in 1940, Kosei is the only surviving daughter of Saga Hiro and the Manchu prince Pujie. She lived with her parents in Manchukuo as a member of the imperial family until she was five years old, but with the Japanese defeat, she fled with her mother to Japan. Eventually, she married a Japanese and had five children, settling down for good in Japan.

While Kosei determined years back that she would aim for anonymity and domestic quiet, leaving a life as a Manchukuo princess behind, she has not always been able to keep her past at bay. When she speaks, Fukunaga is still an aristocrat, always showing extreme politeness and tact. And when she gazes ahead, there is the fragility of a woman who cannot believe how much life has battered her.

"My mother had a strong sense of responsibility," Kosei told me, reviewing her Japanese mother's marriage to Pujie. "For her entire life she worked to bring the cultures of Japan and China together. She came from an old Japanese family, related to the imperial line. She was very much aware of the responsibilities that came with her place in society and the position she had been placed in."

The last one left, Kosei is now her family's spokeswoman, though she has no fondness for publicity. She does, however, want to make sure that posterity treats her parents well, and with that in mind, she endures questioning about her closest relatives and encourages memorials in their honor. She supported the placement of commemorative stones in a "Sino-Japanese Friendship Garden" in Nishinomiya, Japan, and contributed a white-flowering *obassia*, an offshoot of the tree that the Japanese empress gave to her mother long ago.

"As you know, my parents' marriage came about under difficult circumstances, arranged by the military for their own reasons. The military's strategy, to forge ahead by linking two countries together through their marriage, was hard for my parents, I think, but my mother realized that my father had a good character, and so they were able to forget about such things and create a relationship between two human beings. For my mother, the society she had been born into played a role. While the marriage was still under discussion, my grandfather—that is, my mother's father—guided her, saying that if she'd been a man, she'd join the military to help her country. If she, as a woman, wanted to serve the country, then, he said, do your duty and marry. That is how my mother steeled herself to face what was ahead."

As part of her efforts for her parents, Kosei agreed to be the focus of a television documentary about her father; this included a visit to her childhood home in Changchun, which she had left sixty years ago. A woman who has reason to see the world, and especially China, as a fount of catastrophe, Kosei clearly braced herself for the journey.

"My Father, Pujie," which aired in 2006, follows Kosei as she contends not only with her own memories but also with elderly Chinese residents, who can still call up their bitterness about the Japanese occupation. "They treated us Chinese workers very cruelly," a Chinese man who labored for the Japanese tells her during the trip. "They'd abuse us and call us idiots all the time, constantly beat us. The Japanese treated us like slaves and so we workers hated them."

Kosei knows that she cannot atone for the wrongs of the Japanese but is eager to emphasize her father's repentance for his role in the Manchukuo regime: "My father served his older brother, Emperor Puyi, like a loyal vassal," she says, in her pained way, "and continued this throughout the war. In that way he also cooperated with the Japanese, perhaps hoping that his participation would build a fine country in Manchuria. But in his later years, he reflected on what he had done and accepted censure, realizing that the mistakes in his thinking had led him to do unforgivable things. This definitely was not the result of brainwashing. From the bottom of his heart he felt that his past history had been a mistake, a mistake that had brought misery to the people of China's Northeast. When he apologized, he was expressing his true feelings."

During the documentary, Kosei was at least allowed a happy moment to look around the site of her old home, which is now on a busy Changchun street.

"Beyond the garden I am pretty sure that there were rice fields. The cook would come out in a long apron, leading a long line of ducks and ducklings— just the way you often see ducks with their ducklings now. It was that sort of scene. Behind them I would come stumbling along. That's the only kind of thing I remember now."

Kosei can recall the pleasant scene with the ducks, but this soon yields to her other recollections of dislocation, terror, disgrace, and tragedy. As a child, she faced the insecurity of being transported back and forth between China and Japan during the war as her father took up official posts in the two countries; after the Japanese defeat, he was imprisoned as a war criminal for fifteen years; she and her mother made their escape from Manchukuo to Japan through vengeful Chinese mobs and measles epidemics; in 1957 her older sister died in a sensationalized double suicide in Japan. The Chinese underwent unspeakable agonies under the Japanese—there are accounts of mass beheadings by sword, humans flayed alive, biological experimentation on prisoners. Beside these, Kosei's troubles can seem tame, a tiny firecracker amid an unstoppable blaze reducing an entire country to ashes. As a result, Kosei is reluctant to bring up her private grief, perhaps wary of accusations that she, a privileged woman sheltered from the worst of it, doesn't know anything about suffering.

By the time of Kosei's earliest childhood years, the true nature of the Manchukuo regime was obvious to its citizens and to her parents as well.

"My mother's ideas about Manchuria before she went there," Kosei told me, "were quite different from the actual conditions she encountered after she arrived, which surprised her. In the beginning the Japanese believed in the idea of establishing harmony among the five races and wanted to create an ideal country there. But then the army, the Kwantung Army, became stronger, and another aspect emerged, one that had no relationship to their ideals. The military treated ordinary people very arrogantly, and this made my mother very sad. Japan was lacking in natural resources like coal, and so the Japanese increasingly looked to Manchuria for such supplies. Human greed is something that changes over time, and so Japan's early plans for Manchuria underwent great changes."

Among other oppressive decrees, the Japanese ordered the citizens of Manchukuo to abandon their native beliefs and follow the practices of Japanese Shinto. Later on, Emperor Puyi claimed that he had no choice but to go along with the Japanese decision to ban Manchu rites.

"Though the Japanese made much of their slogan about the 'Harmony of the Five Races,'" Kosei's mother, Hiro, wrote, "in reality, the Japanese came first in all of Manchuria. . . . Puyi was forbidden to worship his Qing ancestors. They forced Japanese Shinto on him. . . . The Japanese built a plain wood shrine in honor of Manchukuo's founding near the Imperial Household Department. They trampled on the custom of ancestor worship, which was the principal belief of the Chinese, and forcibly installed Shinto as the state religion. . . . Did the arrogant Kwantung Army believe that they could just rewrite history according to their whims? Did they delude themselves into thinking that actions of this sort would stir warm feelings for them among the people of Manchukuo?" Japanese military officials kicked and beat Manchu soldiers if they were not making good progress in their Shinto studies.

As the war situation worsened for the Japanese, most of the basic grains harvested in Manchukuo were shipped off to Japan, to feed the hungry population there; only sorghum was readily available in Manchukuo. Scarcities affected the royal family and even more so the general population, who starved.

"We work hard to produce flour and don't get to eat it"—went one common complaint—"It all goes to Japan. Do the Japanese look down on us so much that they think we can make do with sorghum?"

Or another, "We work and work, but still our life is hard. This is not our fault. Isn't it the fault of the Japanese, who decided to go to war?" The hungry were not appeased when the Kwantung Army scolded them, demanding that shortages be endured until the victory was won.

"We people of Manchukuo are not given any clothes," a visitor told Pujie, "and even if we wanted to make our own socks, we have no yarn. Don't families of Japanese soldiers have more wool socks than they need? Do the Japanese think we can go around naked, like wild animals?"

In 1943 Kosei and her parents went back to Japan, where her father was to pursue further study at the Army War College. Alone in their house, Hiro and her daughters found themselves in grave danger when Tokyo was bombed by the Americans. "But when I thought about it," Hiro reflected, "scenes just like this had become more and more widespread all over China over the past eight years because of the Japanese army. For the first time I felt that I understood the suffering of the Chinese people. Up to then I had tried to understand, but this had been a mere abstraction, and now at last I had come to a clear understanding of what they were going through."

In February 1945, when Japan's defeat was clearly imminent, Kosei and her parents returned to Manchukuo. Still, the persecution of the Chinese continued, and Hiro felt only shame at her origins. "It was very difficult to be a Japanese. If I could, I wanted to become a Chinese. . . . The Japanese were increasingly surrounded by the ferocious hostility of the Chinese in Manchuria."

Although as Hiro's five-year-old daughter, Kosei was too young to understand any of this, Chinese hatred of the Japanese would engulf her after the defeat, when she and her mother would be tossed out into the inferno of their flight to safety.

Much later, in 1960, her father, Pujie, was released from prison after serving his sentence for war crimes, and the following year Hiro left Japan to live with him in China, where she remained until her death in 1987.

Kosei could not bring herself to join them. "I was confused about what to do. I was unable to rid myself of the feelings of panic from my youth. . . . I wanted to live in peaceful Japan. . . . I wanted the happiness of an ordinary, conventional life."

24

CHINA NIGHTS

Her songs came to express the very sadness of those dark days.

—SATŌ TADAO

"**S**he smiled, her face strikingly white, oval-shaped, and showing obvious refinement," wrote Yamaguchi Yoshiko about the first time she saw Kawashima Yoshiko. It was 1937 in China, just when the Sino-Japanese War broke out, and Kawashima Yoshiko had once more changed her profession: she now ran a Chinese restaurant in Tianjin. "She was not tall but had a figure that went well with her size," Yamaguchi continues in her autobiography. "Wearing a man's black Chinese robe, she had the kind of beauty you see in a charming male actor who specializes in female roles." So began a friendship that has been the subject of much analysis, for the two women would seem to have had much in common. The scrutiny has been unflagging, not only because of their common given name but also because of the similar perils they faced—one coming out alive and going on to flourish. The other not as fortunate.

"The two Yoshikos," as they have been called so often, were actually rather far apart in age, with Kawashima Yoshiko older by thirteen years. She took note of her seniority immediately that day they met in her restaurant.

"When I was little," Kawashima said to Yamaguchi, "people used to call me 'Yoko-chan.' So I'll call you 'Yoko-chan,' and you call me 'Older Brother.' "

Yamaguchi calculates that she herself was about seventeen at the time, and Kawashima over thirty, though she looked much younger. Yamaguchi was wary about this new acquaintance, and a reader of her memoir often gets the sense that she was not one to throw herself into a new connection without carefully evaluating what was on offer. And, certainly, Kawashima gave even those less cautious cause for worry.

Yamaguchi Yoshiko was born to Japanese parents in China in 1920 and as of 1937 had not yet set foot in Japan. That was why she could not immediately decide whether or not the man's black Chinese robe that Kawashima had on was some kind of cutting-edge Japanese fashion. "In China," Yamaguchi observes, "there are male actors who take female roles in opera, just like Japanese Kabuki, but there's no custom of women taking male roles like Japan's Takarazuka drama troupe. . . . So I didn't understand what it meant for a woman to dress like a man. The only thing I understood was that this was a strange kind of beauty, her masculine charm drawing people in. I felt that I was looking at a living doll."

Although still a student on vacation when she met Kawashima in the restaurant, Yamaguchi had already absorbed complex elements into her life, and these would multiply as conflicts between China and Japan intensified. While everything about Yamaguchi was consistently female, she could match Kawashima when it came to clashing loyalties and beliefs. The commentators like to equate her mixed-up background with Kawashima's in other ways too, but they leave out deep psychological distress, which beset Kawashima frequently, while Yamaguchi, adept at adjustment to a churning landscape, seems to have been less vulnerable. Yamaguchi presents on the whole a hardier case, less likely to be shattered by anything that came her way, and certainly she was, over the years, pelted from many directions.

Yamaguchi's father, a sinophile since his youth, taught Chinese to Japanese employees of the South Manchurian Railway. According to Yamaguchi, he was enraptured by Chinese culture from the start and carried on with curiosity and wonder, sometimes sounding, in her sweetened-up recollections, like that most winning of characters—an imperialist gone abjectly native. "My father felt we are the younger brother nation, China is the older brother. He would say, 'You can do nothing to change China. China is so big, so deep. It has such a long history.' Or, 'What is the sense of taking one drop of the Isuzu River [a sacred river in Japan] and putting it in the Yalu River [in China]?' "

Yamaguchi's father insisted that she learn to speak Chinese and personally supervised her study of the language. She gives credit to her musical ear for her mastery of Chinese, which she soon spoke fluently. Her health too played a part in her destiny, since she contracted tuberculosis as a young girl and took singing lessons to strengthen her lungs.

When Yamaguchi was thirteen, she made her public debut at a recital organized by her singing teacher. In one of those miracles abounding in memoirs, she tells of how a Japanese representative from a Manchukuo radio station was in the audience. He turned up again at her next singing lesson, bringing along his fateful offer. In order to attract Chinese listeners, the radio station was developing a new program that would feature songs from Manchuria. They had originally sought a Chinese woman singer who spoke both Chinese and Japanese, but in the end they could not find any Chinese who met their qualifications.

Giving up on the real thing, her Japanese sponsor decided to pass this young and lovely Japanese singer off as a Chinese, sure that she could sing about Manchu fishermen with all the conviction and linguistic proficiency of a native speaker. Yamaguchi was not being recruited to become an ordinary singing sensation, her photo to hang in every home in Manchukuo just to boost her career; rather, her songs would boost those old standbys, "Japanese-Manchu Brotherhood" and "Harmony of the Five Races."

From that time forward Yamaguchi performed as a Chinese, known as the singing star Li Xianglan, whose remarkable voice and popularity would eventually storm across national barriers in a way that the politicians and military could never match. So complete was Yamaguchi's immersion into her Chinese identity that she spent the rest of her long life trying to get herself and her public disentangled from the deception.

Yamaguchi went on to bigger things when she was hired by the Manchuria Film Association, headed by the murderer, opium boss, and zealous nationalist Amakasu Masahiko. The studio's films also extolled the Japanese version of friendship with the Chinese, even going so far as to promote Chinese-Japanese romance. As the faux-Chinese actress Li Xianglan, Yamaguchi appeared on-screen as a Chinese woman who would not only be won over by the beneficence of the Japanese regime in China, she could even fall in love with a fine, high-principled Japanese man. In this way she proved that the Japanese, unlike those pillaging, imperialist Westerners, were lifting the Chinese up from their backwardness and, through patient instruction, bringing two ancient nations together, sampan and cherry blossoms commingled. Enchantment relied not only on Yamaguchi's voice but also on her beauty, which let loose a magic not easily exorcised.

Yamaguchi Yoshiko   *Courtesy Yamaguchi Yoshiko*

With a haunting voice and perfection in a cheongsam, Yamaguchi made her transformation look easy. Who would not want to be persuaded by an exquisite, supposedly Chinese woman, just married to a Japanese man and still in her wedding dress when she sang about evenings in Shanghai:

China nights—oh China nights
Lights from the harbor in the purple night
The junk coming upstream—a ship of dreams
Ah, I cannot forget the sound of Chinese strings
China nights, nights of dreams

*

But fame was still years away when Yamaguchi took a break from school and arrived for a meal at Kawashima Yoshiko's restaurant in Tianjin. In accounts of their meeting that day and those to come, it is easy to see the pathos in

Kawashima's condition: the young Yamaguchi had film star glamour ahead of her while Kawashima's glory days had come to an end. She was finished and seemed to know it.

Either Kawashima's old lover and mentor Tada Hayao or a Chinese warlord was said to have been behind the establishment of the Tianjin restaurant. Preoccupied with management of a war, Tada hoped to keep Kawashima busy and far from where her capricious behavior and criticisms could cause trouble. The building that once housed the restaurant still stands in a seedy, neglected neighborhood, in Tianjin's former Japanese concession. Ramshackle on the outside and evincing a decay that promises more of the same inside, the structure has not undergone the restoration that has improved other old buildings in the city. Still, the restaurant's former cachet can be imagined, despite the grime and the shattered windows of the curved, second floor balcony. Elderly Chinese now congregate below that balcony where Kawashima's customers used to look down onto the street as they dug into their Genghis Khan hot pot. The restaurant also had a less formal section that gained popularity around Tianjin since patrons could eat there standing up.

As an expression of gratitude for their services to Manchuria, Kawashima served Japanese soldiers tea and cake. "Those doing the serving," Kawashima wrote, putting a brave front on things, "had rushed about on the Manchurian plains and fought at the front with the Japanese and Manchukuo troops during the pacification campaign at Rehe. They were heroes of the national army and so they had a good understanding of the hearts and minds of the Japanese army heroes. There was always a pleasant atmosphere in the restaurant and a great sense of military solidarity."

That day when the canny young Yamaguchi Yoshiko walked in and had a look around the restaurant, she did not take long to comprehend Kawashima's plight. At first Yamaguchi was eager to accept the many invitations from Kawashima that came next, attracted by the hedonism of her new friend's social life, which provided a change from the dull routines of school. In her autobiography, written years later, Yamaguchi still captures the cruel accuracy of youth taking measure of a spent and ruined elder. "Kawashima Yoshiko gave me the opportunity to feel liberated from my family, school, and the monitoring of my activities," Yamaguchi writes. "But I could also sense the sinister decadence and desperation around her. She wore her male military uniform only when she attended parties or ceremonies in her role as Commander Jin Bihui. Otherwise she wore her man's black satin Chinese robe and cap. She always looked slightly flushed. She had a sickly pallor on her face, arms, and skin, so she put on light makeup and lipstick and made her eyebrows a little darker. She was always accompanied by a group of fifteen or sixteen women who were like her bodyguards. . . . Of course Kawashima was the queen of the group. No, she was always in man's clothes, and so maybe she should be called the 'prince.'"

Yamaguchi describes Kawashima's daily life, which began when she woke up in the afternoon. "In Kawashima's life, night and day were the exact opposite of what they were for an ordinary person." Coming alive at night, Kawashima ate late with her entourage and then headed out to the dance halls and mahjong parlors, or any other distraction that suited her fancy.

Fascinated at first, Yamaguchi took it all in, but soon wearied of the pace and the company. "I gradually realized that Kawashima's life as Commander Jin Bihui was over, and she had become utterly dissipated. The curiosity she had inspired as 'Mata Hari of the East' and those glory days when she had been praised to the skies as 'Joan of Arc of the East'— all that was gone. The Japanese army, the Manchukuo army, and the right-wing China *rōnin* would have nothing to do with her anymore." As Yamaguchi makes these assessments, her mental calculations are swift, and it is no surprise that Kawashima comes up short. Yamaguchi was soon heeding warnings that she distance herself from Kawashima and return to Beijing.

But this was only the first chapter of a connection that could not be severed so easily and is still invoked to contrast the fates of two women unable to figure out which country was their own. The China-born Manchu princess Kawashima Yoshiko who was brought up in Japan was caught in a similar muddle about where she belonged as Yamaguchi Yoshiko, the China-born Japanese woman brought up in China. They recognized in each other a bewildering patch of fog in the mind where others had the clearest skies. As they both discovered, this blur could affect confidence and judgment. By the time they met, Kawashima was merely seeking solace from a fellow sufferer, but Yamaguchi, just starting out, was keen to learn about the pitfalls ahead.

By the time Yamaguchi next saw her counterpart in Beijing, she had taken in enough information and had no interest in acquiring more. Crouching down in her seat in a movie theater, she succeeded in avoiding Kawashima,

Yoshiko (seated) at her Tianjin restaurant, around 1937. Chizuko is standing at the left.

Courtesy Hokari Kashio

who arrived in her male attire with two soldiers. On Kawashima's shoulder was a pet monkey. Fortunately for Yamaguchi, Kawashima did not have a lot of time to scan the audience for familiar faces since she stormed out at intermission, military escort and monkey in tow, loudly proclaiming that she was bored.

Yamaguchi was not fooled by the display of bravado. "Later I found out that the two men with her were not part of her army but her household help, whom she had outfitted in uniforms and brought along with her."

Yet Yamaguchi kept being drawn in, unable to resist the lure of this shade of her being, who was drug-addled and needy, confused and undone. Next time, as Yamaguchi walked down the street in Beijing, she was spotted by Kawashima, who was riding around in a Ford with the monkey on her shoulder; Yamaguchi did not refuse the dinner invitation. "A fondness for Kawashima Yoshiko welled up from somewhere inside me and so I got into the car." Though reassured by the respectable appearance of Kawashima's residence, which came complete with a guard at the gate, Yamaguchi was nonplussed by other aspects of the evening.

"I'll never forget that strange scene. In the middle of the meal, Kawashima Yoshiko suddenly raised the hem of her robe just like that, exposing her thigh. Next she took a syringe out of a drawer at the side and deftly gave herself a shot. It was a white liquid. . . . She had a brother who was an opium addict and so there were rumors that she did not only use opium but also injected herself with other drugs. I also heard that it was a painkiller for her traumatic spondylitis. And then there's the statement from her youngest sister, who said that she only injected herself with morphine."

Yamaguchi does not mention that Kawashima's career as a restaurateur came to an end when she got caught in the middle of a friend's murder. The victim, sister of the Manchu warlord Su Bingwen, had become intimate with a member of the anti-Japanese resistance forces. When the relationship ended, the resistance feared that the woman would spill their secrets, and so they decided to kill her. She had already been attacked once but survived and was near death in a hospital when several attackers broke into the room to finish her off.

Kawashima, who happened to be at her friend's bedside that night in late 1938, tells of her own matchless bravery and reflexes.

It was about eleven o'clock at night, and Mrs. Wang was holding my hand as she dozed off. . . .

Then three Chinese men stormed into the room with axes in their hands. I only had time to shout out in surprise, when those thugs bashed Mrs. Wang's forehead with their weapon. Blood flowed onto her white pillow.

"What are you doing?" I yelled, rushing over to the man who was attacking her. As I fought with the assailant, trying to get the axe out of his hand, I was slashed deeply on a finger of my left hand. Now look what's happened, I thought to myself as I fought with all my might to topple that thug. After that another attacker came over and hit me on my forehead.

Instinctively I let out a cry of shock, and as I recoiled, the second attacker saw his chance and assaulted me two or three times with his axe. Under attack front and back I continued to fight when yet another man assaulted Mrs. Wang with the death blow and fled, followed by the other two.

Mrs. Wang died, but Kawashima Yoshiko, though seriously wounded, survived after more than two months in the hospital. The newspapers erroneously reported that she had perished, and so she had the opportunity to read her own obituary. "The ancients proclaim that 'only when a person is carried off in a coffin can you judge whether he was good or bad,' meaning that a true evaluation of someone can't be written until the person's dead. In my case the newspaper and magazines attempted to size up the worth of my life and printed the obituaries even before my coffin had been readied. . . . They called me strange, flashy, romantic, adventurous, always after the bizarre."

While she was in the hospital, her restaurant was shut down for nonpayment of rent.

25

EMERGENCY HELP

In a 1978 interview with The Associated Press, Mr. Sasakawa said,
"All my critics are red, or jealous, or else spiteful because I didn't give
them money."

—*NEW YORK TIMES*, JULY 20, 1995

A s she faced uncertainty once again, Yoshiko had much to learn from
Sasakawa Ryōichi. Like Yoshiko, Sasakawa sought regime change at
various times and devoted himself to this cause, yet Yoshiko could
not compete with him when it came to cash and luck. Sasakawa could have
easily been shot in the Shanghai twilight by a Chinese patriot or hanged at
dawn by assorted governments. Instead, Sasakawa survived, moving from
fervid ultranationalist to ubiquitous fixer to prisoner, and finally settling
down as philanthropist with a past.

After the war, he was arrested as a suspected Class A war criminal and
spent three years in jail. Yet in the end Sasakawa sat on a throne not ordinarily available to such wily wheeler-dealers, establishing a foundation with
his fortune and challenging the high-minded, who struggled with their
principles as they accepted his money.

Sasakawa began his career in 1918 as a pilot in the Japanese navy, and
after a two-year stint, he learned enough to apply his aeronautic expertise
in a spectacular fashion. He would use airplanes to influence the course of
major events, including the Second World War. Rice speculation increased
his riches, and he became a supporter of extreme right-wing movements.
He formed his own political party, outfitting his fifteen thousand followers
in black shirts to pay homage to his idol, Mussolini. Too big an operator
to be termed a mere China *rōnin*, Sasakawa's endeavors fanned out widely
as he lent his private fleet of twenty-two planes to the Japanese navy and

flew in supplies for Japanese troops in China. After serving time in prison for extortion, a charge that was eventually dropped, Sasakawa flew off to Rome, where he met Mussolini and gave him a sumo referee's fan. Profiteering in China's precious stones and other materials is said to have brought him millions.

Sasakawa's money and contacts made him a natural choice as consultant when the military became fed up with Kawashima Yoshiko. To be precise, Tada Hayao, by then chief of the North China Area Army, ordered Yoshiko's assassination. Sasakawa remembers the day he was asked to intercede in this matter, and the Japanese conversation is one of those gems of linguistic magic, difficult to capture in English, that make learning Japanese worthwhile. It was June 1940 when the army's Major General Yuri, an old friend, broached the topic with Sasakawa in a Beijing hotel.

"I have something that I must ask you about."

"And what may that be?" Sasakawa looked back at Yuri.

"Sasakawa-san, do you know Kawashima Yoshiko?"

"I've heard talk about her, but I've never met her in person. Has anything happened to Yoshiko?"

"There's been some trouble with her. It's giving me a headache." Yuri lowered his voice. "She's under house arrest now, but the military brass has ordered me to dispose of her."

"What's this all about?" Sasakawa raised his voice without thinking. "Didn't she work for the military during the Manchuria and Shanghai Incidents?"

"That's true. She worked for Major Tanaka Ryūkichi in Shanghai and accomplished a lot when she was a member of the information division of the Special Service Agency, but recently she's become a bit more than the military can handle."

"You mean she's become a nuisance?

"Yes, that's right. . . . These are His Excellency [Tada's] orders. When I think about it, I feel sorry for her. The military exploited her as long as she was useful, that's all, and now that she's done something slightly bad, they want to be rid of her. It's immoral. I can't bring myself to kill her."

Sasakawa had his ideas about how a war should be waged, and though he could tolerate the broader savagery of the Japanese military, he was a stickler for honorable behavior in lesser things. As Sasakawa saw it, Tada Hayao showed manners unbecoming an officer in the Imperial Japanese Army when he asked a hit man to murder Kawashima Yoshiko, who had, after all, toiled on behalf of Japan.

Mustering his characteristic can-do approach, Sasakawa immediately volunteered his services. "What a cruel story. Just leave it to me. I'll meet with Yoshiko and take care of everything."

And so Sasakawa was soon off to visit Yoshiko, wielding a personal power that flew above the petty rules of national governments. At her Beijing home, Yoshiko was being kept under guard by two Japanese military policemen, who checked on all visitors.

"Thank you so much for coming to visit," Yoshiko told Sasakawa. "These days no one comes to see me because they're afraid of Papa." "Papa" was her way of referring to Tada, who wanted her dead.

Yoshiko, wearing flashy Chinese clothing with gold touches, led him to a Chinese-style chair. Sasakawa says that she looked "pale and listless," with the refined though melancholy air that struck others who saw her during this period. She perked up when he expressed concern about her situation, and, according to Sasakawa's adoring biographer, she immediately discerned his upstanding nature and intentions. Rising to denounce the injustice, she railed against being kept in her home under constant surveillance.

"Sensei, you have a look at them," she exclaimed, pointing at the military policemen.

"I'm being treated like a criminal. This is all at Papa's orders. Sensei, they say that I've done bad things. But isn't it Papa who's the betrayer? He makes use of me, showing no mercy, and then tells me that he can't stand the sight of me and throws me out like some old rag. . . . Those guys, they wouldn't hesitate to kill their own parents and brothers to protect themselves. You take Tada or Tanaka, they both were after my body. But they're just worthless. You call them generals? They're nothing but two-bit generals. A bunch of ungrateful thugs."

She issued these denunciations in a loud voice and then turned toward the policemen.

"Hey, when you go back, you tell those two-bit generals that Yoshiko doesn't give a damn about the Japanese military."

Sasakawa endeavored to impose calm on the encounter. "Yoshiko-san, you have every reason to be angry. . . . They make use of you and then turn around and threaten you. It's outrageous. His Excellency Tada's way of dealing with this problem is definitely mistaken. Outrageous. But you have to remember that you are dealing with the highest level of the military. You are going to have to resolve this in a way that maintains their honor and credibility. If you go on like this, they will get upset, and you'll lose your life."

At this Yoshiko—at least according to Sasakawa's besotted biographer—was again overwhelmed by his virtue. "No one understands how I feel," she told him. "You are the only one who truly understands me. I am so happy. Really happy. You are a true Japanese who loves justice."

Sasakawa took charge of her case, and in no time he had her out of Beijing and resettled at the Dalian home of Kawashima Naniwa. Her adoptive father's reaction to her sudden return to his home is unrecorded. Eventually Yoshiko was shipped off for a long stay in Fukuoka, Japan, where she remained Sasakawa's financial responsibility.

It is easy to understand why the Japanese military sought to eliminate Yoshiko, whose dedication to the task at hand had served them well in the past. When she put that same passion into tasks destructive to their aims, her former bosses felt obliged to reconsider her status. Sasakawa's biographer describes one of the rumors, about her method of acquiring funds: "She'd use her troops to inform on people to the military police, who would arrest merchants and rich people. Next Commander Jin would go to the prisoners' families and tell them about how she was well acquainted with the higher-ups in the military police. She told the families that she'd negotiate and so raked in a load of money and property." She was in cahoots with an official of the military police, who received part of her take and then released the prisoners. Such gossip alarmed Tada, who feared that he might be damaged if word of these transactions leaked out.

While such behind-the-scenes deals, if true, certainly complicated the military's view of Yoshiko, they were likely more alarmed by the growing boldness of her public criticisms:

"The Japanese go around spouting all kinds of noble slogans, but the fact of the matter is that Manchukuo is like a Japanese colony," she was heard to say.

"In his heart Puyi hates being emperor even now. He's been cut off from contact with the outside world. It amounts to house arrest. . . . The Kwantung Army is the real emperor."

Sasakawa's recollections of Yoshiko in this period must be viewed as the accounts of a man who saw himself as soaring above ordinary creatures in his morality and vision. He is blatant in spinning the facts for his own enhancement. Still, his portrait of Yoshiko, as recorded by his biographer, in many ways agrees with the portrayals of other contemporaries. Her ravaged appearance began to be apparent to everyone, and her lies, previously crafted with care, were easily seen through. Most often she was desperate—desperate for companionship, limelight, cash, and the drugs that kept her going.

Sasakawa's biographer tells of how, one eventful night, Yoshiko went to Sasakawa's hotel room, rushed into his bed, and refused to leave. Later on, she woke up to give herself an injection in the thigh.

"Hold me," she told him, "I want to be held by a real Japanese."

Her attachment to Sasakawa became so intense that she could not bear any separation. When he had too many commitments to see her, she sent him a telegram announcing her death. Despite a schedule filled with lectures and memorial services for fallen soldiers, he rushed off to see what had happened, only to discover her alive at a hot springs.

"Don't get so angry. . . . I wrote to you but you didn't come. So I sent that telegram."

Although he had no trouble understanding why she would love a rare man like himself, Sasakawa conceded that part of her devotion might have been fueled by her drug addiction. Repeatedly, he saw her injecting herself, and when he urged her to stop for the sake of her health, Yoshiko lapped up his concern.

"I can only depend on you," she whimpered. "You are my only ally in Japan."

Sasakawa's biographer solemnly points out that she had up to then been involved with many men, but all these were "impure" loves, based on a desire for power. "Sasakawa was the first and last of her men whom she could truly depend on, whom she loved from the bottom of her heart, who made her feel a woman's true happiness."

Still, Sasakawa saw that too much of Yoshiko meant mayhem constantly coming his way, and when she offered to become his secretary so that they could be together all the time, he turned her down. He did try to use her skills as a lecturer, scheduling her to speak before members of his political party. This plan too went nowhere. "She would promise to lecture, but on the day of her talk, she would oversleep and not show up. Or, in the middle of her talk, she would step down from the podium and go off to a secluded seat to give herself a shot." Still thinking big, she pestered Sasakawa to join with her to broker a peace between China and Japan.

"I'm thinking of going to see Chiang Kai-shek," she wrote to him. "We don't have time to wait for a better opportunity. You come along with me. We'll have a good long talk with him. . . . If we do that, then we can say that we have at least done something good in our lives."

Although Sasakawa managed to avoid getting involved in this scheme as well, he avows that his loyalty was steadfast and his concern about her welfare unremitting. "Sasakawa supplied all the money required to clean up the mess created by her dissolute life," the biographer writes. "His heart had been greatly moved by Yoshiko's pure passion for her unfinished dream of an imperial state, which she had staked her life on."

26

AN OLD LOVE

I wonder what Yamaga-san and Kawashima-san's lives would have been like if there had been no war and if they had lived in different times? The word "fate" is always on my mind whenever I think about this.

—YAMAGUCHI YOSHIKO

Kawashima Yoshiko next started stealing her old boyfriend's clothes. This comes straight from Yamaguchi Yoshiko, who disapproved.

Yamaga Tōru, Kawashima Yoshiko's first love, reenters the story in China around the time that she was managing her restaurant in Tianjin. Since Yamaga was last seen, he has adapted to changing times and resurfaces as a kind of cultural plotter for Japan's Special Service Agency. Yamaga seems an unlikely member of such an outfit since he had an intense attachment to China, an unhealthy quality in a spy from the occupying army. He loved Chinese culture, as well as Chinese women and opium, and these indulgences certainly detracted from his performance as a ruthless and tight-lipped undercover agent.

Another person plagued by fluid allegiances, Yamaga was responsible for collecting information from the Chinese artistic world; this was an assignment suited to his particular skills. His spoken Chinese was excellent, and his acceptance into arty social circles was facilitated by his passion for Chinese actresses, who reciprocated the admiration. He knew the best out-of-the-way places to eat, like the restaurant that served only the thinnest and most tender slices of lamb. It is clear that Yamaga lived out the classic story of cross-cultural confusion—he had gone to China with the Japanese army, aiming to conquer and rule. In the end China affected his love life, his dining preferences, his loyalty. "The Chinese people seem to go along with what the Japanese tell them," he once said, "but none of them believe what the Japanese military says. The Japanese have no idea how much the Chinese hate the arrogant Japanese. I'm sick of them too."

There is a photograph of Yamaga as he was in those days, standing in front of a Chinese house with a curved roof and lattice windows. Wearing a Chinese robe and holding a fan, Yamaga does not look like a Japanese army officer after the rewards of a conventional career. Though he could claim that this Chinese attire was necessary for his official duties, he does not display the discomfort of a man walking around town in disguise. Rather, he seems to be trying to disguise ebullience, allowing only a faint smile on his round face.

Yamaguchi Yoshiko, who had known Yamaga since her school days, reports that Kawashima Yoshiko and Yamaga resumed their love affair when they found themselves in China at the same time. "I found out much later," Yamaguchi writes, "that Kawashima considered Yamaga her first love. . . . The two of them met again in Beijing and became lovers. I sometimes wondered about their relationship. They were joined together by heart-wrenching feelings that sometimes came out as hate. They had to pursue their love against the background of those times, and both met violent ends."

This description is tantalizing, inviting speculation about how and when these former intimates were reunited, but no hard evidence exists about their rendezvous. What we do know is that Kawashima Yoshiko had seen more of the unruly outside world than would have been predicted of the sequestered young woman who had once hung around Yamaga's room in the Matsumoto bathhouse. Over time, they had come to share certain qualities, for Yamaga had also acquired risky habits, as well as subversive opinions about Sino-Japanese relations.

Yamaga did not abandon his other women for Yoshiko, and she could not abide his unfaithfulness. She became so enraged that she started swiping his belongings, entering his home when he was away. "I never knew what Yoshiko was going to do," Yamaga confided to Yamaguchi. "Once I came back to my residence from headquarters and found the whole place empty. She'd apparently come in a car and removed everything." Still, he preferred to avoid a row. "I can always buy new stuff. Thanks to her I bought myself this new suit and shoes." Associating with Kawashima Yoshiko apparently invited many such incidents, and so Yamaga told Yamaguchi: "Better not to have anything to do with her. She's poison, I tell you."

The jealous Kawashima Yoshiko showed how poisonous she could be when she told the Japanese military police that Yamaga and Yamaguchi were having an affair, and moreover, that he was sharing military secrets with the Chinese. Having fits of jealousy over Yamaga's relationships with other women was one thing, but making false accusations about traitorous activities to an organization known to torture and kill suspects on much less evidence was quite another. The police did not take her accusations seriously, but such condemnations of Yamaga surely made an impression on military officials, who acted on them later.

Not only had Kawashima mistakenly decided that Yamaga and Yamaguchi were romantically involved, she was jealous too of Yamaguchi's success and liked to claim credit for this good fortune. "When she was a schoolgirl," Kawashima complained about Yamaguchi, "I looked after her and really treated her well, but even so she's betrayed me. I bought her a piano and even had a house built for her. Now that she's become a star, she won't give me the time of day. I'm the one who asked Yamaga to get her hired by the Manchuria Film Association. Because of that she became an actress. She's just an ingrate."

Yamaga had more reason to regret his connection to Kawashima Yoshiko when he joined the queue of military men ordered to assassinate her. Apparently Japanese officials were having a hard time finding someone to carry out this assignment. In the end, Yamaga managed to remove himself from consideration for this job, a refusal that could not have been easy.

"She wrote letters critical of the Japanese military's operations in China," Yamaga said, "and sent them to [Prime Minister] Tōjō Hideki, [Foreign Minister] Matsuoka Yōsuke, [ultranationalist leader] Tōyama Mitsuru, members of Japan's political world, and top officials in the military. She called for a peace plan with Chiang Kai-shek. In addition to this, she was extremely critical of Lieutenant General Tada. . . . And she also caused me a lot of trouble. But when they told me to get rid of her, I couldn't get myself to do it. After all, I had known her for a long time, and she was a Qing princess as well as a relative of the emperor of Manchukuo."

In 1943 Yamaga was summoned back to Japan, where he was arrested. Some said that Kawashima was to blame, but others accused one of his discarded Chinese actresses of fingering him as a double agent. Found guilty of charges that included disclosing Japanese state secrets and drug use, Yamaga was sentenced to ten years in a military jail.

Yoshiko clasping the hand of Tōyama Mitsuru. To the left is her assistant, Ogata Hachirō, around 1943

Courtesy Hokari Kashio

"Yamaga certainly had traits that were not suitable in a military man," Yamaguchi writes. "And maybe there was something that justified the guilty verdict at the military court. But I also knew how Yamaga suffered. . . . He had many deep relationships with the Chinese and felt that he knew every aspect of the Chinese people's feelings like the palm of his hand. But as an army officer in charge of 'Yamaga's agency,' what exactly did he feel about his work against the Chinese? He seemed to be suffering as he asked himself such questions."

Yamaguchi did not see Yamaga again until he appeared at her Tokyo doorstep in 1949, after the war was over. He told her that he had escaped from prison during a bombing raid but had kept himself out of sight, fearing the he would be charged with war crimes. He was in debt, and although she could not lend him the sum he requested, Yamaguchi did agree to take care of Yamaga's daughter. Soon after, Yamaguchi learned that Yamaga had committed suicide with a female companion in a mountain hut; his corpse had already been mutilated by dogs by the time it was discovered two months after his death.

★

Yamaguchi's last encounter with Kawashima Yoshiko was just as grim, beginning in a Fukuoka hotel around 1940. Yamaguchi was by then a cinema idol in China and Japan, while Yoshiko was idling away her days far from the center of the action—just where military officials wanted her after they failed to get her murdered. The meeting of these two acquaintances did not begin well, for Yoshiko chose to lift up her robe in the hotel lobby, to show Yamaguchi the scars and fresh needle marks on her thigh.

"This is how I've suffered," Yoshiko declared. "I've gone through hell thanks to my fighting for the Japanese army. These scars prove it."

Yamaguchi did not warm to this kind of intense personal chat, and her displeasure drives the sentences that describe how she excused herself and retired to her room. A persistent Kawashima, who had reserved herself a room in the same hotel, came calling later on. She explained that she had come to town to take care of her adoptive mother, who was recuperating from some mental problems. "She didn't know that I was aware of the truth," Yamaguchi writes, "that in Beijing, orders had been issued expelling her from China, and so she was confined to Unzen."

Struggling for equality in their exchange, Kawashima asked Yamaguchi to star in a film to be made about her life. When Yamaguchi, who had not heard anything about such a project, did not commit herself, Kawashima came up with another, grander suggestion. "I am planning a big national enterprise that will endure in the years to come. Kawashima Yoshiko will join hands with Chiang Kai-shek. I have formed a new political group with Sasakawa Ryōichi. . . . Please join us."

Yamaguchi begged off, citing her busy schedule.

Yamaguchi was able to escape to a meeting, but she had not heard the last of Kawashima Yoshiko, who crept into her room late that night and deposited a thirty-page message by her pillow. Kawashima described her despair in purple ink, her rough written Japanese mimicking her spoken style.

It was wonderful to meet you after a long time. I don't know what will happen to me after this. Maybe this is the last time we will meet. . . .

As I look back, I wonder about my life. I get a strong feeling that it's all amounted to nothing. When much is made of you in the world, you are truly a flower. But during that time there are also people who come to you in reckless throngs, hoping to make use of you.

You shouldn't let yourself get dragged along by such people. You should stick to your beliefs. This is the best time for you to speak up about exactly what you want for yourself. You do what you truly want.

Here before you is a good example of a person who was used by others and then thrown away like garbage. Have a good look at me. I offer this warning to you based on my own experience.

Now I feel myself in a wide field staring out at the setting sun. I am lonely. I wonder where I should walk all by myself. . . .

You and I were born in different countries, but we have much in common, even our names. I've always worried about you.

27

ADRIFT IN FUKUOKA

The Japanese scare me. I want to leave Japan.

—KAWASHIMA YOSHIKO

Because Yoshiko had been marked as a security risk by Japanese authorities, she found herself unable to leave Fukuoka, the Japanese city where she was not welcome. Formerly, Yoshiko had been enraged at only the Japanese military and their cohorts, but with her movements restricted, she was now furious at all Japanese. She never forgot being scorned as a "Chink" when she was young, and with Japanese incursions into China increasing by the day, she heard more slurs against the Chinese.

For their part, Fukuoka's Japanese residents were offended by Yoshiko's scathing attacks on Japan's policies and questioned her allegiance to Japan. Even Fukuoka geishas asked her if she was a double spy for China. Beijing was not promising her a warm reception either: a Chinese assassination squad had posted a threat at her home there, demanding to know why a Chinese like her was a "running dog" of the Japanese.

Shibata Takeo, a Fukuoka detective, has described the havoc wrought by Yoshiko's sojourn in his city. His account, composed decades later, evokes the sorry, troublesome woman he was assigned to guard. According to Shibata, Yoshiko had been designated a "state guest" with a constant police escort. This of course was not the courtesy of a government seeking to honor an important visitor but the vigilance of a police state intent upon tracking a suspicious person's activities. Yoshiko made sure that she kept the police occupied as she flitted around, settling for small-scale disturbances in place of the big productions of the past.

Yoshiko also adjusted her attire for Fukuoka, aiming for a different sort of impact. She discarded her military uniform for a white silk kimono, which some took as the attire of a person preparing for death. An apparition in white who frequented the hot spots around town, Yoshiko succeeded in gaining some notice. This was especially so at the hospital where she went for treatment. "I visited the hospital and saw her lying there in her white kimono" was the sort of comment heard around town. "I was shocked out of my wits."

In her many free moments, Yoshiko besieged the police with her complaints—about the hotel overcharging her or appropriating funds she had left in their care. Not only had she been cheated by the hospital pharmacist, she said, the chief of the hospital had kissed her. Detective Shibata wore himself out in disproving all these claims, and in addition he and his colleagues lost sleep because of her late nights. On another occasion she claimed that her diamond watch had been stolen, but Shibata followed the clues to her dentist, whom she had entrusted with a sealed envelope. "Since I couldn't open the envelope without her permission," Shibata remembered, "I took it over to Kyushu University Hospital and got it X-rayed. Sure enough, the diamond watch was inside." Called in for questioning in the middle of the night, Yoshiko gave the police a jolt when she arrived in the white kimono, a wraith spewing excuses. She was shown the evidence about the watch but wasted no time coming up with a story about how she had two identical watches, and it was the second one that had been stolen. At this, Shibata picked himself up and left the room.

"She wasn't a bad person," said Ogata Hachirō, who became her assistant around this time. "She liked causing a fuss. Maybe to dispel her loneliness. It's hard for me to understand."

But Detective Shibata had no use for such a sympathetic analysis even more than four decades later when he spoke about those days. He said that Yoshiko eventually sent him a letter of apology, confessing that she had misled him with her lies about the watch. Still, he saw no reason to revise his opinion of her motives: "Yoshiko really had bad feelings toward Japan, didn't she? She made fools of the Japanese authorities when she had nothing better to do. I think that her whole purpose was to make a nuisance of herself."

Fukuoka did provide Yoshiko with some pleasant diversion, however, for in the spring of 1939 she became acquainted with Sonomoto Kotone, who was then a high school student. Their passionate acquaintance, punctuated by letters and poetry, provides another view of Yoshiko trying to comprehend her own decline; it also demonstrates once more Yoshiko's need for intense female relationships, an erotic element clear in her declarations of friendship to this young woman. "If we go to China together it will be difficult for you to get married . . . , your schooling, too, will be affected. You'll have to live apart from your parents. I have thought this over a lot. Even so, I wish that we could always be together."

Sonomoto returned the affection. "The room was somewhat dark," she writes, remembering her first meeting with Yoshiko, "and along with the strong smell of musk, there was a freshness that seemed to filter out the noise of the world outside. Warm emotions enveloped her, and she had the gentleness that made one forget those days of vanished glory. There was the sorrow of longing for a distant homeland; there was a quiet meant for a person who wanted to cry alone."

Sonomoto extols her stoical though melancholy friend, and Yoshiko in return told of her dreams of Sino-Japanese solidarity. "Japanese and Chinese are all Asian sisters and brothers," Yoshiko wrote to Sonomoto. "There is nothing so foolish as sisters and brothers killing each other. All people love their homeland. I have dreamed of making my homeland China stable and free of war, with Japan's help and guidance, and seeing it become, along with Japan, a great Asian nation." In mawkish poems, she repeated the theme: "Both Japan and China have been reduced to skeletons. Why do they attack and kill each other?"

While Yoshiko sorrowed for herself and for China, she could still summon the old restlessness, particularly when it came to the possibility of getting out of Fukuoka, and, with luck, Japan. "Beijing is a big city but the people there have much bigger hearts than the Japanese," Yoshiko wrote to Sonomoto. "They are warm. . . . I shouldn't say such things to you since you are Japanese, but I don't like to hide anything. . . . There are really a lot of scary people in Japan. This surprised me. . . . They still often talk about 'Chinks,' and this makes me sad."

At last Yoshiko did receive permission to depart, perhaps with the help of Japan's foreign minister Matsuoka Yōsuke, whom she had known since childhood. Gaunt and obviously ill, she met Matsuoka at the Fukuoka airport in April 1941 on his way back from a triumphal visit to Berlin, and to Moscow, where he had concluded the Japanese-Soviet Neutrality Pact. Just the year before, the mercurial, garrulous Matsuoka had been the driving force behind Japan's signing of the Tripartite Pact with Germany and Italy, a diplomatic decision that damaged Japan's relationship with the United States and helped bring about the attack on Pearl Harbor, the United States' entry into the war, and, eventually, the destruction of Japan.

The nation's ruin was nowhere on Foreign Minister Matsuoka's mind that day at the airport, where Yoshiko shocked onlookers by hugging him in public, a most un-Japanese sort of greeting. During her trial, Yoshiko would have to defend this closeness to Matsuoka, but in April 1941, she was focusing only on the benefits of such an important connection. It is said that she asked Matsuoka to get her travel ban rescinded. Two weeks later, she was allowed to leave Fukuoka for Tokyo.

28

HOPEFUL TO THE END

She didn't have anything to do during the day. And since she liked animals, she bought three monkeys in Asakusa and took care of them in her room. Another one was born, and so . . . there were four monkeys in the end.

—OGATA HACHIRŌ

Yoshiko called her pet monkeys Fuku-chan, Mon-chan, Deko, and Chibi; they lived with her in the Sannō Hotel, then one of the rare Western-style hotels in Tokyo. In addition to tending to her monkeys, Yoshiko busied herself in Tokyo with more urgent projects, like arranging for a cease-fire between China and Japan. She repeatedly phoned the home of Tōjō Hideki, then army minister, to offer her services.

"I would like to serve as the bridge of peace between China and Japan," she told Tōjō's wife. "If they will escort me to Japan's front line, I can help. I know a lot of Chiang Kai-shek's generals."

Tōjō refused to take her calls, telling his wife, "Japan is not so far gone that we need to depend on help from a feeble woman like her."

Yoshiko says that when she heard the news about Pearl Harbor on her radio, she "immediately realized that Japan would lose." In a memoir she supposedly concocted in prison—its authorship has been widely questioned—Yoshiko cited the reasons why Japan was doomed: "Because of the arrogant, blind conceit of the military, they did not understand the true facts about the United States. And at the same time they had excessive faith in their own abilities."

Yoshiko continued to make trips back and forth between Japan and China, unable to settle down. Meanwhile, Sasakawa Ryōichi arranged for the sale of the open-air market in Dalian, which had long been a source

Yoshiko with one of her monkeys

of income for Prince Su's family members and for Naniwa—as well as the source of the family's accusations about Naniwa's plunder of their assets. The sale provided Yoshiko with some cash for expenses in China and Japan, and while she had once proclaimed herself safe in both places— "If I am arrested either by Chinese soldiers or by the Japanese military, I will not be killed"—clearly both sides now suspected her of spying for the enemy.

Her sister Jin Moyu reflects the family's disgust in reporting that Yoshiko ran around with an unsavory crowd in Beijing. Their daily lives in shambles because of the war, her relatives had little patience to spare and tried to keep their distance, though Yoshiko clearly needed to maintain contact with them. Yoshiko is said to have taken up with the Chinese head of the Japanese military police in Beijing, and while others accused her of swindling money out of a Chinese opera star, she later said that she had not cheated him but instead received money owed to her brother.

Kawashima Yoshiko decided on Beijing in the end and established her final residence there, together with her monkeys and Ogata. At last, once Japan's defeat seemed inevitable, the perpetual traveler Yoshiko refused to budge. The dangers awaiting her in China after Japan's loss were obvious to anyone who cared to think about her welfare, but she either could not take in simple facts anymore or had made the astute judgment that once the war was over, she would not find a refuge in Japan either.

A fortune-teller long associated with her family had another suggestion: "I know a way to escape to Mongolia. I will show you the route."

But Yoshiko clung to the idea that her righteous heart would override any accusations and ensure her safety. "I have opposed Chiang Kai-shek's government but I have always devoted myself with great sincerity to the Chinese people. I won't run away. I won't hide." She summoned a blind *biwa* player to play songs in her house and indulged in afternoon naps. All signs point to a forlorn existence as the end of the war approached.

Later, at her trial, a judge asked why she had returned to Beijing, and she offered another explanation: "I came back because one of my monkeys had diarrhea."

29
NARROW ESCAPES

This morning we made a trip to the Temple of Heaven. . . . Here the emperor used to kneel, once a year, on a three-tiered, open-air marble altar, to worship Heaven on behalf of himself and his people.

When we arrived, the outer grounds looked much as we remembered them, but inside, what a depressing spectacle! All the buildings, including the Temple of Heaven itself and the approaching gateways, are filled with hundreds of young men (also, in certain quarters, girls). They are wartime student refugees from Shansi, some of whom seem hardly older than twelve or thirteen. Most of the stone terraces outside, as well as the floors of the temple itself are covered with their thin sleeping pads and meager possessions. . . . As one mounts the steps toward places once reserved for the emperor and his followers alone at the most solemn of religious ceremonies, one can but turn from this scene of human misery and degradation to look at the unchanging Western Hills on the horizon. . . . The mental condition of these boys is far worse than that of the poorest coolie. There is no trace of leadership or organization. Portions of the courtyard, and even the lower tiers of the Altar of Heaven itself, are littered with their half-dried excrement.

—DERK BODDE

After Japan was defeated on August 15, 1945, China simmered in colossal chaos. The Nationalist government's war against Japan may have been over, but there was still one more war to go, with the Communists, who were gaining strength by the day. "In an instant," wrote Jin Moyu, "the Kuomintang and American soldiers as well as MPs in white helmets replaced the Japanese soldiers in the city. . . . Once the Kuomintang came into Beijing . . . the situation was even more turbulent than under the Japanese. Not a single day was calm. Prices quickly skyrocketed, the currency changed, all over the city there was a thriving black market in day-ang (the one-yuan coins made from silver), and people were rattled by the approach of the Communists."

Chiang Kai-shek's forces scrambled to take over the regions formerly controlled by the Japanese, before the Communists could get there first. Many leaders of the puppet regimes set up by the Japanese were kept at their posts for the time being, on the assumption that a government run by former collaborators was preferable to total bedlam or rule by the Communists. "A few of the puppets have been tried and shot; most have been forgiven and taken back into the National Government." Keeping the puppet leaders in place may have made sense at military briefings of Chiang's forces but did not placate those Chinese after quick and thorough revenge. Chiang's assumption of rule was disorganized, his officials corrupt. He might declare that peace had come to China, but scores would reply that his peace had arrived elsewhere, where they were not living.

In addition to the fighting between the Nationalists and Communists, the Japanese surrender brought another kind of pandemonium to the Northeast. There were those hundreds of thousands of Japanese settlers spread out over Manchukuo, many of course sent to distant regions close to the border with the Soviet Union, in case the Soviets got any ideas. Once the war ended, not only did the Soviets have plenty of new ideas, but the local Chinese also seized their moment. On August 8, 1945, the Soviets threw aside the Soviet-Japanese Neutrality Pact, and their troops came pouring over the border, lusting for land, women, and, in particular, wristwatches, which they liked to line up on their arms. Chinese joined in, seeking a more sweeping kind of retaliation.

Japanese settlers throughout Manchukuo found themselves abandoned, without the military might to defend themselves. Japan's Kwantung Army—hitherto so feared that babies were said to stop crying at the sight of them—had quickly arranged for trains to evacuate their ranks from Manchukuo, leaving the settlers behind. Japanese families tell of rushing to the homes of their military protectors in Manchukuo only to find that all had left in a big hurry, with meals sometimes still on the table. Once their army vanished, the Japanese settlers were left alone to face the Soviets, the Chinese, the cold, and deadly infectious diseases.

"Even if Japan loses the war," a settler in a novel declared, reflecting one complacent belief, "that will have no effect on Manchukuo, which is a firmly established, independent country. As proof, isn't it a fact that not a single American plane can fly over us? It's the Soviets who can stir up trouble. But there's the Soviet-Japanese Neutrality Pact, and Soviets are not likely a country that will easily break a treaty. And even if the Soviets attack us, the impregnable barrier of seven hundred thousand crack troops of the Kwantung Army will prevent their approach."

Born in Shenyang in 1939, Yamamoto Takeo tells of his father, who had been in Manchukuo since 1935. Extremely idealistic and immersed in Chinese culture, the father had tried to live just as the Chinese did. His complacency at the end of the war took another form:

After the war ended, my father thought that he and the rest of the family could stay on in Manchukuo, happily, without the Japanese army and Japanese authorities to bother them. He wasn't going to leave. Then Japanese officials came and told him that he should at least send his wife and children to the city.

"They can always come back," the officials said, "but it may be dangerous for them here now."

So my father sent us to Tieling. I was six years old then. We departed on an open truck, leaving my father behind.

My father set about enjoying himself with his Chinese friends, but then one of them told him that the Soviets were coming, and he should leave right away. The Soviets were rounding up Japanese men and sending them to the Soviet Union as POWs. My father's Chinese friends dressed him as a Chinese peasant and told him that if he spoke, the Soviets would know he was Japanese. So pretend to be a mute, they instructed him. He started walking and soon saw the highly mechanized Soviet army roaring down the streets. He stayed away from the highway and hid.

Several weeks later, he suddenly appeared at our refugee camp in Tieling dressed as a Chinese peasant.

Japanese settlers had to make the terrible flight from far-flung homes to cities, where, lacking money and supplies, survivors had to scrounge around for essentials until their government found ways to repatriate them. Approximately eighty thousand settlers died along the way. The settlers' escape from Manchukuo to Japan has given rise to a Japanese literary genre that often focuses on this horrific mass evacuation and the settlers' victimization by the Soviets, Chinese, and the Japanese government and army. The settlers were doubtless victims when it came time to flee, but a reader may wonder whether their prior activities in Manchukuo had been as blameless.

Like any tale of a holocaust miraculously survived, life or death during the escape often hinged upon chance happenings—Chinese clothing offered as disguise by sympathetic Chinese; the ability to fend off measles and typhus; money sewn into clothing. The lust of the Soviet soldiers and Manchuria's cold were constant hazards of the journey.

The royal family of Manchukuo also had to make a hasty exit from Changchun before they too were overwhelmed by the Soviets and Chinese. As for the getaway of Emperor Puyi and his entourage, it was brief and disastrous. Once the Japanese emperor broadcast the news of Japan's surrender, Puyi announced his abdication as the emperor of Manchukuo.

"Chang Ching-hui and Takebe Rokuzo came with a group of 'ministers' and 'privy councilors,'" Puyi writes. "As there was one more farce to be played out, they had brought with them a new composition by the Japanese sinologue Sato—my 'Abdication Rescript.' They looked like so many lost dogs as I stood before them and read it out."

Puyi and his entourage next boarded a plane to Japan, but on August 19, 1945, they were captured by the Soviets during a stopover in Shenyang. "The next day," Puyi wrote, "I was put on a Soviet aircraft and flown to the U.S.S.R." He would remain imprisoned, first by the Soviets and then by the Chinese, until 1959. Hiro's husband, Pujie, who had accompanied his brother Puyi, was also jailed and would not be free until 1960.

Hiro meanwhile was left behind, part of a group of over two hundred remaining members of the Manchukuo court who began their own flight through vengeful Chinese mobs and soldiers. More than the other members of the royal family, who had to contend with the crowd's hatred, Hiro faced additional perils since she was a Japanese. "Outside, the rioters used fire axes to attack the Japanese they found. They even searched the clothes of the children," she wrote. "The rioters didn't just steal the possessions of the Japanese, they marched the Japanese along with only the clothes on their backs, one tied to the next. The people of Manchukuo had been persecuted during the war, and their fury erupted in such looting and assaults."

Nonetheless, she rallied and, once again, was able to summon extraordinary strength. "Once we realized what we faced, moaning about our fate was a waste of time. We had expected to have help from our husbands, but they were gone, and so we women had to think hard about what to do and somehow find a way to get to Japan." She was determined to protect her five-year-old daughter, Kosei, and also the opium-addicted empress.

Her group headed to Linjiang, where they were soon captured by the Communists' Eighth Route Army. Around about here, Hiro's story starts to sound like the imperial version of the escape sagas written by other Japanese settlers who fled Manchukuo. Her companions were more illustrious, and since she was considered a trophy prisoner by her captors, she was not liable to be raped or murdered on the spot. Still, she faced the same freezing cold and crushing change in circumstances that bedeviled all the fleeing Japanese. As in the other accounts, her horrible flight takes prominence—weather, illnesses, marauders from all sides—and diminishes all that has gone on before.

Capture by the Communists meant forced peregrinations, sometimes taking them up steep mountains in primitive vehicles and on long marches in an always cruel cold. Hiro, interrogated countless times, was forced to explain such things as why she had married Puyi's brother, whether she had been an agent of the Kwantung Army brought in to extort money from her husband's family, and whether she was in fact the Japanese emperor's daughter. Remnants of the Japanese Kwantung Army learned of her group's incarceration in Tonghua and, joining forces with the Nationalists, attempted a rescue, which ended in their defeat and the deaths of many Japanese.

Driven mad by these events, the empress became a filthy wreck. She was dragged around from place to place but, deprived of her opium, gradually sank into stink and delirium. Hiro made efforts to tend to her but in the end lacked the strength to keep this sister-in-law alive.

"The empress," Kosei recalls, "had become extremely thin. Sometimes she thought she was still in the palace. She'd call out as if talking to her servants, 'Bring the hot water.' 'Have you prepared my bath?' She would say all this in a very loud voice. My mother always made sure she had the empress's opium in her bag. But when that ran out, the empress suffered a lot. That voice of hers was very frightening to a little child like me."

While captives of the Communists, the empress, Hiro, and Kosei were forced to ride in a horse-drawn cart with a large white flag that labeled them as "The traitorous imperial family from the false nation of Manchukuo." By then the empress was too far gone to bother about the derisive crowds that watched the procession. Finally, the Eighth Route Army had had enough, and the empress was taken to another town, where she died alone.

Hiro was finally released by the Communists, who could find no proof of her collaboration with the Kwantung Army. Next she tried to pass herself off as a settler's wife when she joined a Japanese settlers' group fleeing to Jinzhou. Soon enough, she was betrayed by a Japanese who revealed her true identity to Chiang Kai-shek's forces.

Now she became a prisoner of the Nationalists, who were delighted to have her in their custody. They could proclaim that, because of their vigilance, another prime enemy of the Chinese people had been seized. After taking Hiro and Kosei off to Beijing and then Shanghai, where Hiro was declared a war criminal, the Nationalists refused to free her, despite the protests of Japanese officials. At times the Nationalists claimed they were her "protectors," not her captors; or, they said that she was now a Chinese and so the Japanese authorities had no right to tell them what to do:

"We'll put her on trial like Kawashima Yoshiko and send her to Suzhou Prison if we feel like it."

At last, stealth and negotiation brought this part of Hiro's ordeal to an end: she and Kosei were able to board a ship and return to Japan. During the voyage home, Hiro had plenty of time to reflect upon the sixteen months that had passed since she had parted from her husband.

> My life has been threatened by gunfire, I have suffered through starvation and cold, I have felt my heart torn apart by despair within the walls of a cold prison. How many times have I seen people betray each other, cheat, and kill each other? At the mercy of a cruel fate, I have drifted through a world that was the very picture of hell. . . . Since the Russo-Japanese War, how much Chinese and Japanese blood has been spilled on the Chinese soil I just left?
>
> Why didn't the Japanese try to join hands and make efforts to get along with the Chinese?

30
POSTWAR JUSTICE

QUESTION: State your, name, age, and address.
ANSWER: I am Jin Bihui, thirty-two years old, from Beijing. My address is
34 Dongsi Jiutiao.

—FROM THE TRIAL OF KAWASHIMA YOSHIKO

According to a trial record, Yoshiko was arrested by the Nationalists on October 11, 1945, almost two months after the Japanese surrender. "Is Jin Bihui here?" the police asked upon barging into her Beijing home. When Ogata said that she was sleeping off an illness, they went to get her.

"I was taking a nap at about one in the afternoon," Yoshiko later wrote, "when a man suddenly came into my bedroom and jumped on me. I woke up with a start and found that he was a forty-year-old man with a round face, wearing a white shirt and black trousers. He looked like a laborer or a spy. He let out with a roar, pulled me out of my blanket, covered my head with a tablecloth, and forced me to walk on my bare feet. This was despite my repeated pleas to let me change my clothes and put on shoes since I was sick."

Yoshiko was brought out in her blue pajamas, but as Ogata hurried to find something to put over her, the police thought he was going for a weapon and pointed their revolvers his way. Both Ogata and Yoshiko were taken to a waiting car, their faces covered and hands tied behind their backs. Ogata says that Yoshiko showed no sign of surprise as they drove off, and he always remembered the droll expression that he had glimpsed on her face. Even when the interrogations began, she made a point of mocking her questioners by ordering them to light her cigarettes.

"Ogata is a secretary in name only," this former Qing princess haughtily informed her captors. "He is actually my loyal servant. Arresting a good person like that is a violation of human rights. Release him immediately."

Yoshiko's prison cell was primitive, and treatment by her jailers, harsh; a jeering reporter took pleasure in noting that these quarters were "completely different from her previous luxurious, extravagant way of life." Eventually she tried to spruce up the décor by hanging up a photo of Yamaguchi Yoshiko, a reminder of another, happier time. Food would remain a problem until the end since she found the prison fare inedible. But her possessions had been confiscated upon her arrest, and so she had difficulty paying for meals brought in from outside restaurants. "Please help me," she begged reporters.

In a country exhausted by wars and the struggle to survive, the trials of traitors provided diversion from the calamities of daily life. As the accused were rounded up, there was no consistency about who would be brought to trial and who would be allowed to remain free. While laws were cited in the trials, punishment was random, and, no matter how heinous wartime activities may have been, good contacts in Chiang's regime could mean better treatment. Even Japanese army officers, who had laid waste to China since 1931, were able to get off given the right connections. Okamura Yasuji, commander in chief of Japanese forces at the time of Japan's defeat, had instituted the brutal policy of "kill all, burn all, loot all," which is said to have killed two million Chinese. Once the Japanese surrendered, Chiang took Okamura on as his military adviser and made sure that he was not prosecuted for war crimes by the Allies.

If the Nationalist government sought theatrical tribunals to divert the public's attention from a failing economy and the uncertainty of China's future, the trials of people like Ding Mocun served well in stirring up a lust for blood. He had been responsible for the torture of prisoners in that "palace of horrors," his much-feared headquarters at 76 Jessfield Road in Shanghai. Ding had gained such a reputation for cruelty in the collaborationist regime of Wang Jingwei that a newspaper labeled him Wang's Himmler. It is no surprise that the courtroom was packed when the five-foot, one-inch "Little Devil Ding" appeared in court.

As in all matters involving publicity, Yoshiko could compete with anyone, even the most despised defendants. The Nationalists continued to demonize her as a member of the reactionary Qing imperial family, a woman who had dedicated her life to bringing back her family's oppressive regime and overturning the wonders of the Nationalist revolution. In addition, her close association with Japan made it easy to pile on accusations about her treachery. Then there were her love affairs, her hair, her mannish clothing, all making for grand titillation. "With her assistance," read one rabble-rousing newspaper article,

> some areas in Northeast China were occupied, and she agreed to give up Chinese lands to the Japanese. Everyone felt most gratified to see her in legal custody. No one apparently knows how many of her handsome male "concubines" lost their lives in her residence at 34 Dongsi Jiutiao. After making love with Yoshiko, those men became laborers in the production of heroin, eventually dying of exhaustion. This was the reason why millions of citizens crowded in to get a look at her on her way in or out of court, to see what kind of a "rare and beautiful woman" she was.

From the start, Yoshiko's conviction was a foregone conclusion, but she incriminated herself beyond hope when she was bullied into confessing. She later told her lawyers that she had been lured into producing false accounts of her activities under much duress and after promises of better treatment.

"The court official told me, 'Look, even if you don't know anything, just write down what other Japanese have said or what the people from those fake puppet governments have said. Then the chief will be happy. He'll be able to say that you helped the government and then he'll send you back to Japan.' I was happy and believed them. I agreed to give them what they wanted. I didn't sleep the whole night thinking that if I went back to Japan, I wouldn't leave out a thing in telling all about those military men who had treated me so badly."

Seeking sensational revelations, Yoshiko's interrogators were not satisfied with her initial efforts and made their displeasure clear.

> The next day, having read what I had written, the court official's gentle expression of the day before was gone.
>
> "I don't believe any of it," he angrily told me. "How can you write such a thing? I received big orders from the chief and so I cannot pass this along to him. First of all, this won't help you. We have treated you as an important

Yoshiko at her trial, October 1947 *Associated Press*

person. If I show this document, which is full of empty words, to the chief, you'll be considered completely uninteresting to us, a useless person, and we'll give up on you. You'll have to stay inside here forever. Write something, it doesn't matter what. The chief has especially kind feelings for you and so has sent me all the way over here to talk to you. I don't want to feel that I've been wasting my time. I would like to save you. You have to confess to as much as possible and show the chief that you are a very important person. Otherwise, there's no way to get you released. You'll be imprisoned here forever just like everyone else."

Yoshiko complained about being humiliated in jail, forced to kneel on the ground with a plate on her head, subjected to constant abuse, and fearful of rape and starvation. Such hardships made her amenable to a female official's promises of food and clothing if only she submitted a report about her past deeds. "I thought that since I am a woman, she sympathized with my plight and so I told her, 'I'll just make up something to give to them.' . . . I told her that I was in trouble and cried."

Trying to please, Yoshiko let her mind wander and came up with the sort of thrilling vignettes she had so often fashioned for her public. Only this time she was on trial for her life, and boasting to Chinese officials about parachuting into Manchuria to help the occupying Japanese army or about her indispensable aid to a high-ranking Japanese officer was not the same as telling these same cooked-up stories to a reporter from a mass-market women's magazine in Japan. She implicated herself in wartime activities that had been detrimental to China, even when she had played no role at all, but anyway she apologized for any harm done, explaining that it had turned out badly because she too had been double-crossed by the Japanese.

Hyperbole her medium, she rehashed one of her most publicized, but made-up, stunts—her supposed attempt to get the Manchu warlord Su Bingwen to cease his rebellion against Japanese control and also release his Japanese hostages. "I piloted the plane myself and went to Qiqihar," she wrote.

Upon arriving there I sent a telegram to Commander Su. He replied that very day. Commander Su never answered the telegrams sent by the Japanese military headquarters, the provincial government, or the emperor. Strangely enough, Commander Su always replied to my telegrams. The Japanese newspapers published articles about this every single day. Before I knew it, I became well-known in the Japanese press as a person capable of doing anything. But after I rescued the Japanese held by Commander Su, the Japanese deceived me again. I was left completely alone there at the mercy of Commander Su. Once all the Japanese had been rescued, the Japanese army launched its all-out assault. I completely lost face with Commander Su and did not dare see him anymore. I just waited to be killed, but I did not die.

There is often a disjointed flavor to her confessions, reminding us that she was not only hungry and beset but also withdrawing from a drug addiction and could not keep her mind focused on the main points of her defense.

Interrogated repeatedly, her accounts expanding and tilting in different directions, Yoshiko did not seem to understand what she was up against and, disdainful of the authorities, believed that the charges of treason could not be corroborated by the facts. But, as it turned out, where the facts were lacking, the court would point to the evidence found in Muramatsu Shōfū's novel *The Beauty in Men's Clothing* as well as in Mizoguchi Kenji's 1932 film *The Dawn of the Founding of Manchuria and Mongolia*, which also featured a fictionalized character modeled on Yoshiko. With incriminating proof provided by noted Japanese creative artists, the Chinese judges saw no reason to look further. Astonished that fiction would pass for evidence, Yoshiko ridiculed this legal approach: "They say that novels tell of outlandish events. You take that famous *Journey to the West*. Only Xuanzang is a real person. You're not going to tell me that Monkey and Pigsy actually existed?"

Still, Yoshiko's scattershot confessions, though wanting in coherence, do succeed in conveying the mixed-up but true emotions she had tried to organize throughout her life. It was already an old story, for she had repeated these sentiments time and again, but at this critical time also, she insisted that, as a Chinese, she hated the Japanese for mistreating the Chinese. "My father taught me to promote goodwill between China and Japan, but he didn't say become the slave of the Japanese." And remember, she told her interrogators, she herself had been mistreated by the Japanese. "I was sometimes so furious that I could have died. I am considered the daughter of Kawashima, but I also have Chinese siblings, sisters-in-law, and other family members. The Japanese ignored my opinions. They used me as they wanted. To this day I can't get along with such people, and anyway they are cold to me. That is why I am always alone."

Yet her attachment to China was complicated by her inadequate mastery of spoken Chinese (she insisted upon a translator during her trial), which made it difficult for her to form intimate bonds in her place of birth. "I couldn't understand what was happening in China. I couldn't speak Chinese very well. I didn't have a clue about the names of important people in China nor about Chinese culture. How could I do intelligence work?" She did not feel a part of what was going on in her Chinese family, on the Chinese streets, in the Chinese newspapers, and so, in her telling, it was natural to drift toward the Japanese side. Communication was easier; also it was no secret that she liked certain Japanese individuals, even though they were committed to destroying China.

"I've worked as a secretary for Matsuoka Yōsuke. I've known him since I returned to China at age sixteen. He worked for the Japanese military and often complained to me about his great distress. There are some kindhearted people among the Japanese."

*

The Associated Press correspondent in Beijing wrote a rare, measured account of the opening day of Kawashima Yoshiko's trial on October 15, 1947, in an article headlined "Asia Mata Hari on Trial for Jap Espionage." The AP reporter estimated the crowd in the hundreds, and described the site of the court proceedings as "held in the open in what resembled an improvised stockade. The once-glamorous woman drove up in a heavily-guarded automobile. Her hair was chopped close like a man's." But the crowd was raucous and unruly from the moment Yoshiko arrived in the warden's black car.

More common was the excited tone of a Chinese report:

The flood of local citizens who did or did not have tickets surged through the iron gate. Like a flood from a broken levee, more and more citizens without tickets joined the flow and rushed into the square. People of different classes and professions mixed together along with crying babies and yelling mothers. All faces turned purple, bathed in sweat.

"Why did we bother to come?" some of them loudly complained.

The people who jostled into the square stopped to catch their breath. Those who couldn't enter had to climb trees to watch the trial from a distance. Everyone seemed to enjoy joining the commotion. When they saw Jin Bihui enter the square, the crowd pressed toward her, surrounding her so she couldn't move.

"The judges don't know how to control the situation," went the shout. "If there is no way for Jin Bihui to enter the square, what will they do?"

The hot-tofu vendor was asked to monitor one of the parking areas, where he had set up his cart, and he estimated that 120 bicycles had collected there in just a few hours. Stars from the Beijing opera mingled with the crowd, as did a man who had adopted Yoshiko's pet monkey. "After she was arrested," the monkey's new owner told a reporter, "no one wanted to take care of him, so he was sent to my place. He is now living in a passageway in my house and eats steamed buns and rice with some vegetables every day. He is very well behaved and helps to look after my house and catch lice. He enjoys smoking, and sometimes he goes off for a while to meditate."

As the trial commenced, the defense tried to present its case, despite the commotion stirred up by the spectators, including those hanging from the trees "like watermelons" to get a better look. The court was adjourned when a group of observers broke through the fence and poured into the open space where the proceedings were being held. "Since the judicial staff members were concerned about their personal safety, it was impossible to continue, and the head judge announced the suspension of the trial." On the second day, the trial was moved inside the prison with a smaller group of observers present.

In this more private session, Yoshiko fared no better. She had been charged as a "traitor" (*hanjian*), a capital crime that specifically applied to a Chinese who had aided the enemy. In an argument crucial to her defense, her lawyers insisted that she was exempt from being considered a traitor since she was not a Chinese but a Japanese citizen, having been adopted by the Japanese Kawashima Naniwa when she was a child. As a foreigner in China, she should be tried as a war criminal, and if so charged, her lawyers believed that she would escape execution.

Yoshiko's defense team also wanted to convince the court that she was actually about eight years younger than she actually was, making her too young to carry out the crimes cited by the prosecution. Consistently and fruitlessly, her lawyers objected to the quality of the court's evidence—its reliance on false assumptions, fiction, and cinema.

> Novels and movies describe fictional events. Just as in the folk songs sung by the blind, there have always been many examples of virtuous people being portrayed as crafty evildoers in novels and plays. Is it possible to take these as the truth? The sages of the holy books in fact sometimes write that it is better not to read books than to believe what is written in books. Using vague, made-up stories and rumors as the basis for a judgment in a trial, and, worse, a death sentence will not only confuse people but also seems to treat human life carelessly.

In one of her statements, Yoshiko denied everything and insisted upon the preposterousness of the charges. "My father is of Chinese blood. If China had been defeated, I also would have become a slave in a conquered nation. Why in hell would I help the Japanese defeat the Chinese? . . . I seek only peace in the world. Not only my adoptive father but also the father of the nation Sun Yat-sen emphasized this. How can anyone call me a traitor because of this? If I ever worked as a spy, then tell me, what was my number? Did anyone actually see me doing anything?"

When she had difficulties explaining away certain activities, she blamed her brother Jin Bidong, a prominent official in Manchukuo who could not defend himself since he had died in 1940. "I have many brothers and sisters, and people often get confused about who did what."

In their rebuttals, the prosecution swept aside the points raised in Yoshiko's defense:

> The accused, Jin Bihui, also known as Kawashima Yoshiko, is the daughter of the late Prince Su of the Qing imperial family. She was adopted by Kawashima Naniwa and lived in Japan from her childhood. Influenced by her schooling in militarism, she likes to dress in male attire and admires the ways of chivalry and Bushido. Because of her relationship to Kawashima Naniwa, she came to know important military and political figures in Japan. Submissive to the whims of an enemy country, she allowed herself to be used by them. According to our evidence, after the September 18 Incident of 1931 [when Japan invaded Manchuria], she participated in traitorous acts against her native land in Shanghai, the Northeast, and other places. For these reasons, we believe that the guilt of the defendant is consistent with the Traitor Punishment Ordinances, Article 2, Paragraph 1, Subsection 1 of the Criminal Code.

Against this condemnation, Yoshiko could make only a feeble response: "I don't understand why the prosecutor says such things about me. I became Kawashima Naniwa's adopted daughter not because of my own wishes but because my father sent me there. I didn't know I was a Chinese until I was sixteen. I was extremely sad at that time and hoped that conditions in my country, China, would improve with each passing day. . . . Do you really think that my conscience would allow me to help foreigners attack my native land?"

The prosecution's case seemed particularly shaky when they brought in personal qualities that, they claimed, proved beyond a doubt that she had been involved in nefarious deeds:

The accused is a descendant of the Qing imperial family and has devoted herself to the restoration of the Qing dynasty. She has been brainwashed into supporting Japanese militarism since her youth. She is good at horseback riding, shooting, swimming, running, skating, dancing, driving cars, and piloting airplanes. Though over thirty years old, she is not married. In short, she has all the qualities required for espionage work.

Her lawyers naturally disdained such conclusions: "The prosecution concludes that the defendant is proficient at various languages and has certain skills, so she has all the prerequisites to be a spy. I would like to provide an example to rebut these ideas. In the old days in China, there was a popular story that said that a man who owns sex toys must have committed rape. I would like the judge to think of this story when making his decision."

As scholar Dan Shao points out, Yoshiko's lawyers emphasized her Manchu ancestry in their desperate bid to prove that she was not a traitor. Everything she had done—aiding the Japanese, supporting Emperor Puyi's rule in Manchukuo—came from her attachment to her Manchu heritage and her wish to improve the Manchus' lot. "I am Manchu, and people living in the interior of China are not able to acquire a proper understanding of us Manchus," she had told reporters months before her trial.

Driven by such ideas, Yoshiko's lawyers explained, her actions had caused conflict within the one vast Chinese family but did not rise to broad-based treason against the entire Chinese nation. She had, in short, merely been on the losing side in a civil war. "The indictment states," her lawyers argued,

that the defendant, taking on the dreams of her father and following Kawashima's teachings, dedicated herself to the restoration of the Qing dynasty. But such an intention amounts to nothing more than her involvement in internal strife and therefore does not merit convicting her of treason. And anyway, the defendant took no action that would have brought about the restoration of the Qing.

Less memorably, her lawyer sought to excuse her because of her unhappy childhood, which he decorated with various untruths. "Finally, we ask the court's sympathy and compassion for the defendant. She was born in Japan; both her father and mother died when she was three years old. She was sixteen when she learned for the first time that she was Chinese. We must really sympathize with the plight of this girl, who lost her native country's protection and then was deprived of her parents' tender love."

On October 22, 1947, Kawashima Yoshiko was sentenced to death, found guilty of aiding the enemy and betraying China. The verdict condemned her for such activities as becoming a dancer in Shanghai in order to gather information for the 1932 Japanese onslaught there; bringing the empress to Changchun, with the help of her brother Jin Bidong, to install her as the female ruler of Manchukuo; serving as adviser to Tada Hayao in building up the military in Manchukuo and other military plots; trying to get Su Bingwen to surrender; leading bandit troops to establish a puppet regime in Rehe with Puyi as head; plotting to bring Puyi to Beijing in order to revive the Qing dynasty and overthrow the Nationalist government—and so on.

The judgment was patchy, ranging from those deeds she may have undertaken, definitely did not undertake, confessed to undertaking but later denied. As proof of the cavalier approach to the facts, she was also found guilty of heading an organization backed by the Japanese military that had actually been headed by another Japanese woman. In a 2012 documentary, her sister Jin Moyu expressed the skepticism of many when she reviewed the accusations. "A spy needs to be very intelligent and well educated. Yoshiko was not up to that level. . . . She was extremely bold and often made daring remarks. She could get carried away. I knew that but I don't know if she knew that too. I don't think she had the qualifications to be a real spy."

Most devastating to Yoshiko's defense was the court's determination that even if she had been adopted by Kawashima Naniwa and officially taken Japanese citizenship, she was still a Chinese citizen because her birth father was Chinese; she could therefore be labeled a traitor to China and executed. Her Chinese blood meant more than any document pointing to foreign citizenship.

Yoshiko herself realized that others had collaborated with the Japanese in ways more damaging to China and still survived, but she also realized that the public's anger, stoked by damning media accounts, made her exoneration unlikely. "Apparently a newspaper here wrote that they should put me on show, charge admission to see me, and give the money to the poor."

31

GO WITH A SMILE

I'd rather die soon than spend all these useless days in this prison.

—KAWASHIMA YOSHIKO

Awaiting the results of her appeals, Yoshiko spent the whole day inside her six-foot-square prison cell, except for thirty minutes of exercise. Although she awoke while it was still dark and had nothing to do until the end of the day, she tried to keep her spirits up, especially when writing to Naniwa, whose aid she still sought in a series of emotional letters.

> I feel that it's truly a good thing to be here in this cell in this cruel, tumultuous China. It is truly a perfect protective box, an exceedingly safe paradise. Thanks to you, I have experienced a spiritual awakening regarding various matters. I sit and eat, following the rules, and at the appointed time, my food (cornmeal) arrives. But because it bothers my tongue, they give me water. I am grateful that I am given my food without any trouble. Every day all I do is rack my brain, trying to come up with some bit of cleverness, which must make everyone in the world of mere mortals quite envious.
>
> A court official interrogates me over and over. "You don't give us serious answers," he tells me. "All you talk about are your monkeys, feigning innocence."

She made friends among the women prisoners but in general was repelled by their behavior. "The racket created by women is the same everywhere. They're crude and argue with each other a lot. I'm surprised at how many have killed their husbands." Still, these women were devastated when the guilty verdict was announced.

"I received the death penalty," Yoshiko wrote in a letter to Ogata. "I think that there's no one in the whole world as unconcerned as I am. Everyone is extremely impressed with me. The day the death sentence was announced, I ate two big bowls of noodles. My friends in the prison were very sympathetic, and all of them wept. Even though I kept a smile on my face for the others, I felt like crying."

Her Chinese relatives, who had problems of their own, did not come to visit. In danger of being arrested for their own wartime cooperation with Japan, they did not need to remind everyone about their ties to a traitor. "I have received neither letters nor visitors since being detained in prison. Receiving mail is one of the happiest things that can happen to a prisoner. When I see that other inmates get letters from their family members or friends, I feel quite sad."

Always, she longed for her pet monkeys: "Even today my heart aches when I think about how cute Mon-chan looked when he twisted his head and looked down from the Sannō Hotel's second-story window, watching the road below where the streetcar ran. When I remember the dead Fuku-chan's face, tears come to my eyes. Sometimes, as I think of these things, I turn to the blue sky above and call out to them in a loud voice, 'Fuku-chan, Mon-chan, Deko, Chibi! You were all so unlucky. If I knew that we were going to be separated so quickly, I wouldn't have hit you like that.' It really makes me feel terrible."

Only her assistant, Ogata, tried to help her once he himself was released from prison. Selling some blankets for cash, he collected items that she needed—socks, tooth powder, towels, cakes, smoked pork—and delivered them to her prison through fierce wind and snow. He apologized for not visiting her often but said he could not afford the trip. Next he borrowed money from a Chinese friend and again gathered supplies for her, but when he reached her prison, he found out that she had been flown to Nanjing. "It was really a shame," Ogata wrote to her. "I was so upset that I wept."

Yoshiko tried to maintain her concentration, hoping to save herself no matter what. She realized that she would not be freed, but at least she hoped to avoid execution on appeal. While repeatedly stressing her acceptance of death, she wrote letters full of instructions and was in a fever as she attempted to galvanize Ogata and Naniwa. To the end she believed, wrongly, that if she could produce proof that she was a Japanese citizen, she would be spared the death penalty.

Yoshiko's hopes depended entirely upon Naniwa, whom she urged, in cryptic Japanese meant to elude the prison censors, to get cracking in her defense. Cajoling, flattering, and begging her adoptive father, she was desperate to get her point across.

> How are you? The matter I am most concerned about is your health. I am feeling better and better, so please don't worry about me. This time I require a copy of your family registry. If I can show my name in a Japanese family registry, then I will be cleared. As quickly as possible please send me that copy you sent to Tianjin. This is my sincere request. I think that it's too soon for me to be killed, so I ask you to do this as fast as possible.

She wanted his family registry in order to prove that she had been officially entered as his adopted daughter and thus had Japanese nationality. But as she knew, her name had never been entered into Naniwa's family registry, and so she urged him to falsify this document by substituting her name for the name of her niece Renko, whose name did appear.

Falsifying the registry would have been a delicate operation at any time, and it is speculated that Naniwa did not venture to do this because he did not understand what Yoshiko was trying to tell him or because he feared for his own safety in Japan. He too was under scrutiny, from U.S. Occupation authorities investigating his wartime activities for possible war crimes.

Yet, apart from any of these considerations, Naniwa does not sound like a frantic parent who will do anything to save his child. Perhaps this is not surprising since he had, after all, endured more than he could have anticipated when he ushered Yoshiko into his household, including the innuendoes she had encouraged about their incestuous relations. In his response to Yoshiko's pleas, Naniwa seems collected and detached, a father who washed his hands of his wayward daughter's shenanigans long ago and does not intend to have his life shredded by her again.

Naniwa did not send a falsified family registry but instead wrote an extremely polite letter to Yoshiko's Chinese lawyer, describing his own past services to her family and assuring the lawyer that no young woman was as Japanese as she was. "Since her youth, Yoshiko has received a pure Japanese education. Her speech, customs, and habits have all been Japanized. And of course as a result, she has virtually no sense that she is a member of the Qing royalty. All Japanese recognize her as a daughter of the Kawashima family." But Naniwa did not provide any concrete evidence and settled for a lie about the existence of an official family registry with Yoshiko's name duly inscribed, but lost "as a result of the great earthquake in Tokyo on September 1, 1923, when all the documents in the town hall were destroyed by fire." With much courtesy, Naniwa expressed his hope that the Chinese authorities would be so kind as to release his daughter from confinement. "This year I will reach the advanced age of eighty-three years. My mind and body are growing weaker. I do not have any children, and so in my lonely old age, I fervently wish for Yoshiko's release and her return home."

Naniwa smashed more of Yoshiko's chances when he contradicted her claim that she was eight years younger than she actually was, the point she had been stressing with her jailers. When Naniwa briskly noted the date of her adoption, he was also providing proof that Yoshiko had been lying to Chinese authorities about being too young to have carried out the crimes cited in the guilty verdict. "At the time," Naniwa wrote, "Prince Su felt sorry that our household was a lonely place since we did not have any children. And so in 1913 he sent Yoshiko to my home in Tokyo. She was six years old at the time."

Aghast at such a blatant refutation of her testimony, Yoshiko pleaded with Naniwa to revise his statement. "You've made a mistake in your letter. Please think this over again now. At the time of the Manchurian Incident [1931], I was just sixteen years old. This year I am thirty-three without a doubt. You've got it wrong, I think. . . . If you make a mistake in the year, it causes me all sorts of problems. They'll say that I am telling lies to suit my own purposes."

Still hoping for a reprieve, she continued to beg Naniwa for the quick dispatch of the documents that might save her. But, at last, she realized that all was lost, and her mind sought the exaltation that would see her through.

"After I finished writing," went a letter to Ogata, "I threw my brush away. I thought to myself, 'Will all this deceit do any good?' I had planned to distance myself from all attachments. But I could not do it. Attachments are power, and at the same time they are death. Only when you are dead do attachments fall away. While you are alive, they amount to nothing for all but outstanding people, crazy people, and fools."

Yoshiko granted a last interview to Spencer Moosa of the Associated Press, who would be one of the two Western reporters allowed to witness her execution. "Penniless and bereft of her once disarming beauty," Moosa wrote in an article published just days before she died,

> the "Mata Hari of Asia" is awaiting with resignation her imminent execution. . . . She no longer looks the part of the Oriental siren who used her charms to help Japan in the war. At the age of 33, her upper teeth are gone, her hair is cut in a mannish bob, and she wears a padded gray jacket and slacks that make her small figure look bigger than it is. Some clues to vanished beauty remain in her fair skin, large dark eyes and small, delicate hands.

He told of her "barren" cell and her request that the execution be speeded up so that she did not "freeze to death in jail." She had also requested a private death, because she would be "greatly embarrassed" if she were killed at the public execution grounds near the Temple of Heaven. "Only real traitors and other criminals are usually shot there," she said. This request was granted.

Moosa added that many Chinese "say that the death penalty is too harsh since she was reared as a Japanese, regardless of her technical nationality." Nonetheless, she had little hope of being granted a reprieve, especially since there were stories about how at least one Nationalist official, alarmed that she would spill secrets he had indiscreetly shared with her long ago, wanted her executed immediately.

"I don't like men," Yoshiko told Moosa. "They only make trouble for women."

Though toothless and weak, Kawashima Yoshiko died as she had vowed, in a manner that did not shame her ancestors. "Arguments are just the stuff of this ephemeral world," she had written in one of her last poems. "Go with a smile—that is the proper way. I am my father's daughter."

Refusing the assistance of her jailers, she walked out to the frost-covered prison yard on March 25, 1948.

NOTES

ABBREVIATIONS

Aida	Aida Tsutomu, *Kawashima Naniwa-ō: Denki Kawashima Naniwa* (Tokyo: Ōzorasha, 1997)
Hiro	Aishinkakura Hiro [Saga Hiro], *Ruten no ōhi no Shōwa-shi* (Tokyo: Shinchōsha, 1984)
Kamisaka	Kamisaka Fuyuko, *Onnatachi ga keiken shita koto: Shōwa josei-shi sambusaku* (Tokyo: Chūō kōronsha, 2000)
Jin Moyu	Aishinkakura Kenki [Jin Moyu], *Shinchō no ōjo ni umarete: Nitchū no hazama de* (Tokyo: Chūō kōronsha, 1986)
Niu	Niu Shanseng, ed., *Chuandao Fangzi de jingren miwen: Guomin zhengfu shenpan Jin Bihui mimi dang'an* (Hong Kong: Jinjian zixun jituan youxian gongsi, 1994)
Shōfū essay	Muramatsu Shōfū, "Dansō no reijin," in *Nanairo no jinsei* (Tokyo: Mikasa shobō, 1958), 185–91
Shōfū novel	Muramatsu Shōfū, *Dansō no reijin* (Tokyo: Ōzorasha, 1998)
Terao	Terao Saho, *Hyōden Kawashima Yoshiko: Dansō no etoranze* (Tokyo: Bungei shunjū, 2008)
Yoshiko	Kawashima Yoshiko, vol. 1, *Dōran no kage ni: Watakushi no hanseiki*; vol. 2, Hayashi Mokubē, ed., *Kawashima Yoshiko gokuchūki* (Tokyo: Ōzorasha, 1997)

1. BORN TO CHAOS

I don't want to die: Yoshiko, vol. 2, 98.
On March 25: Niu, 600.
They'll probably execute me: Yoshiko, vol. 2, 91.
I am truly calm: Ibid., 90.
For me: Ibid., 92.
Poor Yoshiko: Kawashima Shōko, *Bōkyō: Nitchū rekishi no namima ni ikita Shinchō ōjo Kawashima Renko no shōgai* (Tokyo: Shūeisha, 2002), 125.

2. LITTLE SISTER

I'm Chinese: Jin Moyu, 94–95, 98–99.
The Eighty-eight-Year-Old Princess: "Bashiba sui de Xiao Gege—Jin Moyu" (Hong Kong: Fenghuang weixing, 2007).
I never met Yoshiko: Jin Moyu, 32.
Yoshiko had her hair: Ibid., 33.
One day I went: Ibid., 33–34.
What's this all about?: Ibid., 36.
Why, Chizuko: Ibid., 38.
Come back soon: Ibid.
Yoshiko invited me: Ibid., 8.
A little while later: Ibid., 8–9.
I looked at the newspaper: Ibid., 12.

3. ROYALTY IN EXILE

The clean, cool fragrance: Willa Lou Woods, *Princess Jin, the Joan of Arc of the Orient* (Wenatchee, Wash.: World Pub., 1937), 4–5.
Why are you crying: Yoshiko, vol. 1, 3–4.
My father wanted to go: Kamisaka, 44.
I will not tread: Niu, 201.
small, with dark skin: Jonjurjab, *Su qinwang yijia* (1964), 22ff.
At the time of the war: Marius B. Jansen, *Japan and China: From War to Peace, 1894–1972* (Chicago: Rand McNally: 1975), 153.
The Japanese police: Aishinkakura Renshin [Aisin Gioro Lianshen], "Shuku shinnō-ke zakki," in *Tōhoku Ajia no rekishi to shakai*, edited by Hatanaka Sachiko and Harayama Akira (Nagoya: Nagoya Daigaku shuppankai, 1991), 41.
You can say: Jin Moyu, 24.
In the Lushun house: Yoshiko, vol. 1, 24.
Looking back: Ibid.
With the world: Ibid., 24–25.
All around it was quiet: Kawashima Shōko, *Bōkyō*, 38.
Our life in Lushun was simple: Ibid., 44.
The Kangxi emperor himself: Mark C. Elliott, *The Manchu Way: The Eight Banners and Ethnic Identity in Late Imperial China* (Stanford: Stanford University Press, 2001), 179.
Since ancient times: Watanabe Ryūsaku, *Hiroku Kawashima Yoshiko: Sono shōgai no shinsō to nazo* (Tokyo: Banchō shobō, 1972), 29.
They wore Japanese clothes: Harada Bairen, "Shuku shinnō-ke no hitobito," privately printed, 1969, 5.
Prince Su's home: Christopher Dewell, Ph.D. diss., University of California, Santa Barbara.
He told me: Aida, 199.

Yoshiko went up: Kamisaka, 51.

One day I was asleep: Kawashima Yoshiko, "Boku wa sokoku o aisu," *Fujin kōron*, September 1933, 67.

4. CONTINENTAL ADVENTURER

Water, sky; sky and water: Miyazaki Tōten, *My Thirty-three Years' Dream*, translated by Etō Shinkichi and Marius B. Jansen (Princeton: Princeton University Press, 1982), 52.

Kawashima's idea in those days: Wada Chishū, "Kawashima Naniwa monogatari," no. 8, *Taun jōhō*, 2000.

Manchuria is the very nerve center: Aida, 46.

By nature: Ibid., 11.

God can see: Ibid., 13.

You are a child: Ibid., 13–14.

Absolutely naked: Ibid., 15.

those gentlemen who are: "Japan's Foreign Policy," *New York Times*, November 9, 1919.

I imagined myself: Miyazaki, *My Thirty-three Years' Dream*, 73.

Many in Asia: Aida, 17.

Those were the days: Ibid.

Swallows and sparrows: Kuzuu Yoshihisa, *Tōa senkaku shishi kiden* (Tokyo: Kokuryūkai shuppan-bu, 1935–1936), 2:217.

I was the rowdiest: Aida, 15–16.

I'll show you how: Ibid., 18.

blessed with many children: Kuzuu, *Tōa senkaku shishi kiden*, 2:248.

Weeping blood: Aida, 25.

Yoshiko was outstandingly gifted: Kawashima Shōko, *Bōkyō*, 125.

If in the end: Kawashima Yoshiko, "Boku wa sokoku o aisu," 69.

I don't need your help: Kuzuu, *Tōa senkaku shishi kiden*, 2:228.

You just leave me here: Ibid., 247.

Leave the Forbidden City to me: Aida, 72.

The proper way: Wada Chishū, "Kawashima Naniwa monogatari," no. 2, *Taun jōhō*, 2000.

China is like a wrecked car: Yomiuri shimbun, July 7, 1925.

[The Chinese people] are like sand: Aida, 175.

I often say: Kawashima Naniwa, "Shuku ō-ke naikō shinsō," privately printed, 1928, 11.

5. A NEW LIFE IN JAPAN

When I was thirteen: Kawashima Yoshiko, "Boku wa sokoku o aisu," 68.

They took away: Ibid., 67.

Naniwa was loose: Watanabe, *Hiroku Kawashima Yoshiko*, 73.

Once Fuku was back in Japan: Aida, 171–72.

What are you doing: Kawashima Shōko, *Bōkyō*, 73–74.

lost his balance: Kamisaka, 60.

In those days: Harada Tomohiko, "Kawashima Yoshiko o megutte," in *Harada Tomohiko chosakushū* (Kyoto: Shimbunkaku shuppan, 1981–1982), 6:74.

I used to get: Ibid., 84–85.

6. MANCHU PRINCE, JAPANESE WIFE

The Kwantung Army hoped: Aisin-Gioro Pu Yi, *From Emperor to Citizen: The Autobiography of Aisin-Gioro Pu Yi*, translated by W. J. F. Jenner (Beijing: Foreign Languages Press, 1989), 289–90.

I will leave the matter to you: Hiro, 32.

We refused the offer: Ibid., 23.

Unexpectedly, for both of us: Aishinkakura Fuketsu [Aisin Gioro Pujie], *Fuketsu jiden: "Manshūkoku" kōtei o ikite*, translated from the Chinese by Maruyama Noboru and Kin Jakusei [Jin Ruojing] (Tokyo: Kawade shobō shinsha, 1995), 74.

7. SCHOOL DAYS

In this world: Shōfū novel, 44.

Just tell me: A sentiment expressed by Kawashima Yoshiko's nephew Aisin Gioro Lianshen, among others. I am grateful to Terao Saho for showing me the transcript of her interview with Lianshen.

quite a walk: Kamisaka, 53.

What country are you from?: Ibid.

The only person: Ibid., 54.

On a day: Watanabe, *Hiroku Kawashima Yoshiko*, 67–68.

Two student teachers: Tanaka Sumie, "Kawashima Yoshiko," *Rekishi to jimbutsu*, June 1983, 26.

She would one moment: Ishikawa Rin, *Akabane mukashigatari* (Tokyo: Kindai bungeisha, 1988), 124.

It did not look: Ibid., 29.

It was as if a lustrous crane: Harada Bairen, "Shuku shinnō-ke no hitobito," 8.

She really stood out: Nishizawa Michio, *Shanhai e watatta onnatachi* (Tokyo: Shinjimbutsu ōraisha, 1996), 141.

My clowning: Takeuchi Minoru, *Kikō Nihon no naka no Chūgoku* (Tokyo: Asahi shimbunsha, 1976), 60.

The teacher is so insulting: Ibid., 52.

Even though the Qing dynasty: Jin Moyu, 18.

I have a home: Kamisaka, 68.

disruptive to order: Harada Bairen, "Shuku shinnō-ke no hitobito," 8.

That's just a roundabout way: Yoshiko, vol. 1, 37.

Uncivilized Principal: Nishizawa, *Shanhai e watatta onnatachi*, 164.

rid the school: Ibid., 163.

discipline and stoicism: Aida, 297.

That day on the way home: Yoshiko, vol. 1, 32.

Little Dove: Takeuchi, *Kikō Nihon no naka no Chūgoku*, 56.

Tonight is a dark night: Ibid., 57.

Sacrifice: Ibid., 57–58.

I was hit today too: Ibid., 58.

This "patriot": Ibid., 50.

They won't let go: Ibid., 59–61.

8. THE BEAUTY IN MEN'S CLOTHING

I had the best of intentions: Muramatsu Shōfū, "Dansō no reijin wa ikite iru," in *Gin no mimikazari* (Tokyo: Dai Nihon yūbenkai kōdansha, 1957), 232. The paragraphs that follow have been adapted from this essay.

I was with Kawashima Yoshiko: Ibid., 226.

So tell me: Ibid., 228.

I had been interested: Ibid., 230.

So you can say: Ibid., 232.

When it comes to historical fiction: Muramatsu Ei, *Iro kigen: Onna, onna, mata onna: Muramatsu Shōfū no shōgai* (Tokyo: Saiko shobō, 1989), 87.

The specialties of this place: Joshua A. Fogel, *The Literature of Travel in the Japanese Rediscovery of China, 1862–1945* (Stanford: Stanford University Press, 1996), 260; from Kikuchi Hiroshi, Kubota Yoshitarō, and Sekiguchi Yasuyoshi, eds., *Akutagawa Ryūnosuke kenkyū* (Tokyo: Meiji shoin, 1981), 230.

Shanghai has everything: Muramatsu Ei, *Iro kigen*, 113.

Why on earth: Muramatsu Shōfū, *Moeru Shanhai* (Tokyo: Surugadai shobō, 1953), 6–7.

It's a very important matter: Ibid., 18.

The driver was a handsome: Ibid., 19.

You're a writer: Ibid., 24–25.

Why don't you stop: Shōfū essay, 186.

I don't want: Muramatsu Shōfū, *Moeru Shanhai*, 74.

As you know: Ibid., 76.

The author lived: Shōfū essay, 187.

model for the novel's heroine: *Fujin kōron*, November 1932, 163.

She got her second bullet wound: Shōfū novel, 6–7.

Thus, before Mariko knew: Ibid., 41–42.

One day Mariko: *Fujin kōron*, October 1932, 375.

In other words: Aishinkakura Kenritsu [Aisin Gioro Xianli], "Kawashima Yoshiko wa doko ni iru?" *Tokushū Bungei shunjū*, February 1956, 221.

Prince Su's treasure: Wada Chishū, "Kawashima Naniwa monogatari," no. 35, *Taun jōhō*, 2001.

add a zero: Kamisaka Fuyuko, *Watashi no jinsei, watashi no Shōwa-shi* (Tokyo: Shūeisha, 2006), 207.

It is said that heroes: Harada Tomohiko, "Kawashima Yoshiko o megutte," 83.

It is not impossible: Ibid., 85.

When Yoshiko's brother Xianli: Ibid., 85–86.

There's simply no truth to it: Kamisaka Fuyuko, *Kamisaka Fuyuko no oi no ikkatsu* (Tokyo: Sankei shimbun shuppan, 2009), 222.

These people: Muramatsu Tomomi, *Watakushi puroresu no mikata desu* (Tokyo: Kadokawa shoten, 1981), 9.

No doubt he clearly mapped: Muramatsu Tomomi, *Dansō no reijin* (Tokyo: Kōbunsha 21, 2002), 44.

I spent my youth: Ibid.

My grandmother: Ibid., 42.

Don't look at: Shōfū novel, 61.

Isn't the section: Muramatsu Tomomi, *Dansō no reijin*, 73.

9. EXTREME MEASURES

Moriyama is really: Shinano mainichi shimbun, September 10, 1925.

dangerous, foreign ideologies: Joseph Mitsuo Kitagawa, *Religion in Japanese History* (New York: Columbia University Press, 1966), 196.

could see a pure side: Shinano mainichi shimbun (chōkan), September 10, 1925.

I said to him: Ibid. (yūkan).

He only has to look: Ibid. (chōkan).

was murdered in a spectacular gesture: Jansen, *Japan and China*, 208.

I didn't think: Kamisaka, 66.

Chinese the Catalyst: Shinano mainichi shimbun, November 21, 1925.

Story About Yoshiko's Marriage: Ibid., November 22, 1925.

I've had all this trouble: Asahi shimbun, Tokyo, November 27, 1925.

I don't want to talk now: Kawashima Yoshiko, "Boku wa sokoku o aisu," 69.

my farewell to my life: Ibid.

Kawashima Yoshiko's Beautiful Black Hair: Asahi shimbun, Tokyo, November 27, 1925.

Please forgive me: Ibid., November 29, 1925.

10. REPERCUSSIONS

I felt that I had to bow: Kamisaka, 22.

Now it is hard for me: Kawashima Shōko, *Bōkyō*, 334.

The troubled Kawashima Yoshiko: Asahi shimbun, Tokyo, February 18, 1927.

There have been various: Asahi shimbun, Osaka, March 7, 1927.

Yoshiko is abnormal: *Yomiuri shimbun*, March 7, 1927.

could not bear his loneliness: *Asahi shimbun*, Osaka, March 7, 1927.

She really became extremely knowledgeable: Kawashima Shōko, *Bōkyō*, 80.

She accompanied him: Ibid., 111.

They rowed and swam: Ibid., 79.

Yoshiko's selfish character: Ibid., 122.

She made sure: Ibid., 126.

11. ON HER OWN

To put it briefly: Harada Tomohiko, "Kawashima Yoshiko o megutte," 71.

I came to understand: Yoshiko, vol. 1, 36.

I was recovering: Kawashima Yoshiko, "Boku wa sokoku o aisu," 71.

She told me: Kamisaka, 73.

Yoshiko really looked like a bride: Jin Moyu, 34.

If they could plant: Nishizawa, *Shanhai e watatta onnatachi*, 221.

My daily life: Yoshiko, vol. 1, 83–84.

as bright as the noontime sea: Ibid.

These Mongols liked: Ibid., 85.

maintaining law and order: Nishizawa, *Shanhai e watatta onnatachi*, 218.

My troops spent a half year: Zhongyang Dang'an Guan, ed., *Wei Manzhouguo de tongzhi yu neimu-wei Man guanyuan gongshu* (Beijing: Zhonghua shuju, 2000).

Almost immediately after her marriage: Jonjurjab, *Su qinwang yijia*.

She was a small woman: Morita Hisako, "Shinchō ōjo to nisen-en," *Fujin saron*, April 1932, 204–8.

12. POISONOUS DEVIL'S BREW

To appeal to the Chinese mind: Whitey Smith, *I Didn't Make a Million* (Manila: Philippine Education Co., 1956), 25–26.

My great adventure: Ibid., 19.

Confucian morals: Andrew David Field, *Shanghai's Dancing World* (Hong Kong: Chinese University of Hong Kong, 2010), 59.

Competition for the foreign trade: Smith, *I Didn't Make a Million*, 22.

Off to one side: Ibid., 25.

calmed down the Charleston: Ibid., 27–28.

brought more good will: Ibid., 28.

I can't even: Muramatsu Shōfū, *Mato* (Tokyo: Yumani shobō, 2002), 11.

Before I had even: Ibid., 26.

From the bottom of my heart: "Watashi ga futatabi onna ni kaeru hi," *Fujin kurabu*, September 1933, 287.

Grandfather . . . I've been chased: Kamisaka, 77.

That problem daughter: *Shinano mainichi shimbun*, May 14, 1931.

13. ADVANCE INTO MANCHURIA

The Pacific War began: Ienaga Saburō, *The Pacific War*, translated by Frank Baldwin (New York: Pantheon, 1978), 3.

purchased with the blood: Yamamuro Shin'ichi, *Manchuria under Japanese Dominion*, translated by Joshua A. Fogel (Philadelphia: University of Pennsylvania Press, 2006), 261; from Sakurai Tadayoshi, *Nikudan* (Tokyo: Eibun shinshisha, 1906), 36.

Manchuria and Mongolia are not territories: Peter Duus, ed., *The Cambridge History of Japan, Volume 6: The Twentieth Century* (Cambridge: Cambridge University Press, 1988), 292.

The gunfire so frightened: *Walla Walla Union Bulletin*, July 5 1946.

a paradise of benevolent government: Duus, *Cambridge History of Japan*, 297.

price manipulations, coerced sales: Louise Young, *Japan's Total Empire: Manchuria and the Culture of Wartime Imperialism* (Berkeley: University of California Press, 1998), 402.

forced through mercilessly: Chong-Sik Lee, *Revolutionary Struggle in Manchuria: Chinese Communism and Soviet Interest, 1922–1945* (Berkeley: University of California Press, 1983), 271.

Miss Kawashima Yoshiko plunges: *Asahi shimbun*, November 16, 1931.

14. AN EMPEROR IN FLUX

I thought that the talks: Pu Yi, *From Emperor to Citizen*, 235.

rampageous: Secretary of State Henry L. Stimson, quoted in Sadako N. Ogata, *Defiance in Manchuria: The Making of Japanese Foreign Policy, 1931–1932* (Berkeley: University of California Press, 1964), 72.

the tiger's mouth: Edward Behr, *The Last Emperor* (New York: Bantam, 1987), 211.

As soon as I heard: Pu Yi, *From Emperor to Citizen*, 219.

I found a foreign-style house: Ibid., 208.

The economics of the Jingyuan Garden: Ibid., 209.

After I moved to Tianjin: Ibid., 209–10

A stick of Spearmint: Ibid., 210, 212.

I do not know: Ibid., 229.

acknowledge a bandit: Ibid., 228.

I was far too carried away: Ibid.

land where our ancestors arose: Ibid., 220.

Thus it was: Ibid., 247.

15. THE RELUCTANT EMPRESS

Twenty autumns later: Vera Schwarcz, *Place and Memory in the Singing Crane Garden* (Philadelphia: University of Pennsylvania Press, 2008), 70.

All Staff Officer Itagaki: Kamisaka, 84.

Their faces were very small: Pu Yi, *From Emperor to Citizen*, 117.

Few of the royal family: Wang Qingxiang, *China's Last Emperor as an Ordinary Citizen* (Beijing: China Reconstructs, 1986), 18.

Puyi's homosexuality: Kamisaka, 84.

I wore a black suit: Yoshiko, vol. 1, 129.

At 11 o'clock: *New York Times*, November 12, 1931.

Get the dog: Muramatsu Shōfū, *Moeru Shanhai*, 116.

In addition: http://www.chinahistoryforum.com/index.php?/ topic/11804-eastern-jewel-kawashima-yoshiko-.

The central government: Ibid.

I didn't know anything: Niu, 58.

She was a little over thirty: Hiro, 56.

The empress was seated: Ibid., 56–57.

16. POWERFUL CONNECTIONS

Yoshiko: What will you do: Kishida Risei, *Tsui no sumika, kari no yado: Kawashima Yoshiko den* (Tokyo: Jiritsu shobō, 2002), 59.

My expressions in the tribunal: R. John Pritchard and Sonia Magbanua Zaide, eds., *The Tokyo War Crimes Trial* (New York: Garland, 1981), 7:15916.

Much later he claimed: Tanaka Ryūkichi, "Kakute tennō wa muzai ni natta," in *"Bungei shunjū" ni miru Shōwa-shi* (Tokyo: Bungei shunjū, 1988), 2:85.

gas intoxication: *Tokyo War Crimes Trial*, 2:2142.

Yes, I spent: Ibid., 165–66.

professional witness: Ibid., 14:34377–78.

He testified glibly: Ibid., 18:44904–5.

General, aren't you known: Ibid., 6:14339.

We handled affairs: Ibid., 14341–42.

sybaritic and unsavory character: *Life*, January 26, 1948, 89.

To put it bluntly: Matsumoto Shigeharu, *Shanhai jidai* (Tokyo: Chūō kōron, 1974), 2:209; cited in Eri Hotta, *Pan-Asianism and Japan's War 1931–1945* (New York: Palgrave Macmillan, 2007), 152.

After that: Tanaka Ryūkichi and Tanaka Minoru, *Tanaka Ryūkichi chosakushū* (Tokyo: Tanaka Minoru, 1979), 454.

When I met him: Muramatsu Shōfū, *Moeru Shanhai*, 22.

Kawashima was imperious: Ibid., 27.

he had something big: Ibid., 50.

Her voice was shocking: Ibid., 96.

well-known perversion: Ibid., 99.

tragic: *Tanaka Ryūkichi chosakushū*, 570.

She was manipulated: Kamisaka, 90.

bought a house for Yoshiko: Tanaka Ryūkichi chosakushū, 454.

did not forget: Ibid.

While he was living: Ibid.

In other words: Ibid.

She never for a moment: Ibid.

Her talents: Ibid., 455.

expert at dancing the man's role: Muramatsu Shōfū, "Dansō no reijin wa ikite iru," 259–60.

basic beliefs: Kamisaka, 87.

Talk about being: Shōfū novel, 91.

At that time: Terebi Tōkyō, ed., *Shōgen watakushi no Shōwa-shi* (Tokyo: Bungei shunjū, 1989), 1:273.

Even so: Ibid., 275.

The important thing to remember: Ibid.

That incident occurred: Ibid.

The Chinese government in Shanghai: Ibid., 274.

The Chinese refugees: Frederic Wakeman Jr., *Policing Shanghai 1927–1937* (Berkeley: University of California Press, 1995), 190.

While this fierce battle: Tanaka Ryūkichi chosakushū, 457.

With Staff Officer Itagaki: Ibid., 459.

Afterward Xianli remembered: Kamisaka, 86.

17. WOMAN OF INFLUENCE

As we sucked the luscious grapes: Woods, *Princess Jin*, 8.

There were two beds: Shōfū essay, 188.

After a late dinner: Ibid., 187–88.

Once I got dressed: Muramatsu Shōfū, "Dansō no reijin wa ikite iru," 255–56.

Why did T: Ibid., 250.

At that time: Ibid., 251.

gave the military what they wanted: Ibid.

clever gift of providence: Shōfū novel, 352.

I am the one: Ibid., 309.

A woman must protect: Ibid., 308.

Kawashima Yoshiko put too much: Terao Saho interview.

Our hostess suggested: Woods, *Princess Jin*, 6.

disguised as a boy: Ibid., 3–4.

The present Nanking: Ibid., 24.

a little Japanese girl: Ibid., 6–7.

I am always lonely: "Watashi ga futatabi onna ni kaeru hi," 286, 288.

When she went to Rehe: Ibid., 285.

What could be more chaotic: Woods, *Princess Jin*, 18.

She thought of the way: Ibid.

As for the Japanese: Ibid., 24.

She became intoxicated: Tanaka Ryūkichi chosakushū, 461.

From the start: Muramatsu Shōfū, "Dansō no reijin wa ikite iru," 244.

I have definitely: Ibid.

Give us your life: Terebi Tōkyō, *Shōgen watakushi no Shōwa-shi*, 1:280.

I cannot live: Aishinkakura Kenritsu, "Kawashima Yoshiko wa doko ni iru?" 223.

money tree: Muramatsu Shōfū, "Dansō no reijin wa ikite iru," 252.

18. A GROWING AWARENESS

One day a field officer: Aishinkakura Fuketsu, *Fuketsu jiden*, 62–63.

When I heard about this: Hiro, 42.

What did you come here for: Ibid., 72.

Hiro, don't think about yourself: Ibid., 58.

During my first winter: Ibid.

The emperor sent over: Ibid., 66.

How can a mere: Ibid.

My contact with non-Japanese: Katō Toshiko interview.

The children were open: Hiro, 70.

slave mentality: Aishinkakura Fuketsu, *Fuketsu jiden*, 151.

severely punished: Ibid.

Your tenure: Ibid., 153.

This episode preyed: Ibid., 95.

With much emotion: Ibid., 96.

traitor: Ibid. 97.

I understood why: Ibid.

19. COMMANDER JIN

[Rehe] is all mountainous: Edgar Snow, *Far Eastern Front* (New York: Smith and Haas, 1933), 295.

"Gen. Su," reads a vivid: Straits Times, November 17, 1932.

Glittering Joan of Arc: Asahi shimbun, Tokyo, February 28, 1933.

I don't mind dying: Yoshiko, vol. 1, 246.

nervous ailment: Ibid., 248.

He was her supervisor: Hirano Mineo, "Josōshirei Kawashima Yoshiko to sono bakka," *Hanashi*, April 1933, 243.

I must go forward now: Aishinkakura Kenritsu, "Kawashima Yoshiko wa doko ni iru?" 224.

Tada adopted me: Chiya Michio, "Gokusō no Kawashima Yoshiko," in *Shi no kōseki* (Tokyo: Hokuyōsha, 1977), 50.

When she caused him trouble: Ibid., 49.

I was living: Yoshiko, vol. 1, 254.

lessen the spiritual debt: Ibid.

uncharacteristically quiet: Ibid., 255

They were all men: Ibid., 258.

There she was: Hirano, "Josōshirei Kawashima Yoshiko to sono bakka," 246–47.

Although the exact number: Terao, 169–70.

a bunch of toy soldiers: Shōfū essay, 189.

She has no special rank: Hirano, "Josōshirei Kawashima Yoshiko to sono bakka," 243.

I created the Ankoku Army: Watanabe, *Hiroku Kawashima Yoshiko*, 139.

In those days: Terao Saho interview with Aisin Gioro Lianshen.

Perhaps not since the Crusades: Snow, *Far Eastern Front*, 294.

[Rehe] was a debacle: Ibid., 293.

chill, bleak, mountainous: *Time*, January 23, 1933.

The Master of Jehol: *Time*, February 27, 1933.

about as fast: *Time*, March 13 1933.

seemed to be in: Ibid.

20. STARTING OVER IN MANCHUKUO

No matter how much: *Aa Manmō kaitaku-dan*, Equipe de Cinema, no. 171 (Tokyo: Iwanami Hall, 2008), 8.

Immigration to Manchuria: Ibid., 10–11.

An officer from the military: Ibid., 21.

I was ten years old: Ibid., 22.

My father taught students how to sew: Ibid., 18.

My little sister: Takarabe Toriko, *Takarabe Toriko shishū* (Tokyo: Shinchōsha, 1997), 11.

My father gave off: Ibid., 85.

Yamamoto had always: Takarabe Toriko, *Tempu, meifu* (Tokyo: Kōdansha, 2005), 41.

They passed by: Ibid., 14.

21. IN THE BRIGHT LIGHT

An ordinary person: Watanabe, *Hiroku Kawashima Yoshiko*, 265.

My whole life has been formed: Niu, 453.

Perhaps, as these words: Kawashima Shōko, *Bōkyō*, 120.

Up to now: Kawashima Yoshiko, "Boku wa sokoku o aisu," 64.

I led these troops: Ibid., 65.

happiness to the thirty million: Ibid.

the good kind: Ibid., 66.

They are suffering in hell: Ibid., 75.

I speak to you: Ibid., 76.

It was a time: Thomas Abe, "Dansō no reijin Kawashima Yoshiko hiwa," *Jimbutsu ōrai*, December 1955, 74–78.

22. WILD CHILD

No, rather than saying: Kamisaka, 117.

I complained to my father: *Shinano mainichi shimbun*, August 11, 1933.

She had no ideals and no ideology: Harada Tomohiko, "Kawashima Yoshiko o megutte," 75.

Yoshiko had no ideals: Kamisaka, 20.

Behaving in a rowdy fashion: *Shinano mainichi shimbun*, August 30, 1933.

genius of speculation: Hugh Byas, *Government by Assassination* (Hoboken: Taylor and Francis, 2010), 249.

messiah: Kasai Yoshiharu, *Shōwa no ten'ichibō: Itō Hanni den* (Tokyo: Ronsōsha, 2003), 202.

Rescue all Japanese citizens: Ibid., 200–201.

You have returned: Ibid., 200.

The Commander's Room: Kamisaka, 104.

I never have the foggiest idea: *Shinano mainichi shimbun*, January 9, 1935.

You only have to imagine: Ibid.

a pink Yūzen kimono: "Gokuchū ni utau Kawashima Yoshiko no 'Kimigayo'" *Nihon shūhō*, August 1959, 166.

glucose: *Tokyo nichi nichi shimbun*, Nagano Shinshū, June 11, 1937.

At this rate: Fukunaga Kenji, "Joketsu Kawashima Yoshiko," *Nihon keizai shimbun*, May 9 1984.

All of you: *Shinano mainichi shimbun*, March 25, 1937.

23. A DAUGHTER LOOKS BACK

After the defeat of Japan: Aixin-Jiaoluo Pu Jie [Aisin Gioro Pujie], "My Family and Myself," *China Pictorial*, no. 8, 1979, 39.

My mother had a strong sense: Fukunaga Kosei interview.

My Father, Pujie: "Waga chichi Fuketsu: Rasuto emperā no otōto—Haran no shōgai," NHK kyōiku, January 21, 2006.

Though the Japanese made much: Hiro, 74.

We work hard: Ibid., 100.

We people of Manchukuo: Ibid., 114.

But when I thought about it: Ibid., 106.

It was very difficult: Ibid., 116.

I was confused: "Fukunaga Kosei: Aishinkakura-ke saigo no tenshi," *Fujin kōron*, February 7, 2009, 138–39.

24. CHINA NIGHTS

Her songs came to express: Yamaguchi Yoshiko and Fujiwara Sakuya, *Ri Kōran: Watakushi no hansei* (Tokyo: Shinchōsha, 1990), 446.
She smiled: Ibid., 91.
When I was little: Ibid., 93.
In China: Ibid., 92.
My father felt: Washington Post, November 30, 1991.
Those doing the serving: Yoshiko, vol. 1, 264.
Kawashima Yoshiko gave me: Yamaguchi and Fujiwara, *Ri Kōran*, 94.
In Kawashima's life: Ibid.
I gradually realized: Ibid., 95.
Later I found out: Ibid., 98.
A fondness for Kawashima Yoshiko: Ibid., 99.
I'll never forget: Ibid.
It was about eleven o'clock: Yoshiko, vol. 1, 268–69.
The ancients proclaim: Ibid., 260–61.

25. EMERGENCY HELP

Sasakawa began his career: Richard J. Samuels, *Machiavelli's Children: Leaders and Their Legacies in Italy and Japan* (Ithaca: Cornell University Press, 2003), 243.
I have something: Yamaoka Sōhachi, *Hatenkō: Ningen Sasakawa Ryōichi* (Tokyo: Yūhōsha, 1978), 178–79, 187.
What a cruel story: Ibid., 188.
Thank you so much: Ibid., 189.
Pale and listless: Ibid.
Sensei, you have a look: Ibid., 190.
No one understands: Ibid., 191.
She'd use her troops: Ibid., 185.
The Japanese go around: Watanabe, *Hiroku Kawashima Yoshiko*, 173.
Hold me: Yamaoka, *Hatenkō*, 195.
Don't get so angry: Ibid., 196.
I can only depend: Ibid.
Sasakawa was the first: Ibid., 197.
She would promise: Ibid.
I'm thinking of going: Ibid., 199.
Sasakawa supplied: Ibid. 201.

26. AN OLD LOVE

I wonder what Yamaga-san: Yamaguchi Yoshiko, *Ri Kōran o ikite: Watakushi no rirekisho* (Tokyo: Nihon keizai shimbunsha, 2004), 128.

The Chinese people seem: Ibid., 125.

I found out much later: Ibid., 40–41.

I never knew: Yamaguchi and Fujiwara, *Ri Kōran*, 227.

Better not to have: Ibid., 97.

When she was a schoolgirl: Ibid., 227–28.

She wrote letters: Ibid., 230–31.

Yamaga certainly had traits: Yamaguchi, *Ri Kōran o ikite*, 125–26.

This is how I've suffered: Yamaguchi and Fujiwara, *Ri Kōran*, 233.

She didn't know: Ibid.

I am planning: Ibid.

It was wonderful: Ibid, 234–35.

27. ADRIFT IN FUKUOKA

The Japanese scare me: Kotone Sonomoto, *Kodoku no ōjo Kawashima Yoshiko* (Tokyo: Tomo shobō, 2004), 114.

running dog: Terao, 187.

I visited the hospital: Kamisaka, 113.

Since I couldn't open: Ibid., 112.

She wasn't a bad person: Ibid., 113.

Yoshiko really had: Ibid.

If we go to China: Kotone, *Kodoku no ōjo*, 108.

The room was somewhat dark: Ibid., 13.

Japanese and Chinese: Ibid., 121.

Beijing is a big city: Ibid., 97.

destruction of Japan: Satoshi Hattori, "Japan's Gamble for Autonomy: Rethinking Matsuoka Yōsuke's Diplomacy," in *Tumultuous Decade: Empire, Society, and Diplomacy in 1930s Japan*, edited by Masato Kimura and Tosh Minohara (Toronto: University of Toronto Press, 2013), 215–16.

28. HOPEFUL TO THE END

She didn't have anything: Kamisaka, 119–20.

I would like to serve: Watanabe, *Hiroku Kawashima Yoshiko*, 172.

immediately realized that Japan would lose: Yoshiko, vol. 2, 25.

If I am arrested: *Asahi shimbun*, Tokyo, February 8, 1932.

I know a way to escape: Kamisaka, 125.

I came back because: Yoshiko, vol. 2, 97.

29. NARROW ESCAPES

This morning we made: Derk Bodde, *Peking Diary: A Year of Revolution* (New York: Schuman, 1950), 12–13; cited in Odd Arne Westad, *Decisive Encounters: The Chinese Civil War, 1946–1950* (Stanford: Stanford University Press, 2003), 223.

In an instant: Jin Moyu, 7, 10.

A few of the puppets: John F. Melby, *The Mandate of Heaven: Record of a Civil War, China 1945–49* (New York: Doubleday, 1971), 152.

Even if Japan loses: Nakanishi Rei, *Akai tsuki* (Tokyo: Shinchōsha, 2001), 2:145.

After the war ended: Yamamoto Takeo interview.

Chang Ching-hui and Takebe Rokuzo: Pu Yi, *From Emperor to Citizen*, 319.

The next day: Ibid., 320.

Outside, the rioters: Hiro, 140.

Once we realized: Ibid., 138.

The empress: Motooka Noriko, *Ruten no ko: Saigo no kōjo Aishinkakura Kosei* (Tokyo: Chūō kōron shinsha, 2011), 112.

The traitorous imperial family: Hiro, 168.

We'll put her on trial: Ibid., 183.

My life has been threatened: Ibid., 187.

30. POSTWAR JUSTICE

Question: State your, name: Niu, 24.

Is Jin Bihui here?: Kamisaka, 125.

I was taking a nap: Niu, 1–2.

Ogata is a secretary: Kamisaka, 126.

completely different: Xinminbao, July 9, 1947, 18.

Please help me: Zhongyang Tongxunshe Zhengjibu, *Chuandao Fangzi panchu jingguo* (Taipei: Zhengda shezi zhongxin, n.d.), 3.

Okamura Yasuji: John Dower, *Cultures of War: Pearl Harbor / Hiroshima / 9-11 / Iraq* (New York: Norton, 2010), 385.

palace of horrors: Frederic E. Wakeman Jr., *The Shanghai Badlands: Wartime Terrorism and Urban Crime, 1937–1941* (Cambridge: Cambridge University Press, 1996), 85.

Wang's Himmler: Masui Kōichi, *Kankan saiban-shi: 1946–1948* (Tokyo: Misuzu shobō, 1977), 251.

Little Devil Ding: Wakeman, *Shanghai Badlands*, 86.

With her assistance: Shishi xinbao, July 11, 1947, 2.

The court official told me: Niu, 519.

The next day: Ibid., 530–31.

I thought that since: Ibid., 532–33.

I piloted the plane myself: Ibid., 39–40.

They say that novels: "Mokugeki-sha ga kataru: Supai no joō Kawashima Yoshiko shokei no shinsō," *Shūkan sankei*, March 1, 1971, 44.

My father taught me: Niu, 29.

I couldn't understand: Ibid., 30.

I've worked as a secretary: Ibid., 32.

Asia Mata Hari: *Indiana Evening Gazette*, October 16, 1947.

The flood of local citizens: *Shijie ribao*, October 16, 1947, 30.

After she was arrested: Ibid.

like watermelons: *Heping ribao*, October 23, 1947.

Since the judicial staff: Zhongyang Tongxunshe Zhengjibu, *Chuandao Fangzi panchu jingguo*, 32.

Novels and movies: Niu, 430.

My father is of Chinese blood: Ibid., 386, 389.

I have many brothers and sisters: Ibid., 390.

The accused, Jin Bihui: Ibid., 384–85.

I don't understand why: Ibid., 385.

The accused is a descendant: Ibid., 405.

The prosecution concludes: *Xinminbao*, October 19, 1947, 42.

As scholar Dan Shao points out: Dan Shao, "Princess, Traitor, Soldier, Spy: Aisin Gioro Xianyu and the Dilemma of Manchu Identity," in *Crossed Histories: Manchuria in the Age of Empire*, edited by Mariko Tamanoi (Honolulu: University of Hawai`i Press, 2005), 98–99.

I am Manchu: *Shishi xinbao*, July 11, 1947, 2.

The indictment states: Niu, 413.

Finally, we ask: Niu, 419.

Apparently a newspaper: Yoshiko, vol. 2, 103.

31. GO WITH A SMILE

I'd rather die soon: Yoshiko, vol. 2, 102.

I feel that it's truly a good thing: Ibid., 90.

The racket created: Ibid., 78.

I received the death penalty: Ibid., 95.

I have received neither letters: *Dagongbao*, November 20, 1947, 47.

Even today my heart: Yoshiko, vol. 2, 96–97.

It was really a shame: Ibid., 72.

How are you?: Ibid., 67.

Since her youth: Yoshiko, vol. 2, 106–8.

You've made a mistake: Ibid., 115–16.

After I finished writing: Ibid., 122–23.

Penniless and bereft: *Long Beach Press Telegram*, March 19, 1948.

Nonetheless, she had little: The official who feared the spilling of his secrets was Sun Fo, then president of the Legislative Yuan.

Arguments are just: Kawashima Yoshiko, *Shinjitsu no Kawashima Yoshiko: Himeraretaru nihyakushu no shiika* (Matsumoto: Kawashima Yoshiko kinenshitsu setsuritsu jikkō iinkai, 2001), 95; cited in Terao, 218.

ACKNOWLEDGMENTS

First of all, I send enthusiastic thanks to Funado Yoichi, who got me started on this project.

In China, Lang Kehua not only organized my trip to the Northeast but also helped me find my way through numerous documents. She has been invaluable to me, and I cannot thank her enough.

In Japan, Hokari Kashio and Yanagisawa Kazuhiko were generous, gracious hosts during my visits to Matsumoto; they allowed me access to their archive and helped in countless ways. Kawashima Shōko, Yoshiko's grand-niece, also took the time to share her views about Yoshiko and other members of the family. Kamisaka Fuyuko and Terao Saho, Yoshiko's Japanese biographers, were immensely kind as well, supplying vital documents and insights into her character.

At home in the United States, Haruko Aoki Iyer helped me with many problems, deciphering mysterious sources and frequently coming to my aid. Teruko Craig checked through my manuscript and as always contributed much to the final product. Mary Few has again been my vigilant reader, offering firm and crucial suggestions. Nancy Berliner helped out with all things Chinese.

In addition I would like to thank the following people for their help: Abe Yumiko, Joanna Handlin Smith, Makinami Yasuko, Margaret Mitsutani, Lynne Riggs, Sang Ye, Takahashi Chikako, Takarabe Toriko, Takechi Manabu, Wang Qingxiang.

Thanks also to my editor, Jennifer Crewe, and my agent, Victoria Skurnick, for their encouragement and friendship.

INDEX

Page numbers in *italics* indicate illustrations.

Tanaka Ryūkichi, 58–59, 112–20; assassination plot against Yoshiko, 114, 130; break
with Yoshiko, 129–31; later life, 116–17;
Muramatsu Shōfū on, 124; personal
characteristics and temperament, 114,
115–16, 129; relationship with Yoshiko,
114–17, 124, 125, 129–31; and Shanghai
Incident, 119, 120–21; and war crimes
trial, 112–14, 116–17; and Yoshiko as spy,
117–18, 120–21, 125
Tang Yulin, 139, 144–45
Tatekawa Yoshitsugu, 97
Terao Saho, 126
Tianjin: Naniwa in, 30; Puyi in, 100–103;
Yoshiko's Chinese restaurant in, 175–76,
179, 183; and Yoshiko's help in trans-
porting empress to Manchuria, 107
Tōjō Hideki, 113, 192, 200
Tokyo, Yoshiko in, 43–44, 89–90, 152–53,
199–200
Tōyama Mitsuru, 166, 192, 193
Toyotomi Hideyoshi, 25
trial of Kawashima Yoshiko, 4, 209–19, 212;
appeals following conviction, 220–23;
and citizenship issue, 5, 216, 219,
221–23; conviction and death sentence,
219; defense arguments, 216–19; and
"evidence" from The Beauty in Men's
Clothing, 55–56, 59, 60, 152–53, 214;
media coverage, 215–16; prosecution's
rebuttals, 217–18; and Shanghai Incident, 121–22; and Yoshiko's association with Japanese ultranationalists,
166; Yoshiko's claims about her age, 7,
216; Yoshiko's confession, 211–14; and
Yoshiko's obliviousness to Japanese
atrocities, 131; and Yoshiko's reasons for
helping the Japanese, 108–10
Tsukushi Kumashichi, 158–59

Vicissitudes of a Princess (Saga Hiro),
40–41

Wada Chishū, 23–25, 28
Wang Jingwei, 210
Wanrong (wife of Puyi), 105–11, 108; death
of, 208; drug addiction, 105, 106, 111,
207; leaves Tianjin for Manchuria
(1931), 105–8; marriage to Puyi, 105–6;
postwar flight and capture, 207–8; Saga
Hiro on, 110–11; unhappiness of, 101,
106
Watanabe Ryūsaku, 152
West, Japan's perception of, 27–28
Woods, Willa Lou, 13, 123, 126–29
Wu Changming, 132

Xianli (older brother of Yoshiko):
accusations of financial misdeeds,
64; on end of Yoshiko's usefulness to
Japanese army, 160; on family's exile to
Manchuria, 15; on Puyi and Wanrong,
106; on rape of Yoshiko, 63–64; on
Shanghai Incident, 122; on Yoshiko's
marriage to Ganjurab, 85; on Yoshiko's
role in bringing Empress Wanrong
to Manchuria, 105; Yoshiko's visit to,
following end of marriage, 89

Yamaga Tōru, 71–72, 90, 190–95
Yamaguchi Yoshiko, 175–82, 178, 190, 192,
194–95
Yamamoto Takeo, 205
Yamatomaru. See Moriyama Eiji
Yin Rugeng, 137
Yuan Shikai, 15

Zhang Zongchang, 142
Zhang Zuolin, 15, 85, 148

Columbia University Press
Publishers Since 1893
New York   Chichester, West Sussex
cup.columbia.edu

Library of Congress Cataloging-in-Publication Data

Grateful acknowledgment is made to the estate of Saijō Yaso for permission
to reprint an excerpt from his song "China Nights" [Shina no yoru],
copyright © Saijō Yao, and to Takarabe Toriko for permission to reprint
an excerpt from her poem "The Death I Always See" [Itsu mo miru shi],
copyright © Takarabe Toriko.

Birnbaum, Phyllis.
    Manchu princess, Japanese spy : the story of Kawashima Yoshiko, the
cross-dressing spy who commanded her own army / Phyllis Birnbaum.
        pages   cm. — (Asia perspectives : history, society, and culture)
    Includes bibliographical references and index.
    ISBN 978-0-231-15218-1 (cloth : acid-free paper) — ISBN 978-0-231-52634-0
(electronic)
    1. Kawashima, Yoshiko, 1906?-1948. 2. Women spies—Japan—Biography.
3. Sino-Japanese War, 1937-1945—Biography. 4. Chinese—Japan—Biography.
5. Princesses—China—Manchuria—Biography. 6. China—History—
Republic, 1912-1949—Biography. 7. Japan—History—1912-1945—Biography.
8. Manchuria (China)—History—20th century. 9. China—Relations—Japan.
10. Japan—Relations—China. I. Title.

DS777.5195.K39B57   2015
951'.8042—dc23
[B]
                                                        2014021788

c 10 9 8 7 6 5 4 3 2

Cover image: The Asahi Shimbun / Getty Images
Cover design: Catherine Casalino
Book design: Lisa Hamm